IN THE SHADOW OF
MARRIAGE

IN THE SHADOW OF

MARRIAGE

Gender and Justice in an African Community

ANNE M. O. GRIFFITHS

THE UNIVERSITY OF CHICAGO PRESS / CHICAGO & LONDON

ANNE M. O. GRIFFITHS is a senior lecturer in the Department of Private Law at the University of Edinburgh and coauthor of *Family Law.*

The University of Chicago Press, Chicago 60637
The University of Chicago Press, Ltd., London
© 1997 by The University of Chicago
All rights reserved. Published 1997
Printed in the United States of America
06 05 04 03 02 01 00 99 98 97   1 2 3 4 5

ISBN: 0–226-30873–1 (cloth)
ISBN: 0–226-30875–8 (paper)

Library of Congress Cataloging-in-Publication Data

Griffiths, Anne M. O.
  In the shadow of marriage : gender and justice in an African community / Anne M. O. Griffiths.
      p.   cm.
  Includes bibliographical references and index.
  ISBN 0-226-30873-1 (cloth : alk. paper).—ISBN 0-226-30875-8 (pbk. : alk. paper)
    1. Women, Kwena.   2. Kwena (African people)—Legal status, laws, etc.   3. Kwena (African people)—Marriage customs and rites.
I. Title.
DT2458.K84G75   1997
305.3'096883—dc21   97-19579
                                                                          CIP

⊗ The paper used in this publication meets the minimum requirements of the American National Standard for Information Sciences—Permanence of Paper for Printed Materials, ANSI Z39.48–1984.

For S. G. Masimega

CONTENTS

ILLUSTRATIONS

Following p. 105

PREFACE

The movement under the trees caught my eye. There were a group of people sitting around in the open air, talking, gesticulating, engaged in some intense activity. What were they doing? As I moved closer to observe what was going on, I saw a woman with a small baby wrapped in a blanket who was sitting to one side of the group, engaged in discussions with the man seated opposite her. From time to time, an older man who appeared to be in authority addressed questions to both parties and to those who were sitting or standing round about. This, in Botswana in 1981, was my first exposure to a kgotla and to proceedings involving a woman's claims to compensation for pregnancy, which was to become the subject of my research over the years.[1]

The narratives in this book focus on the relationship between justice, as represented by law, and women's experiences of the gendered world in which they have to negotiate their status, on which claims to property and resources in family life are based. They present two interrelated themes, the one highlighting the interconnections of gender, marriage, and other partnerships between women and men, and access to resources; the other underlining the relationship between official and customary law, in theory and practice.

These themes are integrated through a discussion of everyday life, derived from women's and men's life histories and narratives of dispute. This perspective provides for a radically different account of law, one which challenges the legal centralist model that has been canonical to colonial, national, and academic treatments of legal discourse. It also foregrounds the strategies that women pursue in making claims on their male partners (whether married or unmarried) for support, maintenance, or other property rights. Such claims represent a major issue for the study of family law in general. They feature in this book, however, as part of a broader social domain which extends beyond institutional forums such as courts to incorporate networks revolving around kin, marriage, and varying forms of resources. How women are situated

1

within such networks is crucial, as it affects their power to negotiate with men, a power constrained by the gendered nature of the world in which they operate.

One of the classic problems addressed in the anthropology of law and the study of legal discourse concerns the ways in which law is characterized, especially in a colonial and postcolonial context, where a clear distinction is drawn between a Western form of law associated with Europeans and indigenous legal practices referred to under the rubric of customary law. This dichotomy is reinforced by formal studies of law, where the focus is limited to particular written sources and institutions. Such a focus, drawn from a legal centralist model, upholds a division between Western and customary law which is marked in institutional terms by the application of separate court systems and procedures.

But an ethnographic approach to the study of law, based in this case on a study of Bakwena[2] in the village of Molepolole in Botswana, undermines any theoretical distinction that is drawn between Western and customary law. It does so by examining how law works in practice from the perspective of people's understandings of and engagements with it. In this context women's and men's experiences with law are substantially different. The book not only charts these differences but documents, through women's experiences, how the administrative and theoretical separation of legal systems does not extend to people's uses of the law in arranging their own lives.

The traditional academic focus on men's experiences with courts in the colonial context has tended to overemphasize the distinction between customary forums (where men have power) and official courts. What constitutes power for women, however, derives from other factors, and where marriage and partnership are concerned women find themselves integrating customary and Western law in ways which are quite different from, and yet illuminate, men's legal strategies.

But power not only shapes the gendered relations between women and men. While the world in which women and men operate is one in which men generally have better access to resources than women (thereby creating the conditions under which they acquire certain forms of power over women), there are women who are able to overcome the constraints that normally face them in their dealings with men. Their ability to do so depends on how these women are situated within the networks of which they form a part and on a whole range of elements, including class, which are factored into the encounters that take place in everyday life.

Thus, gender represents only one dimension (but an important one) of the differences that arise between the sexes from the inequalities inherent in social relations generally and among members of the same sex. Examining the ways in which new forms of wealth and status are translated into inequalities in the heart of community disputes, around fundamental relationships like child maintenance and marriage, provides new insights into the character of village society at a local level. These demonstrate the ways in which apparently egalitarian decision-making processes persistently reflect and re-create inequalities in postcolonial societies. This focus is one that is rarely addressed in discussions of postcolonial inequality in Africa, which tend to emphasize the ability of bureaucratic elites to use the mechanisms of the postcolonial state to reproduce their power and wealth but only at the level of national and macro-level decision making. The use of life histories not only underpins discussions of inequality but is central to my analysis of disputes. Approaching the study of disputes from this perspective not only challenges a legal centralist analysis of law but represents a new methodology in the study of law, for such life histories yield the narratives in which official and customary law emerge as interconnected in personal experience.

Undertaking this kind of research presented me with intellectual and personal challenges, given my training as a lawyer skilled in the arts of doctrinal analysis. Invited to Botswana to establish a foundation course in family law at the university,[3] I found myself confronted with the inadequacies of constructing a course based purely on statutes and cases in the magistrates' courts and the High Court, the stuff of traditional Western legal scholarship. In a country where this type of law (referred to as common law) was juxtaposed with customary law (allegedly derived from precolonial indigenous legal practice), I soon realized the need to integrate discussions on both systems into my analysis of family law. This was underscored by my visit to a kgotla operating as a customary court and by a reading of Isaac Schapera's *Handbook of Tswana Law and Custom,* which prompted my desire to learn more about customary law.

The question of integration, however, was one that had previously been ignored in discussion of law in Botswana. This was because up until this point scholars had tended to focus their attention on one or the other aspect of law. When it came to bridging the gap, I found there were numerous accounts of customary law (Schapera 1938; Roberts 1970, 1972a, 1972b, 1977a; Kuper 1970; Comaroff and Roberts 1981) and of common law (e.g., Boberg 1977). The latter were based on the kinds of analyses of statutes and cases which occur in law schools all over the world, including Edinburgh. But I could not find any texts which provided a sustained account of the interrelationship between these legal fields, especially where family matters were concerned. The need to explore the connections between common and customary law, not only in the formal sense but through people's perceptions, knowledge, and use of law, was what took me back to Botswana for nine months in 1982 and for follow-up studies in 1984 and 1989.

The importance of this type of research was highlighted for me by encounters with law students at the University of Botswana when I taught there in 1982.[4] These students were very curious as to why a lawyer like myself would want to go and live in a hut in a village (even one the size of Molepolole) or to know anything about customary law. For many of them, who were studying law as a route to enter the legal profession, customary law represented a thing of the past and not the way of the future. Its relevance in a modern society was strictly limited. Although many of them came from villages, their knowledge and experience of life in this context was something which became divorced from their situation at the university, especially as the acquisition of such a university place provided them with access to an elite status in comparison with their rural contemporaries. Eager to participate in discussions over the research as it progressed, which provided me with valuable insights into what was occurring on the ground, these students made contributions which were marked by the fact that they fell into two distinct categories, those concerning their approach as lawyers, within a perceived legal tradition represented by common law, and those representing their views as members of village communities, which were often at odds with the former. In this process, I could not help observing the ease with which individuals switched, unself-consciously, from one persona to the other, thus upholding the kind of rationale underlying the formal legal system—a rationale derived from a legal centralist model of law.

A combination of factors led me to work among Bakwena,[5] in their central village Molepolole, which is in the part of the country known as Kweneng District, gateway to the Kalahari Desert, close to the South African border and railway and about seventy kilometers by paved road from Gaborone (fig. 1). Although it is one of the oldest Tswana merafe (polities, sing. morafe),[6] little research had been done among Bakwena over the years, compared with other Tswana merafe, such as Bakgatla, Bangwato, or Barolong, which feature prominently in the work of

Schapera, Comaroff, and Roberts. Not only would such research provide a comparative perspective, but it was also viable because of access to the community through a number of sources, including support at the time from Bakwena Tribal Administration,[7] the Commissioner of Customary Courts, and the District Commissioner.

To talk of a village that is the central site of a morafe is misleading for those who are unfamiliar with what this means in a Tswana context. It is not the cozy accommodation of a few households and families brought to mind through visions of British country life, but rather a bustling regional center spread out over a wide area, with huts and buildings of all kinds as far as the eye can see (fig. 2). People are constantly moving in and out of the village as they seek to make a living through hunting and gathering, attending to cattle and livestock, engaging in subsistence agriculture, and searching for paid employment. When I first arrived in Molepolole in 1982, the village was spread over a number of kilometers and was recorded (in the 1980 census) as having a population of twenty thousand people (although many were absent for the reasons given above). Since then it has continued to grow steadily,[8] and on my last visit in 1992 it was hard to keep track of all the developments that were taking place.[9] I was also amazed to note how much nearer it was edging toward the capital, Gaborone.

During my field research, my guide to and mentor in Molepolole was Mr. S. G. Masimega (fig. 3). It was he who familiarized me with the village, introduced me to the various communities within it along with their kgotlas and wards (described in chap. 2), acted as interpreter and translator, and patiently took the time to teach me about Tswana and Kwena ways. Trained as a teacher, personal secretary to two Kwena chiefs, and a past member of the district council, he has sat on many key committees, such as the Village Development Committee, the Parent Teacher's Association, the Agricultural Show Committee, and the Independence Day Celebration Committee. He is affectionately known in the village as Mr. Commonsense and was nearing seventy when I first began my research.[10] Throughout his adult life he has acted as adviser and interpreter to generations of researchers stretching back to Isaac Schapera in 1936 and including Gary Okihiro, Tony Trail, Ed Wilmsen, Helga Vierich, Jeff Ramsay, myself, and many others from all over the world. Without his assistance as translator and adviser our research would not have been possible.

It was Mr. Masimega who, with the help of tribal administration (representing the personnel associated with the chief's kgotla), arranged for me to meet with members of the various communities and local people throughout the village, acquainted them with the research and enlisted their support and comments on the kinds of issues that arose in a public forum, and gained permission for me to observe them at work in the handling of disputes. At public discussions women would voice their opinion, but they almost never participated vocally when a dispute was in progress (unless they were a party to it). When it came to family matters, the overwhelming response was that the major issue that arose concerned support for women left with dependent children. It was this issue that local people adamantly insisted "creates tension amongst us as a people" and "causes us a headache." Beginning our research at the local level, Mr. Masimega and I worked our way up to the more formal legal institutions such as the chief's kgotla (in Kgosing ward)[11] and the magistrate's court, where written records (in the official languages of Setswana and English) are kept.[12] We were able to review the records of a ten-year period beginning with 1972 to see what the pattern of cases (including both criminal and civil matters) in general, and in particular the pattern of family cases, had been over the years (see A. Griffiths 1988b).

At this point, the research focused on acquiring knowledge of families' problems in everyday life and how these were dealt with in terms of formal legal institutions. Inevitably, this involved a study of cases and disputes, which provided a main source of data. When I returned to Edinburgh at the end of the research period in 1982, I came into contact with Adam Kuper and Simon Roberts,[13] who paved the way for me to meet Isaac Schapera. Another research visit to Botswana was planned for 1984, in order to do a more detailed study of everyday life and to collect life histories from members of one social unit in the village, Mosotho kgotla. Isaac Schapera very generously provided me with his unpublished field notes on Bakwena. These came as a surprise, as most people were unaware that these notes existed: they had been acquired too late to be included in *A Handbook of Tswana Law and Custom*.

These notes included genealogies which enabled Mr. Masimega and me to trace back the descent of people present in a kgotla from 1984 to 1937. Mosotho kgotla was chosen for this part of the research because it was easily accessible, forming part of Kgosing and close to where we would be following up on the disputes attended in 1982 and updating case records. The headman of the kgotla, Tshenolo, was ready to make himself available during the research period (June–August) together with other kgotla members who were willing to participate in the process of collating their life histories.

Perceived initially as a means for providing the background in which my material on disputes could be placed in context, the life histories of these kgotla members have become more central to my analysis over time, as I have come to appreciate the role they play in shaping the context in which people structure and pursue negotiations and claims or, alternatively, desist from doing so. That is why, in this book, they play a central role in the account of people's access to, and use of, law. These life histories were updated in 1989 when I made another research visit (July–September). On this occasion Mr. Masimega and I also took the opportunity to follow up on what had happened to individuals, disputants, and personnel from previous research periods. In this way, we were able to develop a longitudinal perspective on the research stretching over eight years, thus providing a picture of continuity and change across two generations as well as highlighting the differences between and within the sexes.

During the course of these research visits, people responded to my presence in various ways. Some, knowing of my links with the University of Botswana and the capital city, were suspicious of me on the assumption that I was a government spy. Others welcomed me because of those links: they thought that I had influence and could go back to Gaborone and tell government officials that they should respect and support the kgotla system. Some wondered why a young "girl" like myself had any interest in pursuing these questions. In general, however, people were receptive and open to the discussions that took place. Mr. Masimega and I became familiar figures, walking around the village, and when I returned in 1984 and 1989 no surprise was expressed at my reappearance. We were able to take up where we had left off (sometimes followed by comments such as "There goes the old man again with his shadow"). It is out of these encounters that I present the narratives on procreation, marriage, and law.

ACKNOWLEDGMENTS

Over the years many people and institutions have generously assisted me in my research and with the drafting of this manuscript. Without their ongoing support and encouragement I would not have been able to write this book. I would like to thank all those engaged in this project and, in particular, Mr. S. G. Masimega and all the members of Mosotho kgotla and the village of Molepolole, Ra Tshitoeng Mere, Ra Tshenolo Mere, Ra Motlotlegi Koosimile, Ma Goitsemang Mhiemang, Ma Same Moreri, Ma Diane Moreri, and Ra Herman Masimega (who assisted in the collection of part of the research data). A special word of thanks must go to the members of Bakwena Tribal Administration and to those associated with the District Commissioner's Office and the Magistrate's Court in Molepolole who so generously provided assistance, gave of their time, and made their facilities available for the research, especially Mr. Mac Sechele, Mr. E. K. Sebele, Mr. K. K. Sebele, Mr. Kgosiensho, Mr. P. K. M. Sechele, Mr. Gosalamang, Mr. Diseko, Mr. Roland, Mr. Sekga, and Fannah. Without the support of the Government of Botswana, and in particular of the Ministry of Local Government and Lands, the Commissioner of Customary Courts, the Attorney General's Office, the Office of the President, and the Women's Unit attached to the Ministry of Home Affairs the research would not have been possible, and I am particularly indebted to Kgosi Linchwe II, Mr. Lekgwaiele, Mr. Seboni, Mr. Manga, Mr. Showa, Mr. Kgakole, Mr. Nyathi, Steven Turner, Elsie Alexander, Carol Kerven, Nomtuse Mbere, and Joyce Armstrong for providing me with their knowledge and expertise. I am also grateful for the ongoing support and encouragement that I have received over the years from the University of Botswana and from colleagues and students in the Law Department, particularly Dr. Athaliah Molokomme and Dr. Peter Takirrambudde, who have unstintingly provided me with resources and the benefits of their expert knowledge, as well as research assistants Moupi and Doreen Galetshogethe, who assisted me with part of the collection of data and provided some translation services. I would also like to thank librarians Pat Span and Dr. Kay Raseroka for unfailing assistance in tracking down sources in the library and the National Institute for Development Research and Dr. Ulla Khan for making current research on Botswana available to me.

A number of people have not only provided moral support and encouragement but also given invaluable practical assistance by offering accommodation and transport and by taking pictures and acquiring maps, and I would especially like to thank Doreen and Impoeng Khama, Mrs. Sechele, Alfred and Mary Merriweather, Janis Mullan, John Grierson, Lulu Tobo, Victor Cumming, Diane Marshall, Ozi Nkabinde, and Marianne Enge for all that they have done for me.

I would also like to thank the following individuals, friends, and colleagues who have contributed to the development of the manuscript in its various forms: Isaac Schapera, Simon Roberts, Franz and Keebet von Benda-Beckmann, Gordon Woodman, Adam Kuper, John Comaroff, Karen Hansen, Peter Fitzpatrick, Harald Finkler, Fons Strijbosch, Beverley Brown, Carol Greenhouse, Rick Abel, Fran Olsen, Gay Seidman, Peter Goodrich, Niki Lacey, Anne Bottomley, Peter Young, Jane Connors, Peter Slynn, Simon Coldham, James Read, Costas Douzinas, Anne Hellum, Hannah Petersen, Judith Okely, David William Cohen, William Felstiner, John Eekelarr, Mavis Maclean, Robert Dingwall, Marsali Cameron, Ruth Stewart, and my colleagues in the Faculty of Law and at the Centre for African Studies at Edinburgh University.

I am indebted to the following institutions and grant-awarding bodies for providing the financial assistance that made it possible to undertake the research and to complete this manuscript: the British Academy, the Leverhulme Trust, the Social Science and Research Council (now Economic and Social Science Research Council), the Commonwealth Foundation, the British Council, the Carnegie Trust, the Commonwealth Secretariat—Women and Development, the Centre for Socio-Legal Studies, Wolfson College, Oxford, the American Bar Foundation, the Program on International Cooperation in Africa at Northwestern University, the British Federation of University Women, the International Federation of University Women, the London School of Economics and Political Science, the University of Texas at Austin, and, at Edinburgh University, the Hayter Foundation, the Tweedie Exploration Fellowship, and the University Travel and Research Committee.

I would also like to thank my editors, David Brent, Erik Carlson, and Matt Howard, and all the staff at the University of Chicago Press for their strong support and guidance in seeing this work to completion.

Finally, I would like to thank my mother, Joan Ord Griffiths, and my late father, Harold W. C. Griffiths, for their unqualified support and assistance during this project, and my husband, Ed Wilmsen, for his unfailing patience, encouragement, and dedication in reading and commenting on countless drafts of the manuscript.

ONE

*Academic Narratives: Models and Methods in the
Search for Meanings*

This book addresses the question of women's procreative relationships with men and their access to family law in Botswana. It examines the role that marriage plays in the social construction of such relationships and the ways in which marital status affects the kinds of claims that women pursue with respect to their male partners. Such claims—which include compensation for pregnancy, maintenance, and rights to property—operate at both social and legal levels. They revolve around the links that exist between gender, procreation, and marriage and their relationship with one another. These issues are common to both social and legal studies which are concerned with the construction and regulation of family life. My study underlines the social contexts within which these claims arise. This has particular implications for women, given the gendered nature of the social world with which they are faced in Botswana. In addition, the study analyzes the impact that these social contexts have on an individual's (especially a woman's) ability to access and manipulate a legal system which incorporates Tswana customary and European law. This raises issues about legal identity which revolve around the colonial/postcolonial dimension of law and how it is played out in terms of national, regional, and local domains.

My analysis is based on an ethnographic study carried out in one area over a number of years (1982–89), which is grounded in everyday life and ordinary people's perceptions and experiences of their social and legal universe. The narrative and interpretive form of this book, drawn from detailed life histories and extended case studies, highlights the gendered world in which women and men live and how this affects women's access to law. Access to resources (including family histories) plays a key role in constructing different forms of power which affect individuals' abilities to negotiate with one another and the types of discourse they employ. Such power informs the kinds of claims that women and men can make on one another in both social and legal terms. Given the gendered nature of the world from which such power derives, this creates challenges for women which extend to their use of both Tswana customary and European law. In marking what these challenges entail, my form of analysis not only undermines any remnants of the old model of legal pluralism based on distinctions drawn between customary and European law but forms part of wider feminist critiques of law.

In this book, links are made between legal and social identities. These derive from an analysis of power which is not limited to the study of formal legal institutions, officeholders, or disputes but is grounded in everyday life. How individuals are situated in networks of kinship, family, and community and the features which affect their position within material and symbolic hierarchies is crucial. Such elements form some of the multiple ways in which individuals are inscribed. As such, they have an impact on the forms of expression or types of discourse that individuals employ and that affect their ability to negotiate status and to articulate claims with respect to one another.

This kind of analysis not only highlights the circumstances under which people do or do not have access to legal forums, but also accounts more generally for the conditions under which individuals find themselves silenced or unable to negotiate with others in terms of day-to-day social life. Such an analysis also provides for diverse accounts of power relations, not only between but within the sexes. However, an understanding of what gives rise to power in Botswana and how it operates is particularly significant for women, due to the gendered environment on which social and legal practices rest.

The issues of identity, gender, and power are raised in the context of my research in Molepolole. Moreover, these issues form part of a broader set of theoretical concerns that involve ongoing debates within legal and feminist theory. The book presents and analyzes the results of the ethnographic study within the framework of a number of more general theoretical questions. These questions concern the relationship between gender and power and how this relates to law and legal pluralism.

FAMILIES AND MARRIAGE

These broader debates are situated within discussions on familial relations. Both law and the social studies have stressed the importance of marriage in this context. This raises questions about the significance of marriage, not only in empirical terms, but also from an ideological perspective. With respect to Tswana polities there is a long and distinguished tradition of scholarship on this subject, dating back to Botswana's colonial past as a British Protectorate (1885–1966), involving lawyers and anthropologists such as Schapera, Kuper, the Comaroffs, and Roberts. Their work has, however, focused exclusively on one aspect of marriage, that is, marriage in terms of mekgwa le melao ya Setswana, often referred to as Tswana law and custom or customary law. According to John Comaroff (personal communication, 14 July 1994), much of Comaroff and Roberts's marriage data referred to in their book *Rules and Processes* (1981) derived from his research material, which was gathered mainly in South Africa between 1965 and 1975. At that time most people did not go to official churches or to the Bantu Commissioners to get married, for a whole range of reasons including political and economic concerns. As these types of formal marriages were in practice virtually nonexistent among Africans in practice, Comaroff and Roberts ignored them in their discussion of marriage and dispute processing.

But under the formal legal system of Botswana, individuals have a choice as to how they marry, which includes but is not restricted to customary law. Another option under the Marriage Act [Cap.29:01] is registration of civil as well as religious marriages. My research shows that a significant number of persons opt for marriage under this act, which has legal repercussions, especially where divorce is concerned. Yet my research, like that of a number of contemporary studies in Botswana (Kocken and Uhlenbeck 1980:53; Molenaar 1980:12; Molokomme 1991:1; see A. Griffiths 1989a:587), also notes a growing gap between the incidence of pregnancy and the marriage rate along with a corresponding increase in the numbers of unmarried women with children. This was something that Schapera (1933) commented on as early as the 1930s while at the same time continuing to place marriage at the center of his discussion on family life (Schapera [1940] 1955:225). This raises the issue of how far marriage continues to have preeminence in family life today.

My study is the first ethnography of its kind to handle procreative relationships and marriage within a framework which incorporates customary and statutory law. As such it adds a new dimension to earlier work in that it addresses issues which are pertinent to the postcolonial state, not only of the nature of the formal legal system but also of the role that gender plays in providing access to law. On an empirical level, my data document a whole range of relationships involving procreation. Marriages are in the minority among all such relationships. But this is not to say that marriage is not a powerful force, for at an ideological level it provides the frame of reference in terms of which individuals' relationships are characterized—by the partners themselves as well as others—at any moment, particularly where law is concerned.

The ideological power of marriage is uniformly acknowledged (Schapera 1963a, 1963b; Kuper 1975a; J. L. Comaroff 1980; Roberts 1977a; Comaroff and Roberts 1981), but there is dissension over the form that marriage takes and how it operates with regard to the relationship between rules and processes. Leaving aside such issues for the moment, what is accepted as common ground among these scholars is an account of kinship and marriage based on a certain set of marriage strategies aimed at establishing particular forms of alliance and generating access to or the consolidation of resources. Such strategies encompass both royalty (Schapera 1963a) or politically prominent family groups (Comaroff and Roberts 1981:58) and commoners (Schapera 1963b) or less politically prominent members of society (Comaroff and Roberts 1981:58). With kinship operating in the past as the sole, or at least principal, matrix for social, political, and economic relations, marriage assumed an importance not only for elites within a social group but also for more economically successful if less politically prominent commoners. For this reason marriage took place not only among members of the same social group but between groups.

The ideological component of marriage strategies is derived from a concept of the household founded on male and female linkages, represented by the principles of agnation and matrilaterality, which were used to define the Tswana social world. In this world marriage played a central role in the construction of male and female linkages which came to be invested with symbolic attributes. These attributes were gendered in the sense that networks constructed through men, in terms of agnation, were characterized as hostile, assertive, and competitive relations embodied in the public sphere. In contrast, networks constructed through women, in terms of matrilaterality, were characterized as nurturing, supportive, and nonaggressive sets of relations which operated in the private domain.

This account of social relations is one that depicts a male-centered universe where women's only purpose is to create links in a set of relations that are primarily formulated around men and male access to power. My data endorse this view at one level and contest it at another through the narratives that women present of their encounters in daily life and in disputes. Their narratives highlight the ideological power that this construct of social life continues to wield (with material repercussions) especially with regard to law, while at the same time challenging the foundations upon which it is based.

Such narratives are in tune with a feminist critique of this type of analysis of social life, one which situates men within the public domain of law and politics and women within the private domain of the family (see Fineman 1983; MacKinnon 1983; Minow 1986; O'Donovan 1985; Okin 1989; Olsen 1983; Pateman 1988; Petersen 1992; and Smart 1984). Feminists argue that it is precisely the way in which these two domains intersect that creates the conditions under which men acquire the power that they do, to the detriment of women. A key element here is the sexual division of labor that operates to characterize women's activities—much of which involves unremunerated domestic and reproductive services—in a different manner from those of men, as belonging to the private, internal world of the household associated with the domain of the family. Thus, women's labor, although essential to the maintenance of the family as a unit, becomes perceived in a different way from that of men, both within the family itself and by the external world. Yet feminist scholars (Oppong 1994; Goldschmidt-Clermont 1994; Delphy and Leonard 1992; H. Moore 1988; Harris 1981; Robertson 1991; Vaughan 1985) argue that such perceptions are due to the subordinate status and value accorded to women's work, which are derived from the position that women occupy within the family. So gender inequality within the family comes to be reproduced in the world at large, for the composition of families and the organization of households in which they live have direct impact on women's ability to gain access to resources on which power depends.

For these reasons feminists are critical of analyses that underline a separation between public and private and between male and female domains. Such a formulation creates demarcated and bounded zones that are viewed as mutually exclusive rather than focusing on the multiple links between public and private spheres which render them inseparable in social life. Only by making these links explicit is the role of gender in the lives of women and men made visible. In the context of families and households the relationship between members is not defined by these units in and of themselves but in conjunction with the social, economic, and ideological relations that form part of the broader world to which they belong. Although gender intersects with a whole range of factors which come together to situate individuals in their negotiations with one another, it is one that consistently operates to place women at a disadvantage generally in their dealings with men, except in unusual circumstances. Such circumstances usually only exist where women are able to overcome the normal constraints that face them while their male counterparts are, correspondingly, unable to draw on those sources of support that would normally be available to them.

But while reality undermines any separation between public and private spheres, such a division with all its gendered attributes continues to have power as an ideological construct in Botswana, as it does elsewhere. The dominant male-centered perspective recorded by Schapera, Kuper, Comaroff, and Roberts still operates to shape the contexts in which women's procreative relationships with men and marriage are negotiated. These are highlighted in chapters 4–7, which also document women's strategies for pursing their own interests and their attempts to resist or shift the terms of the dominant discourse.

Legal Analysis: Contested Accounts

Kwena accounts of the role that marriage plays in social relations support those presented by Comaroff and Roberts (1981), which stress the inherently fluid nature of social bonds that renders them open to interpretation in a number of ways. They endorse Comaroff and Roberts's interpretation of how marriage operates, an interpretation that gives rise to the dissension between Comaroff and Roberts and Schapera and Kuper that was referred to earlier. For while all of them agree on the ideological structure on which marriage strategies and preferential forms of marriage rest, they dispute the ways in which such strategies are embodied.

For Schapera and Kuper what is key is the rules that frame marriage preferences and that determine the choice of marriage partners. In their account, rules determine behavior so that the social actors follow a prescribed course of action. In focusing on a set of marriage rules as a blueprint for classifying social relations, they adopt a normative approach in tune with scholars such as Radcliffe-Brown (1950) and Fortes (1962). This normative approach is one that presents a somewhat static and bounded account of social relations. In contrast, the focus for Comaroff and Roberts lies with the social actors who use the rules as a resource and who manipulate them to construct the desired set of social relations at any moment in time.

The debates between Comaroff and Roberts and Schapera and Kuper have been aired extensively elsewhere and will not be repeated here, save to highlight the fact that what lies at the heart of their dispute is an analysis of the relationship that exists between rules and processes (Kuper 1970:466–82; Roberts 1977a:241–60; J. L. Comaroff 1980:161–95; Comaroff and Roberts 1981:17–18); Comaroff and Comaroff 1981: 129–49; Schapera 1983:141–49). Such debates on structure and agency form an ongoing aspect of the social sciences and of academic discussion. What is relevant here, however, is the extent to which the differing perspective of Comaroff and Roberts in contrast to Schapera and Kuper are grounded in divergent understandings of law, in this case mekgwa le melao ya Setswana, and its relationship with social life. Here the power of academic narratives must be acknowledged, for it informs the ways in which these (and all) scholars perceive law. The analysis favored by Schapera and Kuper—where rules determine behavior and outcomes, where rules are segregated in terms of social or legal affiliation, and where legal rules are invested with greater power and authority than social rules—adheres to a model of law that upholds legal centralism. It is this model of law that I along with other scholars (Abel 1973; Allott and Woodman 1985; Benda-Beckmann 1989; Collier and Starr 1989; Comaroff and Roberts 1981; Fitzpatrick 1984a, 1984b, 1985, 1991, 1992b; Galanter 1981; J. Griffiths 1986; Harrington and Yngvesson 1990; Lazarus-Black and Hirsch 1994; Merry 1988; Roberts 1979; Snyder 1980, 1981b, 1983; Sarat and Silbey 1987) contest.

Such a model establishes boundaries between legal and social domains and the rules associated with them. These domains exist in a hierarchical relationship to one another, so that the legal rules are not only set apart from social rules, but acquire greater authority than and precedence over them. Law, according to this model, is removed from the domain of social life and represents an autonomous field with immunity from the kind of considerations that permeate everyday existence. Through its autonomy and immunity from ordinary social processes, reinforced by the creation of specialist sources, institutions, and personnel, law claims to invoke neutrality and equality in its dealings with individuals, unlike the ordinary social world from which law studiously maintains its distance.

Economic and Social Transformations

Before turning to this issue, however, it is necessary to say something about the economic and social transformations which have their foundation in the colonial past and influence family life in Botswana today. They represent the prolonged contact that Tswana polities have had with Europeans in the nineteenth and twentieth centuries. This contact precipitated changes in the structure of such polities through the imposition of colonial overrule and Christianity, as well as the introduction of a cash economy and sustained participation in migrant labor over many years.(For a more detailed historical account of these transformations see Nangati 1982; Ncgoncgo 1982a, 1982b; Parsons 1977; Schapera 1938, 1943, 1947; Shillington 1985; and Tlou 1972, 1985.)

Many of these elements were already in existence prior to the British establishing colonial overrule through the founding of the Bechuanaland Protectorate in 1885. In the precolonial period migrant labor was already being practiced. Schapera noted that as early as 1844 Bakwena were working in the western Transvaal as farmhands employed by Boer Voortrekkers. When the Kimberley diamond mines opened in 1870, a number of Bakwena went to work there spurred on by the desire to acquire firearms. Schapera (1947:26) notes that in 1880 there were 2,135 Batswana at Kimberley, who were mainly Bakwena, Bakgatla, and Bangwato. Unlike in later years, those who engaged in such labor usually went for a limited period, sometimes only once, in order to acquire money for a plow or a wagon. The kgosi, who had the right to demand labor from the morafe, used migrant labor as a means of acquiring resources, as did Kgosi Lentswe, who sent a regiment of men to work on the Kimberley mines in the 1880s. Between 1878 and 1882 Kgosi Sechele annually sent over five hundred men to work at Kimberley and Du Toits Pan (Ramsay 1991:253).

By the 1940s, access to European goods and migrant labor had become consolidated to such an extent that Schapera (1947:8) commented: "The people have been drawn into an elaborate system of exchange economy, through which they are linked up with and even dependent upon the markets of the world. New commodities of many kinds have been introduced, many of which can be obtained only from traders and other external sources of supply. The acceptance of these goods has greatly extended the range of desirable acquisitions, and created new standards of wealth and social status. Money has also become established as the principal medium of exchange."

Dependence on wage labor had become established and created a situation where labor migration became a chronic pattern rather than something that was engaged in from time to time. Dependence on European imports, ecological constraints, and the need to meet newly imposed obligations by colonial administrators in cash, such as the hut tax established in 1899, contributed to the escalation in migration which set the context within which Kweneng, like many other African regions, acquired the status of a labor reserve (Ramsay 1991:242).

No other avenues for the acquisition of money were available for the majority of people. Agriculture was not a viable alternative because of its uncertain yields. Crops were dependent on rainfall and susceptible to drought. In addition, by the 1940s, even in a good year the agricultural sector could no longer sustain the population and imports were required (Schapera 1947:133). This continues to be the case today (Kerven 1982:543). In some areas there was a shortage of good arable land (Kooijman 1978:77), and even where this land existed there was often no surplus to sell.

While cattle might be sold, they also were vulnerable to drought and disease, and in any case many people did not possess them in sufficient numbers for their sale to be a viable proposition. Schapera (1947:8–9) noted that in the 1940s people could not derive a secure livelihood from their environment and that with regard to cattle "nearly one family in every four is too poor in cattle to derive a regular annual income from stock farming, and that one family in every fourteen has no cattle at all" (Schapera 1947:133). This position with regard to cattle continues to exist today (Kerven 1982:549–50). Even where people were in a position to sell livestock, they were hampered in the export market by the South African restrictions on weight, in force from 1921 to 1941.

A combination of all these factors, including the restrictions placed on internal development (Parson 1981:239), the lack of infrastructure for marketing, and vulnerability to world economic fluctuations such as the great depression in the 1930s, contributed to the massive growth in migrant labor in which members of Tswana society from all social backgrounds participated (Schapera 1947:42). Such labor was required to meet the needs of a rapidly developing South Africa, which had been growing since the opening of the mines on the Witwatersrand in the 1880s.

Not all migrants went to South Africa or to work in the mines, notwithstanding that the majority, according to Schapera, went to the mines and were concentrated on the Witwatersrand (1947:49). Some men went to Zimbabwe (at the time, Southern Rhodesia) to work in the mines there or went to work on farms as agricultural laborers. Others found employment in an urban context in South Africa as laborers or municipal employees. Women, who were ineligible for mine recruitment, tended to work as domestic servants or as agricultural laborers, particularly in the western Transvaal. They tended to congregate in the urban and rural areas there or in Mafeking (Schapera 1947:69). Many of these women who went to urban areas made a living through illicit beer brewing or prostitution. However, while women did engage in migrant labor, it was not at the same scale as that of men (Schapera 1947:64).

While regional rates varied (Schapera 1947:70; Parsons 1977:124, 132), the overall numbers engaged in migrant labor had been steadily growing over the years until, by the 1940s, four times as many young men were involved than ten years previously (Schapera 1947:32). These recruitment levels were maintained into the early 1970s (Field 1982: 734). We can appreciate the impact when we realize that as many as 40% of men from the southeastern polities were estimated to be absent from the country at any one time (Schapera 1947:195). Of even greater significance was the fact that over nine-tenths of the migrants belonged to the able-bodied age group, 15–44 (Schapera 1947:71).

One effect of this labor migration was a severe reduction of male labor power in the rural areas. This led dikgosi (chiefs), who had previously been active in the recruitment process, to seek to constrain it. Initially supportive, sending groups of men to work to acquire cash for specific purposes like building schools as well as seeking to benefit from the imposed levy on returning migrants wages, they soon became concerned about the sheer numbers involved in the exodus, which depleted the local population and their traditional workforce. The Kwena Kgosi Kgari Sechele (1931–62), spoke for many in his position when he made an impassioned lament that "the tribe will gradually die, because the men who should build up the tribe are spending more and more time in the mines" (Minutes, N.A.C., 17 [1936], p. 63, cited in Schapera 1947:68).

The response to wage labor was one predicated upon economic necessity (Schapera 1947:121) rather than specific factors such as the need to raise bogadi (marriage payment) or money for tax or because of the shortage of arable land. It was already the case that by the 1940s "wage-labour has become an indispensable source of income for the people, generally, and, since opportunities in the Territory are limited, the vast majority go to the Union [South Africa] where there is a far greater demand for their services" (Schapera 1947:122).

The absorption into and dependence upon a cash economy had repercussions for all levels of society (Wylie 1991). Traditional structures of control and authority became subject to a new set of pressures, reflecting external as well as internal factors. Quite apart from dikgosi having their authority subject to the scrutiny of colonial administrators (outlined at the end of this chapter), the external demand for labor set up a new relationship in which a kgosi needed to renegotiate his position. At first active recruiters for such labor, they changed their attitude as they experienced their control over the adult population slipping. The absence of adult males for long periods of time not only depopulated tribal areas, it also altered the way in which people related to a kgosi's authority.

This concern for control extended to young boys and to women as dikgosi attempted to regulate their migration through a series of measures. These included pushing for adoption of a quota system (Schapera 1947:96) and having a representative at the railway station to check that any woman had her kgosi's permission to leave the area (Schapera 1947:90). These attempts to exert control, particularly over women, were a common phenomenon during this period in other African countries subject to colonial penetration (Channock 1985:145–60). This need to exert control was exacerbated as dikgosi found their powers being eroded by colonial authorities.

Transformations affecting the nature of authority were not only the concern of dikgosi. They also permeated family relationships. Schapera commented on the decline of parental authority, which he attributed in large part to a family's dependence on a cash income of some sort for its existence. This was generally acquired through wage labor which necessitated long periods of absence from home. Under such circumstances the nature of parental control altered as fathers or sons or both were absent from home. While seasonal migration meant family members were separated for periods of the year, this was for much shorter time spans than those encountered in migrant labor, where a minimum contract was nine months.

A new dynamic in family relationships was created by the need for and access to money. The fact that the sole cash earner might be a son or daughter placed parents in a different kind of relationship with their children. They had always been aware that they would be dependent on their children for support in old age, but their dependence became accentuated at an earlier stage when there were children working as wage laborers. A system of mutual dependence still existed, as those who were absent relied on those at home to look after their interests. They were still dependent on acquiring land and livestock and maintaining a home base, particularly when the application of pass laws made it impossible for them to settle permanently in South Africa.

While a wage earner remained dependent on a family network to oversee his interests, his direct control over cash put him in a more powerful position with regard to the older male members of his family than formerly, when all he controlled was his own labor. Acquisition of an asset from an external source contributed something new to the process of exchange in the family context, allowing relationships to be mediated in new ways. This brought its own tensions, with fathers complaining about their lack of authority over sons and brothers acting out the inherent tensions in families through conflicts over what was owed by the migrant to brothers who stayed behind to maintain a family base.

Working under a set of conditions which were external to the family domain provided individuals with new experiences, and in some cases both men and women used the option of wage labor to sever family ties and make a new start elsewhere (Schapera 1947:62).

However, despite these transformations involving the ongoing negotiation of authority and power, social relations continued to reflect the kinds of differential status that existed in the precolonial era. While some elites may have engaged in migrant labor, as Sebele II (1918–31) did before he was elected kgosi, and had to live with the kinds of restrictions placed on their authority by colonial administrators, they still maintained a dominant position over others in their constituency because there had been few changes in the basic political forms and processes or in control over key resources such as cattle and land (Parson 1981; Cooper 1979a). Other members of society who engaged in migrant labor for a source of income were nonetheless still dependent on existing structures because of the need to maintain and develop a home base. Since households could not be supported on the income from wages alone and there were restrictions on living in South Africa, it was essential to maintain an agricultural base. It was this base, predicated upon precolonial structures, which led migrant workers into having continuing "material and ideological affinity with the Tswana governing class" (Parson 1981:240). These workers, oscillating between migrant labor and their agricultural base, have come to be called the "peasantariat" (Parson 1981:240).

Impact on Families, Households, and Marriage

Within this broader picture, marriage was inevitably affected. As a result of sustained labor migration, with young adults, especially men, away had taken a year off to travel, for by then he would have received the first fifty-thousand dollars of a trust fund from his maternal grandfather.

It was during Martin's senior year at college, when he turned twenty-two, that he began to concentrate on just what he would do with the money. He decided that he wouldn't use it to travel through Europe, as his mother suggested, but to find a new home, a place where he could meet different people and perhaps become different himself. New York City seemed a logical place, and as soon as Martin graduated, collected his "reward money" as he thought of it, and said his rather muted good-byes to his parents, he moved there, renting a one-bedroom apartment on the Upper West side.

But he'd miscalculated his capacity to adapt. The pace was too fast for him, the crowds too big and impatient like nothing he could have imagined, and he began to have trouble sleeping. One night he had his blue sky dream and his father was one of the basketball players. His pencil mustache and toothy white smile were the last things Martin saw before he started his ascent in the sky.

When he couldn't sleep he'd try remembering his favorite moments from childhood, like the miniature golf game with his father, but they no longer seemed clear enough to recall or believe in as actual memories. Instead he'd find himself listening to the sounds of the city—random noises that seeped through his shut windows and scattered like insects. Martin very quickly became convinced he'd never sleep well, if at all, in New York and decided he had to move. But where? What he realized he wanted was to be near a friendly group of people, and he thought his chances would be better where the weather was warmer. He eliminated Miami Beach as having too many of the negative qualities of New York, but grew increasingly excited the more he read about California. Soon he supplemented his reading by watching as many movies or TV shows about it as he could. After a couple of more weeks he decided that California represented his best chance, and immediately he began trying to sublet his apartment. While that was being settled he thought carefully about what part of the state to move to before choosing a picturesque resort town eighty miles north of Los Angeles, named Santa Vista.

As soon as he got off the plane he rented a Toyota (which he eventually bought) and started driving through his new town. Martin was stunned by Santa Vista's beauty. With its backdrop of mountains, its palm trees on the beaches, and its exotic birds and flowers on every street, he felt its nickname of Paradise was scarcely exaggerated. The people of Santa Vista were unusually attractive, too, and not just the students at the university. Everyone around him seemed lean and fit—even Santa Vistan women in their sixties were still alluring.

There was something else he appreciated about the town, even more than its physical beauty. He felt a spirit of toleration in Santa Vista, a sense that he could look and behave the way he wanted without being judged deficient or even attracting attention.

After staying in a hotel for a few weeks, he rented a modest apartment whose flower-filled courtyards he grew to love. So far he had made no effort to make friends, but wasn't aware of wanting any. He enjoyed being alone and knowing that the spirit of the town was always around him. Shortly, he established a comfortable routine. He'd have breakfast at Audrey's where the working people of the town ate. He liked seeing the bus drivers and maintenance men before they went to work; their talk about sports, their loud laughter, even their cigarette smoke—a rarity in a Santa Vista restaurant—didn't bother him. In fact, it reassured him in a way he couldn't have explained. Sometimes when he wanted to be near older people, whom he also found comforting, he'd walk up State Street and have breakfast at the Copper Coffee Pot, a cafeteria that catered to residents from the senior citizen homes in the foothills.

After breakfast he tried to read for an hour, not wanting his mind to go slack now that he was out of college; then he'd walk into town and try to spend some time on his finances. He still didn't find it interesting but realized it was important to keep informed. He knew if he were prudent he might stretch his time out to two years before he'd have to get a job, and that, of course, was reassuring.

Generally, he had lunch at either the Presidio or The Bakery. The food was excellent at both places and so was the view of the mountains. Sometimes during lunch he wrote postcards to his parents. After lunch he'd walk down State Street two miles until he reached the town beach. There he'd walk left along the beach, spreading out his towel near a group of people—men as often as women—and listening to their conversation. He was not hoping to join them nor was he listening to the details of their lives. It was that Santa Vistan tone he wanted to hear wafting up to him on a light wind, reminding him that things were going smoothly in his town. Once the people he listened to were lovers so the tone was even sweeter, and he wound up listening to them for hours.

That night Martin dreamt he was alone on the beach flying a blue kite. He ran up and down a series of sand dunes, the kite a hundred feet up in the blue sky. Then suddenly the beach flattened, the dunes disappeared. When he looked again he was in the air a hundred feet or higher in a sky of chalk. The kite, which was now also white, had tricked him. Held down by a heavy rock, it was flying him.

Martin woke up trembling. It was more frightening than the basketball dream, and after thinking about it, Martin decided he needed more human contact in his nights. No longer would he cook for himself; instead he would go out to Chez Charlotte where there were exquisite chicken crepes and some of the most glamorous people in Santa Vista eating them, or else to the Copper Coffee Pot where he could listen to the old people. Then he'd rent a new movie each night to play on his VCR before falling asleep.

For a week his new schedule worked well, until the afternoon when he sat near two lovers on the beach again. This time he looked at them long enough to see they were both blond—he in a white bikini, she in one of those light brown suits that only covered her nipples and the dividing line of her rear end. Apparently oblivious to Martin, who was less than ten feet away, they were talking in normal voices about the things they were going to do to each other in bed as soon as they got home.

On his way home that day Martin worried about not sleeping, which would inevitably mean late-night memories (or attempts at memories) of his old life in Newport. Martin decided to help his chances by going to the video store and renting one of his favorite movies, *Starting Over*, that he'd seen perhaps fifteen times. It was a Burt Reynolds comedy—his best movie, in Martin's opinion—about a fortyish man who unexpectedly falls in love again shortly after his divorce. It had a very happy ending.

Martin made some popcorn and lemonade to have during the movie, but when it ended he still wasn't tired so he turned on TV. There were a number of adult phone ads on, and he found himself transfixed by the woman on the "Hot Talk" ad who invited people to call her anytime by a swimming pool where she wasn't wearing much more than the blonde woman he'd seen that afternoon on the beach. When he eventually closed his eyes he saw a kind of composite image of the woman in the phone ad and the woman on the beach shimmering in front of him, making it impossible to sleep. He thought it was because he hadn't had sex with anyone in so long; in fact, in his whole life he'd done it only twice. Each time it was with a woman from an escort service who'd come to his home while his parents were away visiting relatives. On a Friday night, shortly before Martin's own trip to New York, he had called the service and done it for the first time, after several false starts, with one woman, and the next night, still alone in the house, he'd called the service again and slept with a second woman.

Now he decided he couldn't wait any longer. But the situation was complicated since as far as he knew Santa Vista had no prostitutes—indeed, it didn't even have a slum. That meant he'd have to go to L.A., which he dreaded, and do it there. But with no chance of sleep there was little point in postponing things, so Martin got in his Toyota and drove to Los Angeles, finally stopping to check in at a Motel 6 in Hollywood.

He started walking around Sunset Boulevard but discovered the prostitutes there were suspicious of pedestrians, and after one openly accused him of being a cop he went to his car and finally picked up a woman who approached him. She was a blonde of indeterminate age, named Candy, who wore a ridiculously short pink skirt. She tried to talk him into doing it in the car (no doubt so she could get out on the street faster), but Martin insisted on the motel room. He wanted to simulate, as much as possible, what he imagined a normal couple would do.

After it was over it seemed to be something that his body had done automatically, like drinking a glass of water, and he figured that Candy probably felt the same way, though she was kind enough to pretend it was much more exciting than that—and pretend so well that he couldn't actually be sure how much she'd enjoyed it.

"Hey, you look like you're trying to figure out if you had a good time or not," she said, as she was putting on her pink quasi-transparent bra.

Martin turned away and blushed slightly. "I had a wonderful time." Then he handed her an extra ten dollars, which won him a compliment, as she immediately put it in an opening in her stockings.

"Where will you be tomorrow night?" he said.

"Same place, same corner. Hope I see you there."

But when he returned the next night she wasn't there. He waited until 1:30, then picked up a black woman named Valerie. She wore a bright red dress but seemed tired, and Martin thought she was probably on some drug. He took her to the same room in Motel 6 he'd used the night before and began to undress.

"What you want, man?" she said, standing in her outfit by the door like a guard at a movie turnstile.

Martin shrugged, "Just the regular."

"Regular what? You want to screw me, mister?"

"Yes," he said softly.

"Then pay me now. You got to pay me 'fore I take my clothes off, see? That's fifty bucks, mister."

It had been different with Candy, but Martin complied. While they were in bed he tried to kiss Valerie, but she turned her head away.

"Mister, I don't kiss clients. Just keep grinding an' you'll be done soon."

It was funny, her eyes looked tired, but her voice was strong. Martin closed his own eyes, did what she said, and thanked her when it was over.

Once in his car he thought how doubly absurd it was that she should feel nothing, too. He was on the highway heading back to Santa Vista thinking that the whole world of hookers and their clients was a web of illusion spun out over and over by the mutually addicted. He passed Malibu and Carpinteria. He noticed the stars were shining over the water. Then, as if his dream were happening to him while he was awake, he started to feel his weight leaving him, and he pulled over to the soft shoulder as fast as he could. Why was this happening to him? What did it mean? He tried to remember Candy, as if that might help him feel his body, but he couldn't, nor could he recall anything but the most fleeting image of Valerie. He closed his eyes, gripping the steering wheel for support, and saw an image of his stiff corpse-like father drinking and his mother crying on the couch. Was it because of them? But at least they had provided for him in some sense, he thought, whereas he paid only for his own existence, since he had no one else in it, of course. Maybe it was wrong to look to the past for help. Perhaps he should direct everything toward the future and do something worthwhile in Santa Vista. But when he thought of the town with its restaurants and banks and shining harbor he was afraid he would remain weightless there as well.

While he stayed parked gripping the wheel, cars whizzed by him, their lights roaring away from L.A. Martin's thoughts returned to the streets and the prostitutes. He had gone there for pleasure but his whole purpose may have been wrong. Gradually he got an idea about what he could do differently and how Santa Vista could still be put to good use. As he thought about it his weight slowly returned to him, it seemed about a pound per second. By the time his idea had become a conviction he felt solid, and he turned his car around and drove back to Hollywood.

. . . .

He backed up and headed down another side street off Sunset Boulevard. How many had turned him down? Five? Six? He'd have to be more emphatic in his approach next time. He turned onto Hollywood Boulevard. For fifteen minutes there was no one, just the lights coming out of the dark.

Then he pulled up beside a skinny blonde wearing a half-buttoned red jump suit so bright her pale face seemed to almost disappear.

"Can I talk to you?"

"What about?"

He thought she couldn't be older than sixteen, despite her heavy makeup, and maybe was younger than that.

"How'd you like to get out of here?"

"Depends. How much you got to spend?"

"I have a home in Santa Vista where you can stay."

"My meter says that's about one-fifty."

"You don't understand."

"Oh, really?"

"I'm offering you my apartment to live in."

"Great. Can I sell it?"

"I don't want anything in return."

"You into kidnapping? That's very expensive."

"I'm trying to help you. Really. Give you a chance to get off the street and start a new life."

For a moment she looked at him quizzically. The rest of her face had disappeared so he only saw her two green eyes that sparkled unnaturally.

"Yeah, well thanks, but no thanks," she said walking away from his car. He watched her moving ghost-like down the dark block, then opened his car door and yelled, "You'll die if you stay on the streets, you'll get AIDS and die."

"I'll die sooner if I stay with you," came the disembodied reply.

"Jesus Christ," he hissed and pounded his fist on the dashboard.

He drove down the rest of the block, saw no one, got onto Sunset, and drove down it a few miles and began to think that maybe it was too late now. He passed Hollywood High School and had slowed down to look at it, when a girl with a desperate face suddenly knocked on his window signaling him to let her in. Martin immediately opened the door. She was wearing a black miniskirt and a gold silk shirt tied together in a knot to hide a bad rip. She had long, fluffed-out, black hair and large eyes that looked frightened and were badly streaked with makeup.

"Start driving, okay?"

"What's the matter?" he said, but the girl was twisted around in her seat looking out the rear window and didn't answer him. Martin drove down Sunset looking for the exit that would lead to Santa Vista.

He drove a couple of miles without talking or even looking at the girl, who was still periodically staring at the road behind him.

"You wanna date?" she said, finally turning around and half looking at him.

"No, thanks."

"Mind if I just ride with you a few more miles, maybe you'll change your mind."

"Sure, you can ride. I'm going to Santa Vista."

She didn't answer him. She was fidgeting with her shirt, then with her makeup.

"You in some kind of trouble?"

"Yeah, you could say that."

"Somebody after you?"

"Maybe. Yeah, somebody just tried to break my bones actually. So you want a date or what?"

Martin sneaked a look at her and noticed a cut below her left eye that she'd tried to camouflage with makeup.

"No, I don't want a date."

"Great. Are you a cop? Tell me you're a cop, it'll make my night complete."

Martin smiled. "I'm not a cop." He had turned off the exit and was now on the highway heading north.

"Well, thanks for the ride, but how about letting me out now?"

"I'm on a highway. I can't let you out on the highway."

"Sure you can."

"Is that what you want?"

"I don't want to fight you, okay. I just had one, you know? I don't want trouble. Just let me out of the fucking car, okay?"

"Calm down, will you?"

"It's not about calming down. It's about me getting out of the fucking car."

"You have to calm down first and talk to me for a couple of minutes, that's all I ask."

"Talk is free, ain't it? I don't like free."

"Don't worry. I'll give you money. I've got cash."

"I already asked you if you wanted a date."

"You're missing the point. You came to me. You made a decision to put me in your life."

"Okay. You did me a favor." She turned to him and pretended to assess his looks. "You're kind of cute. I'll give you half price."

"You're still missing the point."

"There is no point. What, you want it free? Okay. Give me some Valium or something, you can have it free. Just pull over now, okay? I ain't got all night."

"Look, let's just talk a minute. My name is Martin."

"Terrific. My name's Martina."

"Really?"

"Whatever. I ain't got no time for this."

"You did involve me in your life. You have to admit that. And now that I'm involved I'm responsible, and I can't leave you on a highway at 4:00 in the morning 'cause there's a lot of dangerous people out there, as you well know. And no matter how tough you talk you could get hurt. You're no older than seventeen, are you?"

"Are you some kind of census taker, or maybe you're one of the dangerous people yourself."

"Not at all. I'm a nice person, or I want to be."

"So what nice thing are you planning to do, Martin? Do you have a nice house you want to take me to?"

"Pretty nice, yeah. It's an apartment."

"So what do you want to do in this pretty nice apartment? You planning to slice up my bones into little bite-sized pieces?"

"What are you talking about? It's a place where you can stay tonight."

"Oh, yeah. Where is this place?"

"Santa Vista."

"And how'm I gonna get back, Martin? You wouldn't want me to ride on a stinking bus or have to hitchhike back to L.A., would you?"

"You can stay as long as you want. You don't have to go back to L.A."

"I get it. Steal the bitch. Then jump the bitch's bones. Then cook the bitch. Hey, Martin, I'll jump out of the fucking car now and take my chances with the traffic. I mean it. I'm in no mood."

"Calm down, will you? Look, you're obviously very upset. I'll get off at the first exit and we'll go to a motel or whatever. I'll pay for you to have your own room, give you the key. I'll stay in a different room. In the morning, I'll drive you back, if that's what you want. How's that sound?"

"Fine," she said dully. She seemed to have calmed down but he couldn't be sure. They rode the next twenty minutes in silence. When he turned off on the exit to Carpinteria, she asked a few questions about him and that made him feel good and increasingly sure he'd made a wise decision.

At the Carpinteria Motor Inn he did exactly as he said he would, charging the two different rooms on his Visa card. He handed her the key and she told him he was a real sweet guy. He said that he was three doors away and that in the morning he'd give her a ride either back to L.A. or to his apartment in Santa Vista.

"I hope you'll choose Santa Vista," he said.

She smiled and said maybe she would. Then she opened her door, and he waved good-bye and went to his room.

It was a standard motel room with a shower. He thought about taking one but decided he was too tired. He knew he would have no trouble sleeping, feeling he had already accomplished something by driving Martina to a safe place. He folded his shirt and pants on the chair in front of the desk, and got under the covers.

But fifteen minutes later there was a knock on his door.

"It's me—Martina. Can I come in?"

"Sure, just a second." He put his shirt on and opened the door. She looked away from him as she walked toward the window.

"I couldn't sleep. I kept thinking about the guy that went off on me."

"Would you like to stay here?"

She sat down on the side of the bed. "I don't want to do anything, okay? Just lie down for a while till I calm down, then I'm going back to my room. All right?"

"Sure, pick a side," Martin said, pointing to the bed. She lay down on the side nearest the door, and Martin, feeling he had won a little victory, made sure their bodies didn't touch as he lay down facing the window.

"It's weird to think how many creepy people there are, you know," she said suddenly. Martin thought of his parents and winced. "I know," he said, but to himself he was thinking that he only felt sorry for his parents now. He was feeling strong and more positive inside.

"Creep streets, every one of 'em filled with creeps . . . make cockroaches look like princes . . . make maggots look like kings. My father hit me, you know, when I was growing up and I came here and now this stranger, this black mother, beats on me . . . some progress, huh?"

"You can stay at my place in Santa Vista. You'll be safe there."

"Maybe I should. I mean what's L.A. got to offer me? So . . . what's it like in Santa Vista?"

Martin felt his heart beat. He described as accurately as he could the harbor and beach, the restaurants with the view of the mountains, and the shops on State Street.

"Sounds pretty amazing. But why'd you want me staying at your place? Don't you have no girlfriend?"

"No, there's no girlfriend. So why should I have that place all to myself when I can share it with someone who could use it, like you?"

"Gee, that's really nice, Marty. But I still have trouble believing you don't have at least one little girlfriend stashed away in Santa Vista."

"No, really."

"'Cause you're an attractive man. When you let me in I couldn't help noticing you got great legs."

Martin mumbled a thank you and felt himself blush, then realized she probably couldn't see him in the dark.

"Hey Marty, you use the shower here yet?"

"No, should I? Do I smell funny?"

"You smell real good. I mentioned it because it's a really fabulous shower. You can vary the water pressure, you know. Personally I like it really hard; it felt great on my body. Made it all tingly."

"I'll take one first thing in the morning."

"Between that shower and seeing your legs, I'm having trouble keeping my hands off you."

"You don't have to."

"Don't tempt me, but I think I ought to take things slow with you at first. See what things are like in Santa Vista."

"If you don't like it, I'll drive you back to L.A."

"Sounds real good, Marty," she said, leaning over and kissing him on the cheek. Martin smiled and squeezed her hand. "But let's sleep on it. I'm gonna go back to my room to sleep 'cause you're starting to excite me too much and I don't want to do something I'll regret later. But can I just lie here for a while before I go?"

"Of course," he said. He wanted to sleep himself and was still sure he'd have little trouble doing it. Positive things were definitely happening. He thought that she couldn't help but like the town and that she'd end up staying—that this could well be a turning point in both their lives, although they didn't know it now.

Martin fell asleep easily and dreamed he was lying in the midst of a group of large jagged rocks that the sea slapped against relentlessly. He was wearing a bathing suit and the sun felt good on his stomach, making him feel cared for, in a strange way, and remarkably satisfied.

A noise completely foreign to the dream he was having woke him up. Martina was by the chair where his pants were.

"What are you doing?" he said, although he knew that she was robbing him and a part of him had always known she would.

"Nothing. Getting some Kleenex."

He thought of simply letting her take the money but his sense of fairness wouldn't allow it. He turned on the bed light and she let out a short hollow scream, her face looking shocked in the sudden light like a Halloween mask. She had been stuffing his money into an opening in her stockings.

He stood up and Martina screamed again. "What you gonna do? You gonna kill me for taking some of your stinking creep money?"

She was trying to backpedal toward the door but tripped and fell to the floor.

"Come on and kill me Creep King. I fell, so here's your chance."

She stood up awkwardly and glared at him, half in rage, half in terror.

"I'm not gonna do anything," Martin said softly. "Take a hundred and leave the rest, okay?"

"The rich fucking creep saint has spoken! 'Take a hundred,' he says. You gotta always feel superior, right? You gotta always win. Here," she said, throwing two fifties at him and running out the door with two hundred dollars.

He didn't chase her. He didn't even pick up the money, just stared at the bills which looked like two dead lizards on the floor.

· · · · · · · · ·

He never knew how much time had passed before he went to the window. Nor did he have any idea what time it was when he lifted the blinds, only that it was mostly black out and that the light he did see came from stores or passing cars.

While he waited he went over everything that had happened between them, and all the words they had said to each other. In particular, he reviewed the last fight a number of times. He thought that if he had meant nothing to her and she just wanted his money, she wouldn't have bothered insulting him. He felt that he had touched something in her and that her anger was proof of it. What happened between them was therefore authentic in its own mysterious way.

He didn't know how long he stayed at the windows that night, either, only that he was never tempted to leave or even to sleep. The sky broke blue quickly, the sun shone out strong over the smog. He was surprised that a tear fell down his face, but let it fall. He kept looking up into the shining blue sky thinking that he had won something, that distorted and brief as it was he had had his first sip of love and so could remember everything that had happened with Martina and look at the sky and not feel weightless. That he, Martin, at twenty-two, had finally created a durable memory, and there was little chance now that it would ever leave him.

·················

GHOST PARKS

His wife, Ellen, had yelled at him, then left to go to work at the museum, somehow implying that he, too, should work on Saturdays to better himself. She thought nothing of his current job, that was obvious. Selling disgusted her. It disgusted him, too, but he couldn't see any real difference between her job and his (wasn't she selling herself everyday to her bosses?), so why criticize? And why yell? She made him feel seven years old again, trembling with rage as if before his mother. Why did he put up with this? He felt he was getting so old now; he was already past thirty and he was still being yelled at by his wife. It was ridiculous, but there it was.

Andy paced in front of the picture window. Outside the sky was almost insanely bright. He looked down repeatedly at the elementary school playground where the basketball court was, but no one was on it. It was cold and he could hear the wind, but the court looked good in the strong sunlight.

There was a line, Andy thought, as clear as the foul line on a basketball court, and she had crossed it. Certainly, there were a number of ways you could cross the line—he'd thought for some time that she would cross it with a single outrageous act like sleeping with her boss. He still thought she'd probably done that, but he couldn't prove it. Instead she'd crossed it with her yelling and the abusive things she said. It was not any single thing she said, but rather the number of times she said them, the number of times she yelled at him until she yelled herself right across that line.

He stopped pacing, looked out the window again, and realized that it was over—that much was certain. There was something pure about knowing this, something as pure as the sky. Still he felt nervous, as if uncomfortable in his own skin, and decided that despite the weather, he'd go outside and shoot some baskets, by himself if necessary.

It was more windy than he expected, and unusually cold that morning even for December, but he was still glad to be outdoors. His first thought was to go to Taney Park five blocks away on Pine Street, but then he remembered that the new Park Commissioner had taken the rims off the backboards to keep blacks away. Just like that, one hundred people disappeared. Some of the white players in the neighborhood even complained, but it came to nothing. Now the single basket on the elementary school playground three blocks from his apartment was the only place left to shoot in Center City. Philadelphia was getting more stupid every day, he thought, destroying its own playgrounds for no reason. This basket, which he was now forced to use, was old with a large gray wooden backboard and a slightly over-sized rim so that you could never even be sure you deserved the shot you made. Most of the time Andy didn't let that bother him, but this morning it bothered him a lot. Moreover, after his first basket he missed his next six shots. It was the wind, it was the sun in his eyes, but most of all he was still stunned by his latest fight with Ellen and the realization that she had begun to hate him, and perhaps had hated him for some time.

That he hated her was completely different. He was sure she didn't know, so as long as he kept it a secret it didn't hurt anyone. Besides, his was not a cold or pure hatred—it had been balanced by memories of happier times with her and by the desire he still felt. He often thought of it as a close and vastly complicated basketball game—a game of streaks. When she got angry or wouldn't sleep with him the Hate Team surged ahead, but if she were nice even for ten or fifteen minutes, the other team would rally. But always it was a game he was officiating, and if it got too lopsided one way or the other he could end it and make it disappear.

This morning while she yelled at him he had seen something in her face that was undeniable. She wasn't playing any secret game; she wasn't ambivalent. She simply hated him and it shocked him, though he knew things had been going badly for some time. She was bitterly disappointed in their marriage and was probably sleeping with someone or soon would. She would never want him again as she once had—his sex life with her was lost. His own complicated game was now over as well. The look in her eyes had ended it in an instant. That look made her cross the line even more than her yelling, he realized. He hated her totally now and only hoped she would leave him soon or else let him go. If she wouldn't, if she were afraid of having to pay alimony or else was insane enough to expect some from him (for he had some money from his parents), he'd do something if he had to, anything to be rid of her.

Finally, he made a hook shot. Andy turned instinctively to see if anyone was watching, and saw a black man coming toward him, wrapped in a cheap green cloth coat that reminded him of the army coat he used to wear in college in the sixties. The man had a thin beard which circled his face and gave him a look of sternness and conviction. Andy thought they were about the same age, that he was maybe an inch or two taller, though it was hard to tell because the man was walking hunched over a little with both arms folded against the cold.

Finally, Andy turned to him. "Wanna shoot?"

The man unfolded his arms and opened his hands to catch the ball. For a few minutes they shot in silence. Andy immediately considered himself a better player and hoped there'd be no challenge for a one-on-one. He hated such situations where he had to determine how hard he should try so that the game could be close, and no one would be too hurt or angry. He'd been the starting off-guard on his high school team and generally was one of the best players on any given day at a playground, though of course he'd slowed up a little in the last few years.

"Damn! Can't get one to go down," the man said.

"The wind's brutal. You gotta play the wind today."

They shot another two minutes without speaking. Andy thought about Ellen and began missing his shots again. When the man hit a couple of jumpers, Andy said, "All right!" with sportscaster enthusiasm.

The man walked over to him carrying the ball and extending his free hand. "My name's Graham."

"I'm Andy." They shook hands and Andy asked if he lived nearby.

Graham said no and Andy immediately regretted his question because Graham looked like he was probably homeless. His chinos were badly torn and his shoes looked like strips of bacon. Ellen had upset him so much he couldn't think right any more.

"Hey, man, I want to show you something."

Graham reached inside the pocket of his coat, which came down to his knees, and pulled out a wallet. "See this? I used to be in a group, man. You know music?"

"Sure, some."

"Here's a picture of my group. We was called 'The Thunderballs.'"

Andy nodded. He had never heard of them. He saw a picture of four black men in tuxedos smiling in front of some palm trees and asked what Graham did in the group.

"Sang, played keyboards, sometimes sang lead. We travelled all over when things was good. Then we hit a down time in L.A. See this dude? Recognize him? That's Quincy Jones."

"Sure." It was a colored Polaroid—all the pictures were—of Graham standing next to Jones in a club. Andy found himself checking for inauthentic details, in spite of himself. Graham showed him similar pictures of himself and Whitney Houston, his group hovering around Danny DeVito (of all people), his group sitting at a table with Luther Vandross, and then one of himself and a smiling Cher.

"Amazing," Andy said, in part to make Graham feel good, in part because he was kind of amazed to see a picture of this street person in such friendly proximity to Cher, who had long been one of his fantasy women.

"Yeah, things were cool for awhile."

"What happened?"

"Give me the rock, man; I've got to stay warm."

Graham hit a jump shot and Andy applauded. He thought that he had to do this to keep Graham talking.

"Income tax problems is what happened. I didn't do it. Just trusted the wrong people. Shoulda stayed with the brothers, I guess. Done three years for it, I know that."

"Prison?"

"Three-and-a-half years' time. Just out a few weeks ago."

"How come you're in Philly?"

"Long story, man. I'm trying to get down to Florida. Got a wife and kid in Jacksonville," Graham sighed. "Yeah, I really miss 'em."

Andy stopped himself from asking Graham why he didn't go to Jacksonville. It was obvious he had no money.

"You gotta old lady?" Graham said with a little smile that showed a chipped front tooth.

"Yeah, but I'm trying to get away from her. Can't stand her anymore. She yells at me all the time."

"That's cold."

"Yeah, it shouldn't happen, should it?"

Graham shook his head. "Come on, check me, man" Graham said. He began dribbling with rapid, low bounces toward the imaginary key.

"Remember Earl the Pearl? Watch this." Graham tried a spin move, but his shot only nicked a side of the rim. Then he insisted on going through the routine three more times until he finally made a basket—Andy all the while playing only token defense. After his basket Graham said, "See that, the Pearl is back. Now I'll turn into Clyde Frazier and check you. You old enough to remember those dudes, ain't you? How old are you?"

"Too old to keep guarding you. You're wearing me out." He still wanted to avoid a game, and besides he'd gotten an idea that was still so vague he didn't know if it was an idea or a dream, but to find out he knew he needed to talk some more to Graham. Andy took a jump shot, missed, got his own rebound and passed the ball to Graham.

"Let's just shoot, O.K.?"

Graham rubbed the ball and smiled. "Long as I get to shoot the rock, I'm happy. Long as you have a rock, you're never alone, right man?"

"Right," Andy said, but he hardly heard him. He was thinking about his idea again and for the next five minutes, while they shot, he tried furiously to remember bank statements and deeds and insurance policies. When he was unable to visualize each document he felt that it might no longer exist, and he'd start to panic. Then he'd turn his back and dribble the ball hard on the concrete with his eyes closed until he found he could see the lease or the last bank statement, could make them exist again through concentration. He turned to Graham. "Where are you staying now?"

Graham smiled ironically and shrugged. "No place particular, man. I'm trying to get enough together for a room but they want all this security shit, first two months, then the last month . . . Maybe they're insecure or something," he laughed. "Course you can't get a job if you don't have an address." He swore and spat with disgust, the wind barely letting the spit leave him.

"Sounds rough. I'm sorry."

"I don't know what they expect when they let you out. They don't give you nothing . . . you can't get a job, that's almost impossible. I'm trying to be good. I'm trying not to slip up and do something wrong, but they're not making it easy. Every day I'm tempted 'cause I got to eat, you know? Yeah, I'm tempted every day."

Andy looked at Graham closely. His big dark eyes looked angry, and for a moment Andy was frightened.

"You could stay with me for a while, if it wasn't for my wife. She wouldn't go for it. She doesn't care about helping people. She's one of these unconscious racists, if you know what I mean. She doesn't know herself well enough to even understand it, but she is."

"I hear you."

"But look, I can give you a few bucks so you can eat something today."

"Thank you, man."

"I'll have to get it in my apartment, if you don't mind walking me there."

"That's no problem."

They took their last shots, each waiting till the other made a basket, then left the playground, walking up Chestnut Street. Andy lived in a high-rise filled with what he considered yuppie creeps and future yuppie creeps (University of Pennsylvania business students). It was his wife's idea to move there. He'd wanted to stay in West Philly where they'd lived near Clark Park, a playground where there were always lots of games and where he'd earned something of a reputation. But after Ellen's promotion, she'd insisted on moving. She became impossible on the subject so quickly he couldn't muster a defense. She was hot to live at a semistatus address, and also, Andy thought, hot to get away from black people. Their new building fulfilled both her wishes. Except for the doorman and maintenance men, who were all black, and a prostitute accompanying a blushing business student, he'd never seen a black person *inside* the building. Just another example of apartheid Philadelphia-style, he thought. That Ellen loved the building convinced him she was a racist and made him hate her all the more. As they climbed the steps to his building, he wondered if he should introduce Graham to James, the somewhat supercilious doorman now on duty, but decided to say nothing. So a poor black man in shabby clothes was in the building; let the building make an issue of it. He knew the building wouldn't, that the building would back down.

When they walked into the lobby, James looked at Graham with slightly raised eyebrows, but as soon as Andy looked at him, James buzzed them both in. On the elevator the presence of Margaret, the legal secretary who lived on the same floor, temporarily inhibited them, but as soon as they began walking down the hallway, they started talking again.

"You got a nice building, man."

"The accommodations are nice, but the people are a different story."

Andy turned the key, and they walked into his apartment. "Make yourself at home, sit down if you can find someplace where there isn't a plant or tree growing. My wife likes to pretend she lives in the jungle—a high rise in the jungle, I guess. But no natives, just her and the trees."

Graham sat in a brown leather chair and laughed. "Reminds me of my time in California."

"Wanna beer?" Andy asked as he opened the refrigerator.

"Sure."

Andy took out two cans of Heineken. "I can't find a clean glass. Is the can O.K.?"

"Sure, man. Can's great."

He handed Graham the Heineken and sat down in a green La-Z-Boy opposite him. To their left a large picture window overlooked Center City. Periodically they looked out the window while they drank and talked.

"That the playground where we was?" Graham said, pointing at the window and then momentarily turning toward Andy. Andy nodded.

"Do you check it out to see who's there before you go down? Is that what you do?"

"Sometimes," Andy said, while Graham laughed.

"You got a real setup man. Yes sir, a real setup."

Andy didn't say anything. He didn't want to begin talking until they'd both had a second beer or something stronger. He was trying to remember where he had hidden his pot (his smoking was another thing Ellen and he fought about), thinking the pot might be what he needed to implement his idea. Meanwhile, Graham was talking about his salad days in California.

"When I was in Santa Monica I was three minutes from the beach. That's three minutes if I ran, and I used to run there at first, just to see how fast I could get there. That was beautiful, man. The waves and the sun."

"What was your place like?"

"Two-room apartment we were renting. Got a little crowded 'cause one of the guys in the group was staying there too."

He felt a flash of jealousy which he tried to stop by focusing on Graham's present condition. Graham was looking at him quizzically.

"Course, even though I could get to the beach in three minutes, I couldn't see it from my window, man. You're three minutes from the park and you can see it too. That's a setup. Yes sir, you're in a real classy building."

"I didn't want to come here. I liked where I was before better, but my wife made me move. She wanted a big deal address."

"Where were you before?"

"In West Philly, in a regular apartment. I was near a park too. I couldn't see it from my window, but there were games there all the time with all kinds of people. I don't have anyone to talk to here. Everyone here is the same, if you know what I mean."

"I hear you."

Andy felt odd, as if he were starting to vibrate inside, and took a breath to steady himself.

"I'm getting another brew," he announced.

"Sure, man. We gonna drink the blues away." Graham laughed and Andy laughed too, before stopping himself in the kitchen. He would get nowhere acting like this; he would lose track of his idea. He decided he should change the mood, so when he returned with the beers he asked Graham about his wife and child.

They were in L.A. with him when he was arrested and had gone back to Jacksonville to stay with her relatives, Graham explained. His son, Tommy, was four-and-a-half years old, and for three of those years Graham hadn't seen him. Andy looked at the pain on Graham's face and felt nervous.

"You and your wife have any children?" Graham said.

"Well, there's the two of us," he said, and Graham laughed.

"See my wife doesn't want to have any children. There's not much happening in our bed these days. She thinks she's so successful now that she doesn't have to deal with the likes of me. Want some of this?" he said, holding out a joint and lighter he'd found next to the steak knives in the kitchen.

Graham gave him a funny look. "With my empty stomach, this gonna go right to my head." But he took the joint, inhaled deeply a couple of times, and passed it back to Andy.

"Like I said before, I can give you about ten bucks or so. Wish I could give you more, but that's all I got on me. My wife makes most of the money, and she doesn't share. She hides all her cash, too." He took a hit, passed it back to Graham, then waited until Graham smoked some more.

"Your woman ever cold to you? I mean one or two times they all say no."

"Yeah, one or two times a week, you mean," Graham said laughing.

"Yeah, really," Andy said, forcing himself to laugh. He waited until Graham stopped laughing, which seemed to take a long time, then said, "No, I mean has she ever shut you down for a long period of time?"

"A long time?" Graham asked.

"Yeah."

"Course that's one of those relative terms. 'Cause sometimes a week's a long time and sometimes a day is. Every damn day I spent in jail was long to me."

"I was thinking more like a month than a week."

"No man, that never happened to me 'cept in jail."

"I hate it when they use their pussies as a weapon to shut you down."

"Hey, better they should shut you down than chop you down, right? Like that Lorena Bobbitt did to her husband while he was sleeping. John Bobbitt was his name, wasn't it? Then she drove off and threw it away like an old useless bone. Cold, man."

"Yeah, she got off with nothing man, nothing but a little counseling, as I recall. Hell, she probably enjoyed whining about herself and having someone there who had to listen. That was probably pleasure for her. I know my wife would rather complain than anything."

Andy inhaled on the last of the joint then said, "What did you say you were arrested for?"

"I told you, man, income tax problems. My manager did it. I trusted the wrong dude, that's all."

"That's a lot of time for income taxes."

"Hey, you ever notice life ain't always fair?"

"Right," Andy said, nodding. "Must have been tough in jail. Was there a lot of violent stuff in there?"

"What you think? Wasn't no tea party. You got to be alert, you got to take care of yourself. That's why I can do it now on the streets. I learned how to survive in there."

"But you said you aren't getting into any fights now."

"No. I'm not fighting anyone 'less they fight me first. I told you that. What you think? I tell you one thing on the playground and another up here?"

Andy made a conciliatory gesture with his hands. "Not at all. I'm just trying to understand. 'Cause you said you were tempted."

"Sure, I'm tempted."

"That's interesting 'cause there are probably other people who are tempted too, who might pay you a lot of money to do something for them."

"You mean, pay me to pull some job for them?"

Andy finished the joint and tried to make eye contact with Graham.

"It could be that or something that might be worth a lot more money to you."

"Like what?"

"Say there was a man who really hated someone he was living with.

Say this man had been stepped on and humiliated by this person and felt he'd come to the end of the line." He felt his hand shake but kept on. "Now he might not be a man who looks like he has money, but he might really have some money plus be absolutely sure of getting some more so he could put, say, ten thousand bucks in your pocket. Let's also say that he already has an excellent plan worked out, and he's only looking for someone like you to put the plan in motion so he can put a stop to the cruelty of this terrible person he happens to live with."

Graham leaned forward in his chair. "Am I reading you right? You serious?"

"Could be, Graham. You might be."

"Well, that person wouldn't be looking for me 'cause I wouldn't be doing nothing like that. I draw the line, see. And on one side of the line is money and property, and on the other side is people, even racist pigs— unconscious or otherwise. They're still on that side of the line."

Graham looked directly at him, and a terrible fear swept though Andy.

"That's a very good answer," Andy said. "That's a really impressive answer."

"There's lots of temptation out there, but that ain't one of them. Never be one either. I'm a father, you know. You can't bring one person into the world and take another out. I'll be going now."

Both men got up from their chairs, and Andy mumbled something about how strong Graham's character was. Then he took fifteen dollars from his pocket and thrust it into Graham's hands, worrying that Graham might realize that he'd had money in his pants all along, but not wanting to lie about it either.

Graham said, "Thanks," and put the money in his coat. He had pulled his coat tightly around himself and was heading toward the door.

Andy rushed up behind him and began asking if maybe they could meet to play ball again. He picked up the basketball from in front of the door and followed Graham out into the hallway, but Graham was already standing by the elevator. "Hey," he said, passing the ball to him, "take it. It's yours."

Graham looked down at the ball he had caught, running his fingers over it for a few seconds as if he were combing an animal's fur before he passed it back to Andy. "You need it more than I do," he said. Then the elevator came and Graham left.

In his apartment Andy paced in front of his picture window thinking that Graham saw right through him, which was why he wouldn't take the ball or even say good-bye. But what would Graham do? Would he go to the police, or try to warn Ellen some way, maybe leave a message for her with the doorman?

He ran into the bedroom and, after searching the room quickly, found Ellen's Ativan in the bathroom cabinet. He took a pill and returned to the living room, letting his head fill with a different voice that the mere taking of the Ativan seemed to have set in motion.

He thought, I've been smoking, which is making everything seem worse. The bottom line is it's his word against mine (and I never even, technically, said anything), plus he's a homeless ex-con who's high. Besides, he took the money so he can eat—he just wants to eat. He doesn't want any new trouble; that'd be the last thing he wants.

He sat down in the brown leather chair and his anxiety began to give way to an immense sadness. He started running his fingers over the leaves of a jade plant. How had he come to this point? He could still vividly remember the time when they loved each other. What had happened to those people? It was like time just took them away and replaced them with two angry ghosts. At any rate, he now knew he wouldn't have gone through with it. It was only a temporary rage he was in and now it was over. When Graham spoke of drawing the line, he'd felt strangely moved. He stopped stroking the plant and stood up to see if Graham might be back on the playground or else walking on the street, but all he could see were buildings and the blinding blue sky. It was too cold to be out walking, much too cold.

A few hours later, he fell asleep in the bedroom. When he heard the door open he woke up instantly, but instinctively stayed still.

"Christ, what a day," Ellen was muttering, either to herself or to him, he couldn't tell which. He could hear her undressing, making more noises of exasperation in the room. Be nice, he warned himself. Things can be made better just by being nice. But he was afraid that if he talked she'd find out he'd been high and pick another fight. Tomorrow he'd be nice first thing, but for now it was best to say nothing and just vanish. So he closed his eyes, pretending to be asleep, but the uncomfortable feeling in his skin returned, and for a moment, he thought again of hiring someone else for the job Graham wouldn't do. His head ached, too, but he'd get no sympathy talking about that to Ellen, so he just kept his eyes closed and soon rolled over to make room for her in their bed.

MERCURY

There was a party in TriBeCa, what Larry thought would be the same group of writers his age or older complaining and consoling each other. The party's host, Aaron Reisman, once had a brief flurry of success with his metafictionist stories, but that had all ended years ago. In fact, Aaron had already, in his own words, "surrendered" to his "bad karma" and now wrote only for an hour or two every other weekend. His one enduring piece of good fortune was the loft he'd bought cheap in the late '70s, which, of course, had now sky-rocketed in value. Every year, shortly before Christmas, he'd have a party in his loft for the writers and sympathizers in his circle who all brought wine or whiskey (Aaron somehow constructed the dip), and each year the humor got a little more desperate and bitter.

Until the last minute, Larry thought that this year he'd skip the party. He was in a writing slump, badly stalled on a novel he'd been working on since his book of stories had been published three years ago. Moreover, he was out of fulltime work now, wholly reliant on substitute teaching to make money. Under the circumstances, with all that was on his mind, how could he stand to go to Aaron's party? Still, there was one reason to consider going. He'd heard a rumor that Kenneth Alters would be there. Initially he'd dismissed it as an attempt of Aaron's to ensure a good crowd or maybe a fantasy of one of the guests. Why would a young, glamorous writer/celebrity like Kenneth Alters attend such a scruffy affair? Yet, such things did happen in New York and he couldn't discount it. The more he thought about meeting Alters, perhaps even being able to befriend him and all that might mean, the harder it got to stay home. Finally, he drank a glass of vodka and soda water, then selected a pair of jeans and a purple wool sweater, trying not to look overly concerned about his clothes but not wholly unattractive either. Then, before he'd gotten halfway to the elevator, he went back to his apartment to get a copy of his book of stories, and his knife. He'd been mugged by three teenagers a few months ago and without telling anyone, had bought a large pocket knife which he generally took with him now whenever he went out at night.

There were dark clouds outside and he nearly ran from the corner liquor store (where he bought a bottle of gin for the party) to the train stop. On the train to TriBeCa he spent the whole trip thinking about Kenneth Alters' sudden and stunning success.

An elevator led directly to Aaron's loft on the fourth floor where Larry was greeted by the familiar scene of men mostly on the edge of middle age in their de rigeur minimalist dress of jeans and tee shirts, men who still looked puzzled as to why their stomachs were sticking out and their hair lines receding, holding their drinks while they talked to each other or to the mostly younger women they were with. But the loud laughter and quasi-hysterical talk that usually filled the air was strangely muted. Larry thought that it was like a theater shortly before the lights dimmed. The glances were mostly directed toward the punch bowl in the right side center of the loft where Kenneth Alters, looking infuriatingly as good as his photographs, was standing alone, cool and self-contained in a gray suit and baby-blue tie.

Immediately Larry went to the bar, about twenty feet behind Alters, and fixed himself a vodka tonic, leaving his bottle of gin on an adjacent table. When he looked up again, Alters was still standing alone. In a bizarre (yet somehow predictable) gesture of collective insecurity or perverse pride the other guests were pretending not to pay any attention to Alters, although, periodically, everyone in the room was actually looking at him. What provincial idiots they are, Larry thought. Someone a little famous comes to their party, and immediately he paralyzes the room. He drank his vodka quickly, deciding that the less he thought about what to say to Alters, the better. He would simply tell him that he admired his work (he had only allowed himself to read a single story of Alters', which he'd considered more precious than precocious) and then at some point tell him about his own book, hopefully giving him the paperback copy he'd brought. It was imagining all the consequences (that never happened anyway) and giving time for anxieties to multiply that intimidated people.

When Larry finished his drink he began walking directly toward Alters, then seeing that he was talking with Aaron, he went to get another vodka from the bar. With his new drink in hand he looked out at the rest of the loft and soon noticed an attractive brunette, a poet he'd spoken to for a few minutes at a couple of downtown parties. For some reason, probably because of his fixation with his former lover Debby, he'd never called her and couldn't even remember her name. Was it Jama, Janette, Janine? Anyway, it was "J" something, so he thought of her as Lady J. She was talking to Morty, a forty-something writer who dressed like a hippie and wrote simple-minded parable-like stories—a third-rate Brautigan. Lady J, wearing a very nicely cut black dress, looked like she was humoring Morty. Larry began to move toward her but before he could make any meaningful progress he was stopped by a less attractive woman, a redhead with darting, almost comically intense green eyes.

Gesturing slightly with her head, she said, "Is that who I think it is?"

"That's Kenneth Alters, himself."

She looked perplexed and astonished. She was overly dressed, Larry thought, and was wearing too much makeup and jewelry.

"Wasn't he on the cover of *People* last week?"

"He wasn't on the cover, but they did a story on him," Larry said.

"Yeah, that's right. It was about this three-picture movie deal he signed. God, can you imagine being that successful at his age and that rich, if you can believe the story."

"Normally, I don't read those kind of magazines but since I'm a writer myself, I was curious to see what they'd say. It's so rare that they do an article about a writer."

"You write novels, too?"

"Yes, and short stories."

"Do I know your name?"

"Larry James."

Larry watched her studying him skeptically for a few seconds as if he might be lying about being a writer. The thought made him bristle and he finished his second drink. She looked like a poor man's Lucille Ball anyway, he thought.

"So have you met Alters yet?"

"No, I haven't."

"Oh," she said with what Larry thought was obvious disappointment. "I was going to ask you to introduce me, but what the hell, he's just a person. I can introduce myself. After I've had a couple of drinks," she said, laughing loudly. Larry tried to supress his anger while he waited for her laughter to subside, then excused himself, still keeping his eyes on Alters who was giving Aaron a lot of time.

He went to the bar and fixed himself a new vodka tonic. It was strange to think that just three years ago Alters was completely unknown. That's when his first book of stories had gotten both extraordinary reviews and sales. A host of articles with pictures of the young, golden-haired writer began appearing everywhere as if he were a movie star. Of course, Alters' youth (he was only twenty-five, ten years younger than Larry) was used to help promote him as a phenomenon. That and the brilliant way Alters himself marketed his California friendliness. Surprisingly, his antisnobbism was seen, even by cynical New Yorkers, not as disingenuous but as refreshing. At the time Larry reassured himself that his own first collection, published the same year, had also gotten some very good, thoughtful reviews, though his small press publisher could hardly compete with Alters' major New York house in getting anything like the amount of attention Alters got. Still he could at least consider himself a part of the same general literary universe. But when Alters' novel, published just last year, eclipsed the success of his first book and became a bestseller, everything changed. Now at twenty-eight, Alters really did inhabit a different literary and social world. He'd been on late-night talk shows, there were articles speculating that he might act in one of the movies that he was writing, and in an interview with the *Times* he expressed an interest in directing. Could one doubt it would happen? When he moved to New York and bought a loft in SoHo, *New York Magazine* wrote about it. Cotation of a relationship is the aspect of social or public recognition (of which patlo represents a visible element). There are relationships where the parties are regarded as married although patlo has never taken place. One such example from Mosotho kgotla is provided by Wamakhyu, who is Otswataung and Shadiko's daughter. According to her mother, Shadiko,

> She [Wamakhyu] did not stay long with us after school. She married Mosimanegape from Senyedimana kgotla. In fact, patlo was not done because he died before it could be carried out. When she became pregnant we [the relatives on both sides] agreed that marriage should take place. The young couple wanted to marry at common law and have the marriage registered. We agreed as parents that they could live together. They stayed with us in Basimane ward until Otswataung [Shadiko's husband] went to live with his nyatsi [concubine] in Borakalalo ward and I moved here to this house that my son Modise built for me. Wamakhyu and Mosimanegape went to live with his parents in their kgotla. They have six children. The eldest child [twenty-one] has just got a job at the Jwaneng mines [in Botswana]. The marriage was postponed for so long because they needed money for the celebrations. Unfortunately he [Mosimanegape] died last year [1983] before they could take place.

Although patlo never took place, the couple's relationship is treated as a marriage. Such recognition is due to a number of factors, which include parental agreement to marriage, the duration of the relationship, the number of children involved, and the fact that Wamakhyu has been living with the man's family in his kgotla for many years. Indeed, it is significant that since Mosimanegape's death, she has continued to live with his family and is treated as his widow.

Shadiko's account highlights a number of elements that are central to processes of social recognition. A key factor for consideration is the degree to which the two individuals' families have become involved in their relationship and accorded it public recognition. Such recognition derives from formal meetings between family representatives, agreements reached on such occasions including acceptance of the parties living together, the giving of gifts, and attendance at significant events in the other family's life, such as celebrations for the birth of a child or funerals. Where the woman has a child, it is essential for the man's family to publicly acknowledge the birth by providing support of some kind, such as soap, napkins, or food for the mother and child. They should attend or contribute to the celebration held to mark the end of her confinement after the birth of the child. If the child dies, they should attend the funeral or send representatives. Failure to act in these ways demonstrates dissociation from the relationship and is to be weighed against prior agreement to marriage or the giving of clothes and blankets to the woman, which may amount to a betrothal gift known as peelela.

It is important to recognize that a relationship is constantly evolving. At one moment the giving of gifts and other features may suggest a marriage or movement toward such a state, but at another, behavior may be such that this impression is undercut by subsequent events which undermine previous actions. This means that status cannot be viewed simply in linear terms, based on the length of time that a relationship has lasted, for what has occurred in that period may be subject to different interpretations at different times.

On the other hand, marriage in Botswana is not confined to the ongoing processes of negotiation associated with customary law. Another option is available through the Marriage Act 1970 [Cap.29:01] which provides for the registration of religious or civil marriages that are conducted according to its terms.

Civil or Religious Marriage

Like other Batswana, Bakwena also engage in civil or religious marriage, which plays an important role in their society, especially for those who are Christians.[14] This aspect of marriage and its relationship with customary marriage is one that is often overlooked. It is not present in the work of Comaroff and Roberts (1981) or in their account of the relationship that they present between marriage and dispute processing, because according to John Comaroff (personal communication, 14 July 1994) their data reflected a marked absence of religious or civil forms of marriage among their research subjects. But the civil or religious aspect of marriage among Bakwena is something that should not be ignored. In her account of Kwena marriage, Mosotho Moreri's widow talks of the feast that used to accompany patlo but is now postponed until the marriage is registered. Her reference to registration underlines the way in which civil or religious marriage is accommodated within Kwena society. Shadiko does likewise. The reference to postponing patlo until a civil marriage can take place indicates for many kgotla members and for the village generally that a civil or religious marriage is a significant form of marriage which often accompanies patlo and which may even affect the timing with which patlo takes place. Molokomme (1991:103) has also noted that marriage is increasingly being associated with civil marriage among the Bangwaketse.

Both forms of customary and civil or religious marriage are legally recognized. Under the Marriage Act 1970 [Cap.29:01] parties may marry according to civil or religious rites [s.7] and their marriage must be registered [s.13]. Where such a marriage is entered into, any prior marriage must have been dissolved [s.15]. This latter provision upholds the concept of monogamous marriage and outlaws polygyny. However, the provisions of the Marriage Act do not apply to any marriages "contracted in accordance with any customary law of Botswana" [s.2]. While the Marriage Act prohibits an individual from engaging in polygynous marriage [s.15], under customary law, it is permissible for a man to have several wives. However, there is nothing to stop an individual from going through a form of marriage with the same person, under both common and customary law, provided that person is his or her only spouse—in other words, provided that the marriage is in fact monogamous.[15] Many of those who celebrate marriage in Molepolole do so according to both common and customary law.[16]

Procreative Relationships and Marriage in Mosotho Kgotla

But while marriage is important, the links between procreation and marriage have become attenuated for the reasons outlined in chapter 1. These reasons centered on the effects of sustained labor migration, a decline in polygyny, and greater freedom of association between the sexes at school and at work, all of which have contributed to the numbers of unmarried women with children in Botswana today. As Comaroff and Roberts have observed (1977, 1981), this is due in part to a move away from polygyny toward serial monogamy, where both women and men tend to engage in a series of relationships investigating the potential of various partners and testing the benefits of such associations before committing themselves to marriage with one partner. The national picture is reinforced by the data from Mosotho kgotla, where a number of procreative relationships are marked as marriages, either through patlo, or registration, or a combination of both.[17] These marriages, however, by no means predominate in numerical terms among procreative relationships in general. Collected from the life histories of members of Mosotho kgotla, the overall figure for procreative relationships was 195. Of these, ninety-two fall within the definition of formal marriage. In other words, the relationships encompass ninety-two marriages and 103 other types of relationships.

At first sight, the figure of ninety-two might seem a high proportion

for relationships representing marriage. But the figures take on a different meaning when they are broken down in terms of generation and
gender (app. A). Men account for almost two-thirds of the marriage figures, that is, for sixty-one out of the ninety-two marriages. Given that
there are seventy-three men associated with the kgotla who are or have
been involved with women in childbearing relationships, the marital
figures for men are extremely high. However, it should be noted that a
number of these marriages are accounted for by men in the older generation who married polygamously or who remarried when a wife died.[18]

The picture changes dramatically when the women's position is examined. Out of the seventy-seven women associated with the kgotla
through descent who have had children in 111 relationships there are
only thirty-one marriages. In other words, there are thirty-one marriages
in contrast with eighty other types of relationships. In contrast with
men, there are over three times the number of types of relationships
other than marriage in which women have had children. Of added interest is the fact that the numbers of women marrying over two generations
have remained relatively constant.[19]

How is it that women compared with men find themselves in a more
plural set of relationships? To some extent the data on men are more
incomplete because knowledge of their procreative relationships was
harder to gather where they were not present or willing to divulge it.
The presence of a child, the most obvious marker, is not readily apparent
in the same way as it is with a woman. Unless a man admitted to the
existence of such a child or family members had knowledge of such a
child a relationship could pass unnoticed. Historical and demographic
considerations also come into play. There are demographically more
women than men living in Botswana (Botswana 1991a:11), a situation
which has been exacerbated and replicated through the years due to the
high numbers of adults, particularly men, involved in migrant labor.

There is, however, another issue at stake. To what extent do those
relationships which do not fulfill the criteria for formal marriage (in
terms of patlo or registration) qualify as marriages on the basis of general
social recognition? In other words, how many may be considered actual
or potential customary marriages, which need not be marked by the
occurrence of any specific event? The life histories make it clear that
even in these terms the majority of such relationships have few if any
of the features associated with customary marriages or relationships in
the process of becoming a marriage. They lack the basic elements, such

as familial agreement and exchange of gifts, out of which social recognition as a marriage might be constructed.

An analysis of all 103 relationships other than marriage reveals a pluralism which represents varying degrees of personal and familial involvement and of social and public recognition. At one end of the scale are those relationships where there was minimal involvement, while at the other there are a few relationships which existed on a lifelong basis with some degree of mutual support and recognition from both families. In between are a number of relationships which reflected something more than minimal involvement but which never quite reached the level of recognition and involvement exhibited by those relationships at the other end of the scale.

Each relationship has its own particular characteristics and meaning for the individuals concerned, but in order to acquire a general perspective on these relationships, each was classified on the basis of factors such as the length of time that it had lasted and the number of children involved. However, these factors had to be read in the context of the degree of public recognition accorded to the relationship by the individuals and families concerned. This was important because in some cases a relationship may have lasted for many years and produced a number of children, but if the man never formally presented himself to the woman's relatives and his family did nothing to publicly mark its recognition of the relationship, then the relationship could never fall within the marital orbit regardless of how long it lasted or the number of children concerned. Indeed, many of these types of relationships involve concubinage, which clearly sets them apart from marriage-type relationships.

Bearing this in mind, I devised a rough system of classification which covered five categories. Four of these categories covered relationships which had ended, and the fifth one represented relationships which were still current. Those relationships which had ended were placed within the fleeting, brief, intermediate, and lifelong categories. The fleeting category, which lies at one extreme of the scale, represents those relationships with no social recognition and minimal involvement. In the brief category are those relationships displaying some contact but still involving minimal social recognition. Moving on from here are those relationships with more substantial involvement and recognition, which fall under the intermediate and lifelong categories. Some of these relationships in the intermediate category represent potential customary marriages which never materialized. Finally, at the end of the scale are those relationships in the lifelong category, which represent those relationships with the highest degree of social recognition and which lasted until the death of one of the parties. For example, Same, Robert Moreri's daughter, had a lifelong relationship with a man named Busang which lasted over thirty years until his death in 1984.

Such categories can never fully capture the essence of a relationship, but they are useful for providing an overview from which to assess marriage. Do most relationships tend toward Same's type of relationship or do they tend toward the other end of the scale? Are there any differences between the generations in this respect? Leaving formal marriage aside, two-thirds of the other types of nonmarital relationships have come to an end.[20] Of these relationships, the overwhelming majority fall within the fleeting and brief categories, with only a minority within the intermediate and lifelong categories. The picture is one where the majority of procreative relationships fall within the ambit of those with little or no social recognition and ostensibly different in character from the kind of relationship represented by Same.

Women, rather than men, predominate among the other types of relationships.[21] The numbers involved in both generations are roughly equal and considerably outnumber those of men.[22] What is interesting is that among the older women in G.3, the relationships are roughly split between those with little or no social recognition and those with a higher degree of social recognition.[23] Among the younger women in G.4 this has altered. Almost all the relationships now fall within the fleeting and brief categories.[24] This suggests that while divergent types of relationships have existed over two generations, and are not therefore a new phenomenon, among the younger generation there is a tendency toward a more tenuous type of relationship.

Current relationships account for less than one-third of the total number of other relationships.[25] Where they exist, they involve twice the number of women in the younger generation as in the older generation.[26] This is not surprising, as the older a woman becomes the more chance there is of a relationship breaking down and the more difficult it becomes to find another partner. Older women find themselves competing with younger women, and the situation is often exacerbated by the lack of available men. Where current relationships exist, they tend to have lasted over a number of years, and by 1989 five out of the fifteen current relationships existing in 1984 in G.4 had been converted into formal marriages through patlo or registration.

What can be deduced about marriage from this information?

Among women in both generations there are a mixture of relationships which include formal marriages and other types of relationships. In some cases the marriages have broken down and the women have moved on to other types of relationships. Of those in other types of relationships some are current and others have come to an end.[27]

Clearly, marriage is only one of a number of types of relationships which exist in practice. However, while it does not predominate in empirical terms, it is still important because it provides a major reference point for assessing relationships. This is demonstrated in chapter 4, which deals with the way in which negotiations over pregnancy are conducted according to relationships' potential (or lack of potential) to become marriage. Relationships, whatever their nature, develop in the shadow of marriage. Within this shadow people find themselves differentially situated with regard to family connections, their access to resources, and their position in the life cycle. While it may be "natural for Batswana to marry"—an observation that was regularly made by men and women in the village during the course of my research—there are those who do not, either because they have an element of choice (often based on access to alternative resources) or because they are not in a position to negotiate. The kinds of choices that are open to individuals, which depend upon a whole range of factors including stage in the life cycle and affiliation with various forms of networks, are highlighted through discussions of life histories that are presented in the next chapter.

THREE

Diverging Families: Social Stratification, Procreation, and Marriage

The differences in ties that bind families and households are not just the product of varying stages in individual life cycles or in family composition, but also represent the product of their histories developed over generations. Such histories play a crucial role in constructing the different contexts in which individuals and their families gain access to resources. This in turn creates access to different forms of power, which affect individuals' abilities to negotiate with one another, including the terms of discourse they employ. The varying networks that underline differing spheres of operation and forms of association are highlighted by the life histories of descendants of Koosimile (see fig. 4c).

These cover two particular family groups, headed respectively by Makokwe and his brother Radipati. They will be presented in detail because they reflect the greatest contrast among Mosotho kgotla families based on diverging means for survival. The disparities in the acquisition of resources and status that they highlight are not only pertinent at a local level but mark the kind of inequalities that are present in Tswana society more generally and that are growing at such a rate that the government of Botswana has openly acknowledged its concern. The types of networks that create and reproduce such inequalities, exemplified by Makokwe's and Radipati's family groups (under the respective labels of peasantariat and salariat) are representative of those networks that are in existence and operate across the country as a whole.

Membership within such networks is crucial to an individual's life trajectory, for the life histories from Mosotho kgotla highlight the range of possibilities that are open to individuals in their lives as well as the constraints which they face, all of which are shaped by the network to which they belong. This is particularly pertinent for women and has implications for their negotiation of procreative relationships and marriage.

Makokwe's family is representative of the majority of families in Mosotho kgotla and of many families in Botswana today because their lives have focused on subsistence agriculture, livestock, and migrant labor of an unskilled nature on an intermittent or contract basis. There has been little attention paid to education, and where it does take place among the younger generation it is at a fairly basic level. These characteristics, which are shared by many other families in Botswana, associate them with what Parson (1981) terms the peasantariat. Members of this kind of group are increasingly distanced from the elite cattle owners and higher-income wage earners (NDP6:8).

In contrast, the members of Radipati's family (see fig. 4c), who are in a minority in the kgotla, have focused their attention on education and the acquisition of skilled and secure employment, which among the younger generation is predominantly government based. These family members no longer engage in subsistence agriculture or in migrant labor of the type entered into by Makokwe's family members. This sets them apart from other families, and, through the position of the younger generation, who represent a growing elite in Botswana, places them among what Cooper (1982) refers to as the salariat.

Before turning to these life histories it is necessary to say something about the context in which Molepolole became established as the central village for Bakwena and the formation of Basimane ward, in which Mosotho kgotla is located. It is not possible to present the complex history of Bakwena in Molepolole in detail here. For that one must consult the pioneering study of Okihiro (1976) and more especially the recent work of Ramsay (1991). Both authors provide richly documented accounts of the coming into being of the Kwena polity and its geographical domain, Kweneng. The present-day Bakwena are descended from a number of small, disunited communities which were consolidated and transformed into a regional power during the reign of Sechele I (c. 1833–92) (Ramsay 1991). Prior to this, there was no overarching Kwena (or Tswana) unity, but rather a number of eponymous Tswana groups including Bakwena and Bangwato, which were small and mobile and in the mid-eighteenth century probably did not exceed one hundred families each (Okihiro 1976:13, 1981:395). Such royals who trace their descent from this time are known as the Sons of Kgabo.[1] It was Kgabo's descendants, including Sechele I, who helped shape the politics of the morafe found in Kweneng today.

The period of wars in the early nineteenth century restructured the geographical and political map of southern Africa (Ramsay 1991; Ncgoncgo 1982a). Bakwena found themselves subject to attack by the Amandebele under the leadership of Mzilikgazi. They also found themselves subject to Boer aggression. When in 1842 the Boers broke away from British rule and undertook the Great Trek to settle in the Transvaal they had a great impact on the lives of Africans. They imposed land and labor policies that altered the social, economic, political, and demographic status quo within their extensive areas of settlement. What Ramsay (1991:50) has termed "the Batswana-Boer war of 1852–53" served to alter the demography of southeastern Botswana, the area in which Bakwena had been settled since the early nineteenth century.

In addition to this, Africans also had to deal with the expansionist tendencies of the British South Africa Company and Cecil Rhodes. Throughout this period and indeed long before it commenced, Africans had exposure to Europeans and to European trade. According to Livingstone and Sebele I, Motswasele I (died in 1790) was the first kgosi to inform Bakwena of the white man. We find at that time a Scotsman, David Hume, as an important figure in the regional expansion of trade in game products. In 1835, Andrew Smith led the Central African Expedition to Kwena country and the court of Mzilikgazi "which was a catalyst for, as well as a consequence of, increased European interest in the interior's commercial potential" (Ramsay 1991:75).

Within this volatile environment, Sechele I was able to transform Bakwena into a regional power through his ability to provide armed resistance to Boer aggression (assisted in part by arms supplied by missionaries such as Livingstone), to build up support within the morafe, and to exploit the commercial potential of the land that he governed through his business acumen (Ramsay 1991). He was able to create a regional power where before there had only been disparate Kwena factions claiming descent from the same eponymous founder, a man named Kwena (crocodile), and each vying for primary position among its collateral branches. Part of the process of creating this power came from Sechele's ability to incorporate his factional collaterals, refugees, and displaced persons from other polities into a single morafe.

The present members of Mosotho kgotla, which forms part of Basimane ward in Molepolole, are the descendants of such displaced persons. According to Schapera (1952:55), their ancestors were said to have come to Kweneng as refugees from Bangwaketse during the reign of Motswasele I (c. 1770–85). They were said to have had commoner status, being batlhanka (servants), and provided the founding members of Basimane ward, which was established during the reign of Motswasele II (1807–21), the father of Sechele I. Basimane is plural of mosimane, meaning "herder" or "husbandmen" (i.e., someone in charge of cattle), and it made sense that such a ward, under Kgosing, would be established at this time because a successful morafe was acquiring large numbers of cattle through raiding and needed capable herdsmen in numbers. The same development was taking place among Bangwato, under the leadership of their kgosi, Kgari (Parsons 1977:115).

During this period (1826–28) Kgari, the Ngwato kgosi, is credited with rationalizing the incipient socioeconomic stratification in Tswana political structure to control the spectacular increase in numbers of people subject to the kgosi and their increase in productive potential through the kgamelo, or "milk jug system" (Parsons 1977:114). Through this system the class ranking inherent in Tswana social structure was strengthened by giving local elites direct economic and administrative control over the lower classes in their sphere of assigned responsibility (Wilmsen 1989:99).

Okihiro (1976:135–36) refers to Sechele I adopting this system for Bakwena soon after he became kgosi in 1831. He also refers to the fact that changes brought about by the great influx of immigrants led to "a reorganization of the labor force, increased participation by women in the external exchange sector, greater investment in house construction, a redistribution of wealth, social stratification, and the rise of crafts and specialists" (Okihiro 1981:396). Sechele took advantage of this situation to strengthen his power base. One of the ways he accomplished this was through using refugees and immigrants to build up his personal following, by placing the newcomers' households under his direct authority within Kgosing, or by allowing them to form autonomous wards, such as Basimane. Sechele not only welcomed refugees (baagedi) and immigrants, but sought to cement their allegiance by giving them mafisa (patronage) cattle from the royal herd, which was then rapidly increasing in size.[2]

It is from the reign of Sechele I that Okihiro (1976:111) marks the beginnings of the large settlements that characterize the central villages of Tswana merafe today (Parsons 1977:115; Tlou 1985:32).[3] He also notes that the majority of dikgotla associated with Kgosing in 1975 were established during the nineteenth-century wars (1981:386–87). He summarizes eyewitness accounts of Kwena growth over fifteen years following 1840. In 1843, Livingstone reported three hundred Bakwena under Sechele, joined in that year by Kwena-speaking followers of Ratshosa—the leader of this Kwena faction was Moruakgomo, the son of Ratshosa, who was the brother of Motswasele II's father; Moruakgomo was thus Sechele's cousin. Up until this period and beyond, Ratshosa and Sechele vied with one another for central power. In 1849, Bakwena under Sechele expanded once more by incorporating 3,600 peoples, including Bakaa. By 1857, Livingstone estimated that there were twenty thousand Bakwena living in Dithubaruba, Sechele's capital at that time. Bakwena established themselves in Molepolole in 1864 when Sechele moved his capital from Dithubaruba.

At the time these settlements were formed and even earlier, Bakwena, like other Batswana, were engaged in foraging as well as agro-pastoral activities. According to Okihiro, food production for the pre-nineteenth-century Kwena consisted of hunting and gathering wild plant foods, herding primarily goats but some cattle, and rudimentary agriculture primarily of melons and beans. Immigration due to war and Afrikaner dislocations stimulated sweeping changes in economic and political life. Apart from restructuring involving the creation of larger administrative units to accommodate a more settled community this also led "to the rise [in importance] of grain agriculture, cattle herding, and trade" (Okihiro 1981:396). Within this environment, access to land, labor, and cattle was important.

The structures which facilitated such access were those of kinship and mafisa (Nangati 1982). Through kinship networks individuals could acquire rights to use land, to participate in reciprocal exchanges of labor, and through inheritance to acquire cattle. This was particularly the case as the political system meshed with the ward structure, whose headmen were perpetuated on the basis of genealogical status and had powers to allocate land.

Within such a system, where power was dispersed throughout the various levels of Tswana society, a kgosi could not afford to act as an autocratic ruler for fear that he would be assassinated (as was Sechele's father) or be deposed. Schapera (1956:143–50) has commented on the precarious nature of a kgosi's authority in Tswana polities, which stems from the diffusion of power, and Ramsay (1991:118) notes that "the royal kgotla remained simply the ultimate forum of appeal." Most decisions were made within the subordinated forums of the client kgotla grouped within Kgosing, or more infrequently, the other four autonomous metse under the direct authority of their senior dikgosana. The autonomous immigrant communities remained under their own rulers, who were generally addressed as "kgosi." The picture of kgosi as "paramount chief" representing a central and absolute repository of power is misleading, as Channock (1985), Roberts (1991), and others have shown. Maintaining a position as kgosi required the ability to manipulate and balance the varying sectional interests within the polity. Sechele excelled at this, creating and maintaining alliances (as, for example, with his cousin Moruakgomo) while at the same time seeking to establish a more centralized form of control through his reorganization of the kgamelo system.

By virtue of his position, a kgosi had large herds of cattle because, inter alia, he was entitled to all stray (matemela) cattle, cattle as tribute or war booty, and those cattle raised through levies or fines. Sechele used his powers of patronage effectively. He did not simply give matemela cattle in mafisa to refugees and immigrants, but also used them to create or to reward support from the commoner ranks within Kwena society. While there were divisions within the society, these were by no means fixed, but remained fluid, so that individuals and their families might move up or down on the social hierarchy. One such example is provided by Segakisa Rampena, who came from the malata, or serf, class; Segakisa was a loyal follower of Sechele and supported him during his wanderings before he consolidated his leadership of the Kwena. As a reward Sechele placed cattle in Segakisa's care, and these cattle became known as difetlhamolelo (lighters of the fire); they provided the material basis for the formation of Segakisa's kgotla, Difetlhamolelo, which today "survives as one of the principal sections of Molepolole" (Ramsay 1991:63).

Just as some individuals could be upwardly mobile, so the opposite was true, and some more remote royal descendants found themselves slipping into commoner status. However, many Kwena royal descendants, Sons of Kgabo, also prospered under Sechele. As leaders of the metse (community) and badisa ba lefatshe (overseers of the land) they shared with the kgosi the right to allocate land and collect tribute from the hunters of the Kweneng-Kgalagadi. Ramsay (1991:127) has commented that in this fluid mosaic of political and economic change, the interest of the Sons of Kgabo lay "in promoting and preserving the role of genealogy in defining access to power."

A HISTORY OF KWENA ROYAL MARRIAGE STRATEGIES

Sechele used marriage as one of the tools in his repertoire for consolidating his power and extending his wealth and status. It was a means by which he sought to create alliances within the polity as well as to extend them through marriage with rulers of other Tswana polities or other influential persons such as traders (fig. 5).

Alliances within the Polity

One of the ways in which he attempted to maintain allegiance was by marrying the daughters of his underchiefs. The missionary David Livingstone remarked on this as a strategy, noting that he had married the daughters of three of his underchiefs, who had on account of their blood relationship stood by him in his adversity and that

> this is one of the modes adopted for cementing the allegiance of a tribe. The government is patriarchal, each man being, by virtue of paternity, chief of his own children. They build their huts around his, and the greater the number of children, the more his importance increases. Hence children are esteemed one of the greatest blessings, and are always treated kindly. . . . A poor man attaches himself to the kgotla of a rich one, and is considered a child of the latter. . . . The circle of huts immediately round the kgotla of the chief is composed of the huts of his wives and those of his blood relations. He attaches the under chiefs to himself by marrying, as Sechele did, their daughters, or inducing his brothers to do so. (Livingstone [1858] 1971:17)

Another way of cementing allegiance was through marriage with close kin. As noted in chapter 2, the most potentially hostile relationships tended to center around one's male kin, as brothers, uncles, and cousins competed with one another for position and property. Marriage to the daughter of a close male relative could transform a potentially hostile relationship into a supportive one. Mindful of what had transpired between his father and his father's elder brother Sekgokotlo (a conspirator in the murder of his brother over the right to chiefship), Sechele sought to make an alliance with his own elder brother, Kgosidintsi, by marrying him to his daughter Ope, much against the wishes of the missionary Moffat, who considered the match between uncle and niece incestuous (Sillery 1954:121).

Although older than Sechele, Kgosidintsi had to defer to Sechele because his mother was not regarded as his father's principal wife (Ramsay 1991:55). This potentially hostile situation never erupted during the brothers' lifetimes because Kgosidintsi accepted his junior status and Sechele in return recognized him as one of his close advisers and gave him the headship of Mogkalo ward, one of the principal wards in Molepolole to this day. Sechele attempted to strengthen this tie by marrying one of his younger daughters, Bantshang, to one of Kgosidintsi's descendants in the first house. Kgosidintsi's influential role is noted by Ramsay (1991:55), who comments that "both he and his descendents have consistently played a role in Bakwena affairs second only to that of the Sechele line." For these descendants, however, the relationship has proved to be the source of some friction, as we shall see in some of the dispute cases we shall examine in a moment.

During Sechele's reign, Basimane ward prospered, and Mhiemang (who became the common ancestor from whom all the founding members of Mosotho are descended) married polygynously and established the three houses of Mere, Moreri, and Koosimile, whose direct descendants established Mosotho kgotla. When Sechele died in 1892, the problems of agnatic rivalry revealed themselves in the form of competing claims to the chiefship. Kgari claimed that as the eldest son of Mokgokong, Sechele's wife in the first house, he should succeed his father. Sebele, however, disputed this on the basis that his mother, Selemeng, although coming after Mokgokong in time, was the principal wife, and that he therefore had a stronger claim to the chiefship. The morafe split into factions of roughly equal weight but along socially differentiated lines. Sebele had the support of his father's brother, Kgosidintsi, and others of the ruling group including the leaders of the autonomous metse, who it is said were wary of appointing Kgari because of his close links to Bangwato.

Kgari, on the other hand, tended to derive support from the more subordinate commoner groups. It appears that Mhiemang's son, Koosimile, attempted to enhance his status by allying himself with Kgari's followers through marriages with members of Kgari's family. Support was also forthcoming from Sebele's younger brothers, Motswasele IV and Motsetsi, who no doubt hoped to improve their fortunes as junior royals under Kgari's patronage. Kgari was, however, unsuccessful in his claim, and Sebele was appointed kgosi. As a result, Kgari split from the group with his followers and attempted to establish himself as an autonomous ruler. After his death in 1895 most of his followers drifted back to Sebele (Ramsay 1991:230).

Early Colonial Context of Sebele's Reign

When Sebele became kgosi (he ruled from 1892 to 1911), he did so within the British colonial context of the Bechuanaland Protectorate. The settlement patterns which had been established in his father's reign became entrenched. Kwena influence declined as Bangwato, able to break free from two decades of Kwena intrusion (made largely because of Kweneng's geographical location outside the main trade routes), established their preeminence (Ramsay 1991). At the same time Bakgatla and Balete emerged as independent polities and Bakwena found themselves deprived of grazing land.

European trade, which had become central to the region, declined as the market for ivory and ostrich feathers in the 1880s progressively deteriorated. It also became subject to competition from ostrich farms established at the Cape. While trade declined, dependence did not. Nangati notes that even in the 1840s there was a great dependence on European goods. He observes, "In no time, foreign articles, such as utensils, brought by traders started to compete with indigenous manufactures. . . . The consumption of imported edibles, such as tea and coffee, luxuries, such as snuff, and ornaments, like beads and trinkets, became habitual. It should be noted that consumption of these goods did not go far down the social hierarchy." (Nangati 1982:142). As Wilmsen has noted (1989:133; see also Schapera 1970:103), this dependence had vastly accelerated by the 1890s. During this period there was growing exposure to missionaries and the reins of external control passed from the ad hoc hands of merchants to the policy-conscious care of colonial administrators (Wilmsen 1989:129). Sebele benefited from the reforms instituted by his father for consolidating his power and was assisted in this by colonial administrators. This is the period to which the creation of a "paramount chief" may be attributed and when indirect rule led to the privileging of the local elite. However, Sebele and the other dikgosi also had to deal with the growing threat of encroachment by the British South Africa Company and Cecil Rhodes, which led to the famous trip to London of Sebele, Khama I, and Batoane to petition the British government not to permit them to be incorporated within the newly founded Republic of South Africa (Ramsay 1991:232; Parsons 1967; Tlou and Campbell 1984:159; Morton and Ramsay 1987).

In this environment, there were changes in the power structure which contributed to a greater degree of stratification by creating an additional group of interests beyond those of royals and commoners and which marked the inception of what was to become a new middle class (Mautle 1986). There was a further stratification of wealth. While much of the wealth in the nineteenth century went to traders, a significant remainder went to indigenous economies concentrated in the hands of chiefs and headmen (Parsons 1977; Wilmsen 1989:11).

While Bakwena had been migrating since the 1840s to work for Boer farmers as laborers or domestics, it was during the 1890s, with the opening of the mines on the Witwatersrand, that the need for industrial labor on a more comprehensive scale, particularly in the context of a rapidly developing South Africa, became apparent. At the same time as these needs were making themselves felt, Bakwena and other Tswana merafe were experiencing an ecological crisis fueled by drought, plagues of locusts, and the great rinderpest epidemic of 1896–98, which swept across the whole of southern Africa decimating the cattle population. It is said that by mid-May 1896 Kgosidintsi had lost all of his cattle and that Sebele's herd of ten thousand cattle had been reduced to seventy-seven head (Ramsay 1991:245). With crop failure came famine, which together with dysentery and typhoid fever greatly weakened the population. Dependence on European imports, ecological constraints, and the need to meet obligations in cash newly imposed by colonial administrators contributed to the escalation in migration (although it did not reach its zenith until the 1940s). In Ramsay's view (1991:242), it set the context within which Kweneng, like many other African regions, acquired the status of a labor reserve.

Sebele I's Alliances through Marriage

Sebele, like his father, favored polygamy, although his marriage to his first wife, Gorileng, was a Christian one. While I have no information on whether he was related to his wives, like his father he married a sister of one of them, Ikaeng, the sister of Gorileng. The complexity and fluidity of sexual relationships is illustrated by his extramarital relationship with Baultwe, or Mmathadi, who was the wife of Mhiko Segakisa, a descendant of the Segakisa who had so staunchly supported his father and was now a prominent member of the morafe as head of Difetlhamolelo ward.

The relationship lasted many years, and they had several children. While Mhiko apparently accepted and even sanctioned the union, Gorileng was vehemently opposed to it, and her spirited opposition led to a split within the morafe along sectarian lines physically manifested by Sebele and Bautlwe living in one part of Molepolole and Gorileng and her supporters in another (Ramsay 1991). Earlier in his reign Bakwena had agreed to move most of the village to Ntsweng Hill, a supposedly healthier, less congested environment than Borakalalo Valley some two miles to the northeast. It is said that Sebele eventually married Baultwe in 1901 with the consent of Gorileng's sons, Kebohula and Kealeboga, who was to become Sebele's successor.

Sebele tended to adopt the same strategies as his father toward alliances through marriage, namely, marriages within the morafe as well as close kin, binding others in allegiance, along with external alliances with other Tswana merafe. His daughter, Khudubanyana, was married to Pisang of Thato ward, an immigrant ward led by seceding royalty from the Tawana. His son, Moiteelasilo, was married to Mpelo from Mokgalo ward, a prominent ward headed by members of the Kgosidintsi family. His second wife, Nanao, came from Basimane ward (and was the mother of Mr. Masimega's wife). His son, Kebohula, was married to Kwenawarona, his father's brother's daughter. His second wife, Motlhaping, of Bamalete origin, came from the royal house of Kudunyabe at Kopong Village.

Sebele's heir, Kealeboga (Sechele II, 1911–18), also married a close relative, Phetogo, who was the daughter of his father's brother, Tumagole. The relationship was not, however, successful in forging internal cohesion within the ruling group. The hostility between royal houses that Sechele and Kogsidintsi had avoided erupted with Kgosidintsi's son, Baruti, who took every opportunity to undermine Kealeboga (Ramsay 1991). This included having an affair with Phetogo, to whom he was related as her mother's mother's sister's son. They had a child together, Neale, who reigned as chief from 1962 to 1970. The friction between the parties was so great that Kealeboga resorted to divorce in 1915.

According to Ramsay (1991), this feud was fueled in part by Kealeboga's desire to marry Lena, who had royal connections with another dynasty, being the daughter of the kgosi of Bakhurutshe who had recently deserted her husband. There is some dispute as to whether Lena was Kealeboga's second or third wife. According to Ramsay (1991:325), she was his third wife, as he had been married to and also separated from Kebue Modietsho, or Mmaletlamma, his second wife. Others, however, do not regard his relationship with Kebue as a marriage. This is another example illustrating the problems surrounding the marking of a status classification.

It is interesting to note that in his encounters with Baruti, Kealeboga received little support from his younger brothers, Kebohula and Moiteelasilo. This is hardly surprising in the case of the latter, as Sebele I had openly expressed the desire that Moiteelasilo should succeed him on his death, a desire which the morafe ignored. The political situation was not improved by the British seeking to extend their influence through the creation of a Bakwena Tribal Council in 1916. Although this council did not last long, Kebohula and Moiteelasilo were active members. Baruti was also a member, but after his fall from grace he was replaced as spokesman for Mokgalo ward by his brother, Motswakhumo.

In the aftermath of Kealeboga's divorce, Bakwena became increasingly polarized between an elite minority opposed to and a popular majority in favor of the kgosi. In order to control the factionalism, Kealeboga moved the site of the capital to Ntsweng in 1915. Members of the opposition, including such prominent people as Kebohula and Moiteelasilo, stayed behind in the valley with most of Ntloedibe kgotla and Mokgalo and Ratshosa wards. When Kealeboga died in 1918, he left the morafe divided. Such divisions have continued to operate, particularly with regard to succession, which became an issue when a number of dikgosi died without children (Ramsay 1991).

Up to about 1916, dikgosi had been able to consolidate their authority. During Kealeboga's reign, with British support and subsequently, the process of dismantling this very authority—now viewed as a threat to colonial interests—was implemented by British administrators through legislation.

THE POSITION OF COMMONERS AND THE FOUNDING OF MOSOTHO KGOTLA

It was during the reign of Kgari Sechele (1931–62) that the chief's kgotla, Kgosing, became established in the spot that it occupies today. Kgari succeeded Kelebantse (Sebele II 1918–31), who was sent into exile by the British in 1931. As part of their program of consolidating support for Kgari the British imposed forced removals in 1937 from Ntsweng and Borakalalo, where many members of the morafe were situated, to a new site which marks the current Kgosing (figs. 6–13). As part of this upheaval, the members of Basimane ward had to move from Ntsweng, and Mosotho kgotla was founded. Our focus shifts now from the history of elites to those less politically prominent members of the morafe associated with Basimane ward and Mosotho kgotla.

At the time of the move in 1937, some junior members of Basimane ward had already settled in the vicinity of the relocated chief's kgotla because of their role as tribal police. This meant that they had already occupied space that should have been subject to ritual cleansing by the most senior ward members (a practice which is followed whenever a new ward is established or a ward is moved). In order to deal with this situation and to enable the more senior members to occupy the appropriate space, the ward was divided into three kgotlas, those of Motlabi, Moitlobo, and Mosotho, with the most senior members settling in Motlabi kgotla. The more junior members congregated in the other two kgotlas, and the first twelve households associated with Mosotho kgotla came into being (figs. 4, 15, households 1, 3, 5, 7–12, and 14–16). These households represented descendants of a common ancestor, Mhiemang, referred to earlier, who married polygamously and established the three houses of Mere, Moreri, and Koosimile, whose direct descendants established Mosotho kgotla (figs. 15–21). Koosimile, like the royalty of that time, was said to practice polygamy and is credited with three wives. His first and third wives are said to have had royal connections with Sechele's son Kgari, who was unsuccessful in the competition with his brother Sebele for taking over the leadership of the morafe on Sechele's death in 1892 (Ramsay 1991).

Koosimile's third wife came from Goomorwa ward, whose members are closely related to Baanami, Kgari's son. These royal connections were said to be more powerful than those of the first wife, which was said to explain why Radipati regarded himself as Koosimile's foremost family representative, although he was only born in the third house. It is not clear what resources Koosimile possessed during his lifetime, but he is believed to have been reasonably well off, one kgotla member commenting that he must have been wealthy in order to have been a polygamist. He was, according to Tshitoeng (see fig. 14a), "a good man. He respected his elder brothers and Bogosi. He would go out hunting and bring back the proceeds to give his family. He had cattle but he was not rich. He had enough for his family but nothing to pass on." As far as anyone can remember, his children did not inherit much, if anything, from him. His sons, Makokwe (in the first house) and Radipati (in the third), were married when the British enforced removals from Ntsweng, where Basimane ward was located in 1937, to its current site next to the chief's kgotla in Kgosing ward. Since then Mosotho kgotla has grown over the years, until by 1984 it had became associated with thirty households (fig. 4: households in the kgotla are numbered according to their spatial position in relation to one another in 1984; see fig. 15).[4] By that time, twelve of the additional households had been established elsewhere due to lack of space in the kgotla.[5] But back in 1937 both Radipati and Makokwe established founding households in the newly created kgotla,[6] where they pursued very different lives from one another.

THE PEASANTARIAT: MAKOKWE'S FAMILY

Makokwe, like his father, was a polygamist. He had three wives with whom he was living when the enforced removal from Ntsweng took place in 1937. Like many men of his generation (G.2) he had no formal education and preferred to stay with his family at the lands,[7] rather than involve himself in village life and participate in kgotla affairs. He is remembered as a man who was aloof from other kgotla members. He maintained his family through lands and cattlepost activities and making karosses for trade, a skill which Radipati's daughter, Goitsemang, maintains Makokwe learned from her father. Such activities only provided support for the family at a subsistence level, and his eldest son, Motlotlegi, commented that when "my father died [he died] a poor man." This was confirmed by Makokwe's other children.

Access to Resources

Like their father, Makokwe's six sons never received a formal education. Instead, they followed the usual pattern assisting at the lands and herding cattle at the cattlepost. By this time, migrant labor had become incorporated into the life cycle, and as adults they shifted to working on contracts at the South African mines. Such contracts took up a significant part of their adult lives, covering much longer periods than those documented as the average for a Motswana (Schapera 1947:54–59).[8] The significance of this kind of labor is such that for many it has replaced initiation ceremonies (now banned or seriously curtailed) and marriage as markers of transition from adolescence into adulthood. In the life cycle as constituted by local people the paradigm for becoming an adult male these days involves leaving home to take up paid employment elsewhere. This action initiates the transition from boyhood to manhood, which will be reinforced by each subsequent period of employment away from the village. For girls, however, the transition is marked not so much by a labor contract as by pregnancy. Through the paradigm of becoming a mother a woman reaches the next stage in her life cycle and makes the transition from being a girl to being a woman. This acquisition of adulthood does not depend on the status of the relationship in which the child is born, on whether it is or has the potential for a marriage. Thus, for local people age is not a main consideration in acquiring adult status for either men or women, and neither is marriage (although it provides an additional element of maturity and authority that accrues to an individual as he or she progresses through his or her life cycle).

While they were migrant laborers, Nkadikang and his brothers maintained their lands and cattle base, following the predominant profile of many families in Botswana, who need to combine these activities for their subsistence. Without the cash input from their employment they would not have been able to engage in agriculture or build up their holdings in livestock. Makokwe did not leave them with a sufficient inheritance to enable them to opt out of such employment. Apart from land, which all the sons acquired on marriage, they had to build up their own livestock and other agricultural resources.

Unlike his brothers in the third house, Motlotlegi was not awarded any land by Makokwe, but acquired it through a maternal relative who was a headman with power to allocate lands at the Marabane plowfields. His position differed from that of his brothers, as his parents were divorced when he was young and he was brought up among his mother's people in Kgaimena ward. While Makokwe allocated land to three of his sons (Nkadikang, Morabane, and Ntlogelang), this land came from Ntloedibe ward and was acquired from the headman Botsabelo, who was a maternal cousin of Makokwe. Another son, Kemongale, acquired the land that he plows from his partner Keselibile's maternal great grandmother. This land was passed down from Tshitoeng's wife's mother, to Tshitoeng's wife, and on to her daughter Keselibile. The youngest brother, Ramojaki,[9] acquired his land from his widowed mother, who lived with him and his wife for several years before her death. Her field at Morabane derives from her mother's family, who were also from Ntloedibe ward.

Cattle and livestock purchased with the earnings from migrant labor were looked after by Makokwe, while he was alive, and by other family members who were not at the mines. When Makokwe died, some of his sons claimed that there were a few goats which were divided, but others hotly denied this. In any event, these goats were said to have perished shortly after Makokwe's death. Memories vary, but they do underline an important point, namely, the susceptibility of cattle and livestock to disease and drought. This makes for a precarious existence particularly where small holdings are involved. Motlotlegi has lost many cattle and has had to rebuild his herd a number of times over the years. Despite these setbacks he continued, with the help of his sons, who remitted money from the mines, to build up his livestock.

The same is true for his younger brothers. In their case, they started with the added advantage of their father having earmarked a heifer for each of them during his lifetime. However, these cattle had all perished by the time of his death, and like Motlotlegi, they had to start all over again in rebuilding their stock. This has taken time and been subject to many setbacks. Ntlogelang, for example, has lost cattle on several occasions, but by 1989 he had been able to rebuild his herd up to twelve, through engaging in various mafisa arrangements whereby he acquired cattle in return for services rendered.[10]

Motlotlegi was born and raised among his mother's people in Kgaimena ward, so his father's household in Mosotho kgotla was not his natal household. This is no doubt because his parents separated when he was very young, and in such cases it is usual for the children to remain with their mother until they are old enough to take up their association with their father's side of the family. What is unusual in Motlotlegi's case is that he claims to have lost all contact with his mother's people on becoming an adult.

Motlotlegi is associated with Mosotho kgotla, but he has not built there (to do so would reinforce his links with his father's side of the family). However, this may well be due to lack of space, as the kgotla can no longer accommodate additional households. Household 26, which Motlotlegi built, is in fact right at the other end of the village from Mosotho kgotla in an area known as Lekgwapheng (located off the aerial map in fig. 2, to the left). Like their father, Makokwe's sons are viewed as having distanced themselves from the kgotla, one explanation being that "when he [Makokwe] died his children scattered to where[ever] they could make a living." Even those sons who grew up in Mosotho kgotla and have built their own households[11] have done so in Lekgwapheng, where they are all reasonably close to one another. Only one brother, Kemongale, has a household in the kgotla, which was acquired from the first cousin of his partner, Keselebile.[12] Over time Kemongale has preferred to settle more permanently at the lands, leaving the household in the care of Keselebile's children. Along with his brothers, he has left his unmarried sister, Olebeng, in charge of the natal household, and she has run it for many years.

Unlike his brothers in the third house, Motlotlegi had no male siblings in the first house with whom he could pool labor, as his half brothers were either unborn or too young to be of any assistance. Instead, he relied on his father, Makokwe, and his own sons to care for his livestock while he worked at the mines. As his sons joined him, his wife, Mosarwa, assumed responsibility for plowing, assisted by their daughters and later by hired help. Motlotlegi earmarked a heifer for the eldest daughter in recognition of her services in herding cattle when no males were available.

This assumption of male tasks by women has already been commented upon and has also been noted in other African countries which were heavily involved in migrant labor (Hay 1982). It is said to have strengthened the position of women, giving them greater authority within their communities which they were reluctant to give up when the men returned (Schapera 1947:185). Not only that, but in some cases it fueled their desire for greater freedom, leading them to reject the family/domestic labor/lands complex of activities in favor of other alternatives such as migrant labor (Schapera 1947:62; Izzard 1985).

Family Life Cycles

Motlotlegi at eighty-nine (in 1989) has progressed through his life cycle from herding cattle at the cattlepost, to working as an adult at the mines, to retirement in middle age and reengagement in full-time agro-pastoral activities. Blind and unable to work any longer, he is now at the end of his life cycle. With seven adult children who have all married and built their own households or become associated with households elsewhere, he and his wife Mosarwa are now at a stage where they rely on their children for support. While this could pose a problem, given that a number of their grandchildren are adult and have young children of their own, the resources are such that they are in fact well supported. Their youngest child, Ntshimane, who works at the platinum mines in Rustenburg, South Africa, plows or hires other people to plow for them, and some of their grandchildren who are attending school live with them and carry out domestic tasks for them. There is still an element of reciprocity involved, with Mosarwa supervising the care of these grandchildren who are too young to look after themselves.

While Makokwe may have died a poor man, Motlotlegi and his children through their lands, cattlepost, and mining activities have accumulated a measure of wealth which is reflected in the fact that over the years household 26 has been built to a modern design. It has become a house with four walls (instead of three, which is the Kwena definition of a round hut). It has acquired a corrugated iron roof, glass windows, and a stout wooden door. However, more significant than these visible manifestations of success is the fact that Ntshimane has a brand-new tractor, which few families in the village, let alone Mosotho kgotla, can afford. He has also been able to acquire the money to set his wife up in business running a bottle store.

The rewards for Motlotlegi's half brothers have not been so great, despite the fact that they have been able to pool resources and share labor. When Makokwe died, the chain for the span of oxen (an item both monetarily and symbolically costly) was shared between Morabane, Nkadikang, Ntlogelang, and Ramojaki. While they have built up their own resources through their own efforts—for example, Morabane acquired his own plow from a Mokgatla man in exchange for two sheep and a bag of sorghum—they have also been able to act cooperatively. So for example, Nkadikang and Ntlogelang shared the same cattlepost when they were younger, and Ramojaki and Morabane used to work together when they were younger, taking it in turns to go to the mines, plow, and look after cattle. However, these arrangements proved unsatisfactory in the long term, and they were abandoned. Ramojaki explained, "At that time [when we were younger] we helped each other but there were problems because when I was at work [at the mines] there was lack of attention to cattle and I had to decide how to go about plowing for myself." He was expressing the kind of tensions that Kooijman (1978:225) described in her fieldwork. Brothers may act cooperatively, but they are also situated in a relationship that has its competitive aspects, which creates tensions. Such tensions may lead to fission, but this may also be seen as part of the normal developmental cycle of a family. It is not surprising to find cooperation in men's lives diminishing as they grow older, create their own households, and seek to establish their own position in the family. Makokwe's sons in the third house are at just such a stage; with adult children and grandchildren accommodated in their households, their responsibilities and obligations shift as the range of individuals to whom they are related multiplies.

Progressing through the Life Cycle: The Male Experience

All of Makokwe's sons have come to the end of their employment at the mines. In some cases they acquired temporary employment on their return to Molepolole, but in the cases of Nkadikang, who worked briefly as a laborer, and Ntlogelang, who worked on the road to Letlhakeng when it was being constructed, this has long since ceased. Both are now engaged full-time in lands and cattle activities. In contrast, their younger brothers, Morabane and Ramojaki, have found other employment in which they are still engaged. The former works as a night watchman for the hospital and the latter as a borehole mechanic for the district council. They continue to combine employment with their lands and cattle activities.

Having spent a significant part of their adult lives in formal employment, they have reached a stage where they have been able to accumulate some livestock; indeed, Ntlogelang and Ramojaki have enough cattle to make up their own teams for plowing. With their own children available to provide labor for herding or plowing and with money to hire such labor, there is not the same incentive to engage in cooperative agricultural activities with their siblings, which might deplete their real or potential resources, compared to returns they might receive by conserving their energies within their own more immediate circle. While not as wealthy as Motlotlegi, in comparison with other households associated with Mosotho kgotla they are relatively well off, having access to cattle, labor, and a cash input. They fit the national profile which points to male-headed households being in a much stronger position with regard to these resources than female-headed households, even where such households have access to male contributions.

It is not only the brothers of this family who have come together in some form of association. Their only sister, Olebeng, Makokwe's youngest child, has received help and support from her brothers and in return has assisted them in agricultural activities. Ntlogelang claims to have plowed for her in the past and to supply water to her in a drum. She seems to have the closest relationship with her brother Ramojaki, who is nearest to her in age. According to him, "We help each other. When I have money and no time to plow I give her money and she plows for herself and me." While her brothers claim that she did not have any cattle earmarked for her by their father, she herself maintains that her parents left her two head. It was not clear if these were her mother's, but in any event these died during a drought a long time ago.

As she is unmarried, Olebeng's brothers still regard themselves under an obligation to assist her, although their ability to do so has become more limited given the number of children they have, particularly when these are young unmarried daughters who have babies and require support. Unlike those of her brothers, Olebeng's children all died at birth or in her confinement so she is not in a position to draw support from them. On the one hand, she has not been burdened with the need to care for young children, but on the other, she has no immediate descendants to take care of her in old age. In such a situation, she is fortunate that her brothers provide what support they can. Like many women of her generation (G.3) she only went to school to learn to read and write and left as soon as that was accomplished to go back to helping her mother with domestic and agricultural tasks.[13] Like her mother, she has never experienced formal employment of any kind, but has spent her life engaged in activities concerned with lands, agriculture, and the domestic sphere.

The pattern outlined above continues to serve, with some minor modifications, as a model for subsequent generations of Makokwe's descendants. These include the acquisition of some formal education for boys in the younger generation (G.4),[14] but only to a basic level, and, in some cases, a shift away from employment at the mines to other areas such as the construction industry, where they are employed as bricklayers or builder's laborers. As such work tends to be intermittent, based on a contract for each job done, this has done little to provide for more stable and long-term employment. There is competition for such work among those members of the younger generation, such as Galefelele (Ntlogelang's son), who at sixteen finds himself ineligible for employment at the mines due to cutbacks in South Africa's recruitment of workers outside the country and a policy of employing only those who have been on previous contracts. Those who are lucky, or who have connections, find work. Keselibile's son, Kabo, for example, found his job as a builder's laborer in Gaborone in 1989 as the result of a recommendation given by his sister's current male companion. Those among the younger generation who cannot find work tend to hang around the natal household or on the periphery of urban areas where they may have relatives.

Procreative Relationships and Marriage

It is within this type of environment that procreative relationships and marriage are negotiated (fig. 14). Among this family group, these range widely from marriage at one end of the scale to fleeting and brief relationships at the other. This diversity reflects a higher degree of marriage among the older generation, with a more fluid and variable set of relationships occurring among the younger generation. Among the older generation, including Makokwe's sons and grandchildren there is a high rate of marriage, in many cases to a relative. In both cases, however, the options open to individuals and the power they possess to negotiate the terms of their relationship depend on where they are situated within their family network and the resources on which they can draw. Such power may enable one to negotiate marriage, as in the case of Makokwe's sons, or to reject it, as in the case of Olebeng, his only daughter and youngest child. In contrast there are those in the same generation, such as Keiphe's daughter, Diane, who are not in that privileged position and have had to settle for whatever kind of relationship is available.

Makokwe's son, Motlotlegi (G.3), married Mosarwa, who was a relative (father's father's brother's son's daughter). Their seven children have all married. Of the five daughters, three married men to whom they were related. The eldest daughter, Gaselefufa, married Gabriel Mere who is her father's father's father's brother's son's son. On their marriage they went to live with Gabriel's parents in Mogogoru kgotla. They inherited household 21 in that kgotla from Gabriel's maternal grandmother. Mosarwa, Gaselefufa's mother, gave Gaselefufa and Gabriel the field that she brought with her into her marriage with Motlotlegi, and it is this land at Lewale that Gabriel and his family continue to plow. Gaselefufa has never been formally employed. Her husband Gabriel's profile is similar in nature to that of Koosimile's sons in the same generation. He went on contract to the South African mines until he was forced to stop in the 1950s because of an accident at work which paralyzed the fingers of one hand. After that, he came home to work on the lands where he and Gaselefufa have focused their activities ever since.

Another of Motlotlegi's daughters, Thatayone, married a cousin of Motlotlegi's from Modibedi kgotla. Her sister, Boikhutso, married a more closely related relative who is a "son born by our father's sister," who is a member of Basimane ward associated with Motlabi kgotla. They have both lived with their husbands' relatives for many years and established their own households.

Another two daughters, Kemolaole and Goitsemodimo, married men to whom they were not related. One came from Tsweneng kgotla and the other from Thamaga, a village close to Molepolole. In both cases, the women remained living in their natal household with their children and in both cases the marriages broke down, due in part to the strain of long separations enforced by mine labor contracts. Deserted by their husbands, whose families showed little interest in maintaining marital ties, the two sisters left Molepolole to search for work in Mafeking. As deserted wives with dependent children, they fall into that category of women referred to by Schapera as likely candidates for migrant labor, that is, those who are vulnerable because they represent a drain on existing family resources. It is interesting to note that Kemolaole and Goitsemodimo's sisters who are still married have never involved themselves in migrant labor or been employed.

Both Kemolaole and Goitsemodimo worked for many years in Mafeking and formed long-standing relationships with men there with whom they have had a number of children. In Kemolaole's case, her partner, Brown, built for her in Lekgwapheng next to her mother and father. By 1989, aged sixty-one, she had reached that stage in her life cycle where she returned to her natal village to live full-time. As Brown has died and she is no longer employed, she relies on her children for support, particularly her eldest son, Stofle, a miner who has built a house for himself next to his mother and his grandparents. Her sister, Goitsemodimo, at fifty-five, is still living and working with her partner in Mafeking. She has not yet managed to build a house for herself in Molepolole but maintains close links with her family.

Makokwe had no children in the second house. In his third house, marriage is present among his sons' relationships. All five have married, and in three cases they are related to their partners. Nkadikang's first wife was Phiriyagae's daughter, who was related to him as his father's brother's daughter. Morabane's wife is a remote relative; she is born of Rantleru, who was one of his granduncles from Moitlobo kgotla (which forms part of Basimane ward). Kemongale, who was first married to Phiriyagae's daughter, entered into a long-term relationship with Keselibile on her death. Keselibile, Tshitoeng Mere's daughter, is related to him as his father's father's brother's son's daughter. Given that second marriages are regarded as less formal in nature, and that Keselibile and Kemongale are related, their relationship is regarded as an informal marriage by kgotla members. In contrast with her six brothers, Makokwe's daughter, Olebeng, has remained unmarried.

Among the next generation (G.4), particularly women, the situation is much more fluid and diverse. This is in tune with the overall findings for Mosotho kgotla and Botswana as a whole. One-quarter of the sixteen women in this generation had to leave school because of pregnancy.[15] These women included Nkadikang's daughter Walebaka (age unknown) and Ramojaki's daughters, Okahune (seventeen), Mmasadi (fifteen), and Mokgarehe (seventeen). As in many cases of this kind, the relationships giving rise to pregnancy came to an end without any serious discussions of marriage between the families concerned. The women, like others elsewhere, have all moved on to other relationships, none of which are regarded as marriages. In the fourth case, the pregnancy had only just occurred in 1984 and it was too early to tell whether marriage was considered a real option or not.

In contrast to these four women, we find six others (of the sixteen women in this generation), ranging from their late teens to their mid-thirties, who have married. In some cases, the women, who are more advanced in their life cycle than those referred to above, have entered into a number of relationships before marrying. Morabane's daughter, Lebalang, for example, had children with three different partners before settling into a marriage at age twenty-eight with her third partner. Her first two relationships, which were in the fleeting and brief categories, had none of the qualities associated with a potential customary marriage. Her situation fits the profile presented by Comaroff and Roberts (1977) of parties trying out various relationships before committing themselves. There are other women of her age, however, who have had a number of relationships, none of which have become marriages or exhibit any of the marks associated with a potential customary marriage.

On the other hand, in a few cases such as that of Peneka, Kemongale's daughter by his first marriage, such experimentation with relationships is unnecessary and marriage takes place at an early stage before pregnancy arises. In between there are those cases, illustrated by Ntlogelang's daughters, Koketso (thirty-four) and Mmupi (thirty), where the woman became pregnant in her first relationship, which progressed over the years until it eventually materialized into a marriage. In both these cases the families met and agreed to the relationship continuing; after the birth of subsequent children, the women moved to live with their partners' families. At the end of this process, which spanned from five to eight years, they finally married.[16]

Where marriage exists among Makokwe's family it reinforces certain connections, creating links and a conduit for resources which are recycled from generation to generation. One example was provided by the land brought into Motlotlegi's marriage by his wife, which was passed on to their eldest daughter when she married. Another is provided through the building of households. All Makokwe's sons, whether in the first or third house, built their own households after marriage and thus extended the family domain not only in physical terms but also with regard to potential political power on a local scale.

What is at stake for individuals and their families in negotiations over procreation and marriage varies according to the stage that has been reached in their life cycles. When the individual is of school age, he or she may be considered too young to be taken seriously as a marriage candidate, especially as his or her potential for development is as yet unknown. However, when children are older, their parents have an interest in their children's marriages as a means of consolidating and accumulating assets through strengthening or establishing those bonds that will ensure collaborative endeavor and pooling of resources among different family groups, especially where land and labor are concerned. Other family members, such as siblings, also have an interest in the creation of marital links, as these will place them in a particular set of relationships with others, thus imposing certain obligations and duties toward those persons. Where children are concerned, their mother's marriage to their father will result in their becoming affiliated with his family group, with all the claims of membership and rights to inheritance that such affiliation establishes. Balancing all these interests is a difficult task especially where the individual couple are concerned. For they may be more interested in pursuing their own agenda than engaging in the broader arena of extended family politics. The kinds of tensions that can arise within families as a result of these differing perspectives, especially between generations, are highlighted by some of the narratives that appear in this chapter and throughout the rest of the book.

Women's Access to Resources within the Peasantariat

Life for the women in Makokwe's family revolves around the village and the lands where they engage in domestic and agricultural activities. Living in the village for much of the year, they are able to attend school, unlike their brothers, who are away herding cattle at distant cattleposts. This means that they are able to acquire a greater degree of formal education than their brothers, who in many cases among the older generation have received none at all. Out of the twenty women (in G.4) who are the daughters of Makokwe's sons, only one, Motlotlegi's daughter, Goitsemodimo, did not attend school at any point, because she was the only one available to look after her father's cattle. The other women, who range in age from fifty-nine (Motlotlegi's eldest daughter, Gaselefufa) to thirteen (Ramojaki's youngest daughter), all acquired some degree of formal education. For the vast majority this represented attending primary school up to levels ranging between Standard 3 and Standard 6. Only four completed primary school by passing Standard 7; only three managed to attend secondary school, none of whom completed their courses.

Within this family group, women's formal education is confined to a basic level, although it is interesting to note that younger women within the generational grouping tend to attain a higher level of education than older ones. For example, Motlotlegi's four daughters only learned to read and write, while three of his youngest brother Ramojaki's five daughters completed Standard 6 and two of them completed Standard 7, with one actually attending secondary school.

Apart from those women whose education was interrupted because of pregnancy, representing 20% of the women overall in this family group,[17] the others in this family group left school to attend to domestic duties, to help their mother run the household, to look after sick or aged relatives, and to engage in agricultural activities. As already noted, young women make the transition from adolescence to adulthood at the birth of their first child, regardless of whether they are married or not. Attaining a particular age, such as eighteen, the legal age of majority for both sexes, is not regarded by the people themselves as a critical reference point. The statistics for Botswana as a whole (Botswana 1989), and the experiences of women from Mosotho kgotla in general, demonstrate a high incidence of pregnancy in women before the age of eighteen.

The women associated with Makokwe's family are engaged in agricultural, domestic, and reproductive activities which compliment the activities of their male counterparts. This has been the case with Makokwe's only daughter, Olebeng, who has been part of a family network exchanging her domestic and agricultural labor for her brothers' assistance with plowing and support. She has never moved beyond this sphere of operations to undertake any form of paid employment.[18] In the course of her life, she has had several children (all of whom died at birth) with a number of male partners but has never married and has remained living in her natal household. Neither she nor her brothers regard any of her relationships as being marital in nature. Olebeng explained that when she first became pregnant her parents (who were alive at that time) had no interest in pursuing the issue of marriage or initiating any kind of discussions with the man's family. Throughout her life she has been engaged in domestic and agricultural activities of the type that link her into a network where she has had to rely on male support from her father, her brothers, and her male partners for her existence. Within this system, she has been fortunate because her brothers have been quite generous in the support that they have given, assisting her with plowing and proving cooperative in other matters. Unlike Radipati's daughter Goitsemang, who is in conflict with her brother David over the natal household, Olebeng has been fortunate to have her brothers quite happily hand the natal household over to her. Compared with other women, she is in a relatively strong position.

The eight women who have married or are in long-standing relationships with Olebeng's brothers have a similar history, although they have, in accordance with custom, established new households for themselves in Lekgwapheng. Only one woman, Odirile, Ramojaki's wife, has had any experience of formal employment, and this was only on a temporary basis working under the drought relief program in 1984. This pattern holds for the younger women in G.4, although a number of them have experienced some form of formal employment.[19] So for example, Ntlogelang's daughters Koketso (thirty) and Mmupi (thirty) have worked briefly as a domestic and a shop assistant. Ramojaki's daughter Akohang (25) also works from time to time as a cook or a cleaner when not at the lands. Like that of their male counterparts in the family, this employment is generally at a level involving rudimentary skills. It is as insecure in tenure and as intermittent as men's work.

In this environment, where the emphasis is placed on subsistence agriculture, livestock, and a cash input from migrant labor, marriage is particularly important for women, who as unmarried daughters and sisters find themselves at the bottom of the social hierarchy in terms of power and access to resources. Such power not only derives from status and point in the life cycle, but also includes an individual's capacity to generate or control resources. Among women, power devolves with age linked to status, so that a young, unmarried, childless woman is in a less influential position than her older married sister who has children. Both, however, defer to their mother and even more to their grandmother, who by virtue of her age and status is considered to be in the most powerful position of them all. It is not age alone but the incidents that mark its passage, such as childbearing, which are an integral part of the life cycle and create status. The combination of age with status feeds the dynamics of power.

The same is true for men. A young, childless man who has never experienced formal employment has less status than his older married brother with children who has worked at the mines. Both should defer to their father and grandfather, who have passed beyond these stages. However, this is not always done, especially when the older generation is dependent on the younger to provide for them, as Schapera noted in the 1940s. The fact that the younger generation relies on the older generation to manage its interests associated with the village and to provide child care does not necessarily correct a shift in power relations.

In addition to these considerations, women find themselves further constrained at every level because of the structured set of gender relations in which women and men are situated. While women may have access to land and livestock, the forms this takes are mediated through men. This is because it is men or young boys who herd the livestock and thus acquire control over them. When it comes to cultivation of land, labor is required, and most people still rely on cattle to work the plow. Those that have a team or can contribute to one control the time of plowing and the sequence it may follow. In Mosotho kgotla, they are mostly married men; they plow their own fields before those of brothers, parents, and unmarried sisters. This is especially the case where recipients can contribute only their labor or are too old to provide even that.

Women have often provided the labor and done the plowing, as Motlotlegi's wife and daughters did in the past, but they have had to enter a male domain to do so, and this requires male consent and cooperation. Where this is not forthcoming there are problems. Women may have cattle but they have to get them to the lands to plow or back to the village to sell; both involve the cooperation of men who control the cattlepost or lands. There are often complaints that such overseers use these cattle for their own ends. Indeed, disputes often arise on this issue in Botswana. Keitatole's widow from household 19 talks of just such a dispute concerning the family team, which the herder claims has died but which her sons believe he has appropriated for his own purposes. This provides a case in point, in that Keitatole's widow cannot pursue the matter herself, but must do so through her sons. So male control is exercised not only in physical, but also in structural terms in that the mechanisms for negotiating these issues are predicated on men. How this operates in terms of the kgotla and how women deal with this situation are demonstrated in the disputes that will be presented in chapters 4 and 5.

Diane: The Vulnerable Position of Unmarried Women

Within this kind of network, an unmarried woman finds herself severely disadvantaged. Although she is part of a group formed of her family and kin who have responsibility for her and thus obligations to plow for her, her position within this network is a vulnerable one in that her interests are subordinated to those of other family members. Schapera (1947:67) noted the problems this caused in the 1940s when he observed that many unmarried women with children and widows became migrant laborers not only in response to family pressure to find support, but also in order to escape their lowly position within the family household. Women had to weigh the advantages of operating in this arena, as a wife or unmarried woman, with the disadvantages that this entailed. In many cases they had no choice. So it is with Diane (fig. 22) from Mosotho kgotla.

How women are linked to the peasantariat is presented through the contrasting profiles of Diane and Makokwe's daughter, Olebeng. Diane and her daughters have not been so fortunate as Olebeng. They have found themselves disadvantaged by the kind of constraints which are inherent in a kinship network. Diane is the eldest of Keiphe and Odibeleng's seven children. Her family background has much in common with that of Olebeng. In other words, her family has also engaged in livestock management, subsistence agriculture, and migrant labor.

Diane's brothers, Jeremiah and Oabona, like those of Olebeng, have never been to school. They herded cattle and worked on a number of contracts at the South African mines. However, the youngest brother, Lazarus, did go to school and went on to the University of Botswana, from which he graduated with a bachelor of arts degree. Unlike his brothers, he was able to bypass the mines and find employment with the Botswana Development Corporation (B.D.C.). Oabona is the only brother who has married (patlo), but Jeremiah has a long-standing relationship with a woman in Molepolole with whom he has six children. Diane's other siblings do not appear to have any children.

Unlike Olebeng, Diane and her two sisters went to school. While one sister, Rosemary, got as far as Form 2 in secondary school, Diane never got beyond Standard 3 in primary school. Like numbers of women in Botswana, they had to leave school because of pregnancy and never returned to formal education. Rosemary managed to put herself through a typing course, which enabled her to find employment in Gaborone with the Nigerian High Commission and then with a company called Business Machines. Although both Rosemary and Diane have children, only their sister, Memme, has married through patlo and a civil ceremony. Rosemary's first child was conceived during a brief relationship in school, and her second child was conceived in a brief relationship in Gaborone. Both relationships have been classified as fleeting because there was no contact with the man's family or any form of social recognition associated with a potential customary marriage. While Rosemary's mother is unhappy with this situation, she says nothing to her daughter because she is the only one of her children who is able to support her in her old age.

Such is the family context within which Diane (fifty-one in 1989) operates. In telling her story, she reveals how her first relationship had the potential for a marriage but after that her relationships took on another character, as she moved from man to man until she ended up in a nyatsi relationship with a married man which lasted a number of years but had ended by 1989. According to her

> I left school in 1955 when I was seventeen years old because I was pregnant. I met the father at my mother's place in Molepolole. His name was Nelson Guwer and he was from Tshosa ward. When I became pregnant my parents took action immediately. They went to his family and discussed marriage. We were both asked if we agreed to marriage and said yes. His parents paid tlhtlhagora[20] and gave me a ring. At that time he was working in Molepolole. After my confinement he went to work elsewhere and he ceased to visit me. My mother went to see his family and when questioned about marriage arrangements they said they were no longer in a position to marry because my father's elder brother Rampole was not in favor of the marriage. That was not true. That was just a lie. I gave up at that stage. I felt the promise of marriage would never be fulfilled.
>
> After that I met another man who proposed marriage. he was from Mosarwa kgotla. His father came to tell my parents that he had seduced me and that he was requesting marriage. They agreed to marriage. We had three children together. Before that third child was born my mother went to see his family. They said that he would marry me when he came back from the South African mines. He never came back and we gave up. He never did anything. He did not support the children. My family supported me. My father was working on the South African Railways and paid for the children's school fees, food, and clothing.
>
> I met another man from Molepolole and had a child with him. He never did anything. Then I met a man from Koodisa ward and had five children with him. He is married. Until he was laid off from the South African mines [in 1983] he supported all the children. We were together over ten years but now he just drops by from time to time to say hello. As he has been without a job for a long while he no longer provides any support.

There is some discrepancy between Diane's account of her relationships and that of her mother, Odibeleng. Odibeleng maintains that the Guwers were entitled to withdraw from the marriage in Diane's first relationship because of her behavior. Odibeleng says that they behaved well, supplying Diane with food and clothing during confinement. After confinement, they were in the process of negotiating marriage when Diane fell in love with someone else and had a child. After this, Odibeleng said "we were discouraged as parents and did not take any action. We felt that she had disobeyed us by mixing with another boy when we were expecting her to marry Guwer's son." While mother and daughter are still friendly and some of Diane's children live with and look after Odibeleng, it is clear that Odibeleng does not approve of the relationships in which Diane has had children and does not wish to discuss the circumstances surrounding their birth beyond the first two children. This disapproval may have encouraged Diane to move away and establish her own home in household 28, which is some distance away from Mosotho kgotla.

As in the case of Radipati's daughter, Goitsemang (to be discussed shortly), there are tensions in this mother-and-daughter relationship regarding men. Both women have established their own households, but they have done so in different ways. Diane's world depends heavily on male support and cooperation to operate the networks necessary for its existence. To a certain extent this was forthcoming during her father's lifetime, but when he died her brothers ceased to incorporate her in their networks. They failed to plow for her and indeed took over for themselves the field that she had been allocated. Although she acquired the use of another field from a male neighbor, she was unable to utilize this resource in 1984 because she could not afford to buy seed or to hire labor. Like many women, she was able to plow for the first time in 1989 only because of assistance provided by ALDEP[21] under a government scheme. In addition, Diane claimed that her brother Jeremiah exerted pressure on her to leave the natal household. Fortunately she was able to buy a plot of land in Molepolole for twenty pula, the money for which was probably provided by her fourth partner.

Her situation fits the profile of the vulnerable female-headed household at risk described by Kerven (1979a; 1984), Izzard (1979; 1982), Brown (1983), and others. Her social context makes her more dependent on men for her existence than someone like Radipati's eldest daughter, Goitsemang, who is only one year older. Given Diane's brothers' lack of interest and their own family commitments she has had to turn to male partners for support. As her life cycle has progressed, she has had to accept what is offered and to be prepared, as with her fourth partner, who had supported all her children, to enter into a relationship that would never lead to marriage or formal recognition of the children by the man's family. She fits the profile for those relationships differentiated from marriage which Schapera (1947:173) noted tended to be entered into by older unmarried women.

Diane's situation is perpetuated in the next generation. All five of her adult daughters have, like her, had to leave school because of pregnancy, although they left with higher grades. The two oldest daughters, Nametso (twenty-nine) and Margaret (twenty-six) (who have since died),[22] each had a second child in another relationship, but these relationships were also short lived. Of the seven relationships entered into by Diane's daughters between the ages of sixteen and twenty-nine only one displayed any of the signs associated with a potential customary marriage. This was Onneile's relationship with a Kalanga man from Central District. She had a child with him when she was eighteen, and the families agreed that they would marry. He supported Onneile before the birth and provided food and money for her and the child while she was in confinement. However, he did not provide any support for her when she was pregnant with the second child, which was born when she was twenty, and he then faded from the scene. This is not an uncommon experience among women in Mosotho kgotla. Onneile's sisters' relationships all fell under the headings of fleeting or brief and involved no more than brief meetings between the families. It may be that Onneile's partner was prepared to contemplate marriage because he came from a morafe that is considered to be subordinate in status to Tswana merafe.

Unlike their mother, several of Diane's daughters have been employed in domestic service or as shop assistants or barmaids. But this work has been intermittent. In 1989, only one, Malutu, aged twenty-six, was working as a shop assistant in Gaborone, where she was living in rented accommodation. Of the other two surviving adult daughters, Onneile, aged twenty-eight, was unemployed but living with Diane's younger brother, Lazarus, in Gaborone; Khone, aged eighteen, was at the lands.

THE SALARIAT: RADIPATI'S FAMILY

Radipati's family members have developed differently, and among the younger generation have come to represent a growing elite in Botswana, the salariat.

Radipati's life history is very different from that of his brother Makokwe. Subsequent generations in Radipati's family have continued to develop along the lines he promoted in his lifetime, which distinguish them from Makokwe's descendants. Like his brother, he does not seem to have inherited anything of significance from his father, Koosimile. However, through his mother's elite connections, as a child he was taken up by Kealeboga (Sechele II) and received an education which was unusual among men of his generation. Mixing with members of the chief's kgotla and participating in their affairs, he acquired a reputation as a good orator, a skill highly valued among the Tswana and which enhanced his public status. When it came to marriage, his first wife Kaojana, born of Meshack Leshona from Moloi ward, came from a well-educated family. Her father was a deacon in the London Missionary Society who read the bible in church on Sundays. While not rich in cattle, he had status arising from his educational attainments and links with the church.

The Christian Dimension

The influence of Christianity propagated by missionaries was something that steadily took hold among the Tswana from the second half of the nineteenth century onward. Sechele I is famous for having been David Livingstone's first convert to Christianity in Africa. His conversion took place in 1848 (Livingstone 1959:260), but Livingstone subsequently "cut him off from fellowship" (Sillery 1954:95) for not adhering to monogamy and having a child with one of his former wives to whom he was polygamously married.

That Christianity was making its mark among Bakwena, despite the hostility noted by Livingstone to Sechele's conversion, may be seen from the fact that a number of Mhiemang's descendants married in church as well as according to traditional Kwena rites. These included Robert and Gasentsima, both sons of Moreri (fig. 14*b*), as well as Radipati, who was married twice in church. It has been said that in the struggle surrounding the succession of Sechele I, his son Kgari attempted to mobilize support by allying himself with the Christian faction within the community while his brother Sebele drew on more traditional sources (Ramsay 1991:226).

Just as Kgari and Sebele may be juxtaposed with one another, so may Koosimile's sons Makokwe and Radipati. While Makokwe, like his father, was a polygamist, Radipati was not. Unlike his brother, he married Mantshadi in church, although he also celebrated the marriage according to traditional rites and most unusually paid bogadi. In this way, Radipati became allied with a different element of Kwena society than his brother Makokwe, one which built on a different set of connections. Like his father, he continued to make influential connections, for Mantshadi's father, Disang, was related to Tawana royalty. When Disang seceded from the Tawana, he and his followers were welcomed by Sechele. In recognition of his position, he and his followers were allowed to establish their own ward, Thato, over which he was appointed headman. Radipati and Disang's daughter, Mantshadi, had a son, Daniel. When Mantshadi died Radipati married Mhudi from Thato ward. As a mark of Mhudi's status, although somewhat unusually according to Tswana practice, Mhudi is said to have brought some cattle and goats with her along with some batlhanka and a plowing field into her marriage with Radipati. Mhudi and Radipati had three daughters, Goitsemang, Salalenna, and Olebogeng, and three sons, David, Pelonomi, and Moses.

Social Standing in the Village

Well connected through natal and marital alliances, an eloquent orator and skilled kaross maker, Radipati was a well-respected member of the community. People remember that it was one of his karosses which was presented to King George VI on his royal visit to the Protectorate in 1947. While seen as a "kind of nephew" to Kgari Sechele, he was highly regarded "because he was an industrious and clever man." According to Goitsemang, Radipati's daughter, he tried to help Makokwe by passing on his skills as a kaross maker and by giving cattle to him and his family to look after under the mafisa system. He tried to provide practical assistance where necessary, for example, by making Makokwe's family the gift of a steel bed.

When Radipati died in 1950, Goitsemang was thirteen years old. She recalls that the older men related to the family were responsible for dealing with the property and that the elder brother of Radipati's first wife took most of it and gave it to Daniel (Radipati's son of the first house). It would appear that before he died Radipati and his son Daniel had not been on good terms, which Goitsemang attributed to constant friction over the issue of education. While Radipati wanted Daniel to pursue an education, Daniel did not, and when he married he went to live with his wife's family at Mogoditshane, where he stayed until his death.

All that Radipati's family in the second house received on his death was the physical property of household 5 and some cattle which had been given out under a mafisa arrangement. Goitsemang remembers that there was a piece of paper that looked like a will, but this was not produced before the kgotla and as a young girl she could not pursue the matter. Her mother, Mhudi, was left to manage as best she could. They had some land but "no uncles to help us plow." Given the way in which people in Mosotho kgotla are related, there were clearly uncles, but they may have been away on migrant labor or unable or unwilling to provide such assistance. According to Goitsemang, "We did everything ourselves. My mother sold two oxen to get money to hire someone to plow. She also sold corn and beans, whatever was produced from the lands, but she never brewed beer." The latter may be due to the fact that some Christians do not drink on principle and would never brew beer.

Through their labor and the sale of some cattle, Mhudi was able to continue the process of education that Radipati had started. Cooper (1982:18) has noted that having cattle to sell was a crucial ingredient for the provision of education among those he worked with. Those that had acquired a level of education that gave them access to a higher level of employment had done so through their family's ability to finance them by selling cattle which had been inherited or bought.

Education and Access to Employment

Unlike many men of their generation, Radipati's three sons in the second house all acquired an education. In two cases, that of the eldest son, David (aged forty-six in 1989), and of the youngest son, Moses (aged thirty-four in 1989), they also went on to have a university education. David went to study law in Swaziland at the University of Botswana, Lesotho, and Swaziland, and Moses took a degree at what is now the University of Botswana. Such educational attainments enabled them to follow a career path different from that of most of their contemporaries, who went on contract to the mines. When David left the university (it is not clear whether he got a degree), he established his own business in Selebi-Pikwe running a bar and bottle store and disco. He then moved to Boputhatswana, where he was reputed to have a job as a law lecturer.[23] In 1989, he was back in Molepolole claiming to work as a lawyer, assisting other lawyers in the preparation of their cases for the magistrate's court and in close contact with the police. He has very much pursued an entrepreneurial lifestyle. Moses, on the other hand, went straight into government employment as an agricultural officer stationed in Hakuntsi in 1984 but back in Gaborone by 1989.

The middle brother, Pelonomi, who was thirty-nine in 1989, did not care for school and did not achieve high enough results to pursue the kinds of options open to his brothers. Like his contemporaries, he did a stint at the mines, after which he came back to Molepolole and found a job working as an orderly at the hospital. He is fortunate, because unlike others in his generation, not only has be been in consistent employment, but he is able to live and work in the village.

These sons of Radipati present a different profile from the sons of Makokwe or from the profile of those generally associated with their generation (G.3). Not only do their educational and employment trajectories differ, but they also appear to have little interest in lands activities. Their sister, Goitsemang, observed, "When my brothers grew up they did not like plowing. They neglected farming. There was no one to tell them how farming should be done. Men sometimes look down on women and don't listen to them when their father is dead."

Their approach is consistent with that of some of those men who fell within the scope of what Cooper (1979a) calls the educated salariat, who were in the top rank of wage earners in his survey. While they represented a minority in withdrawing from agricultural production, they still maintained their interest in cattle. The District Commissioner for Molepolole in 1982 observed that he and his wife no longer plowed and that was not uncommon among their circle of professional people, although they still maintained cattle for status and other reasons.

Radipati's daughters also present an unusual profile for their generation due to the fact that they have all experienced formal employment for a substantial part of their adult lives. Goitsemang, the eldest daughter (aged fifty-two in 1989), was in Standard 4 primary school when her father died. Her mother, Mhudi, managed to continue to find the money for her education. Goitsemang recalls that her mother's contemporaries were very surprised by her attitude: "Many people asked her why she spent money from plowing on education when tomorrow you may have nothing and your children may do nothing for you." However, her mother was not influenced by their views, and Goitsemang was able to complete Standard 6 and go on to train as a nurse in Lobatse. She compares her position with that of Keselibile, Kemongale's partner and Tshitoeng's daughter, who went to school with her but never went beyond Standard 1 "because she was not interested in education."

According to Goitsemang, "Parents did not regard education as important. They are only realizing now that education means a lot. They considered cattle more important." To adopt another view was to set yourself apart, so that "in the olden days if you kept yourself clean and wanted to be educated, people said that you were trying to be like a European." After her training in Lobatse, Goitsemang went to Johannesburg to work in a private surgery "because there were no jobs in Botswana before independence." She met her partner, Charles, who was also from Molepolole, there. Her working life in Johannesburg was interrupted twice by pregnancies, which brought her back to Molepolole. There she was supported by her mother and her sister Salalenna. She finally left nursing in 1969 because Salalenna was very ill and she had to come back and assist her mother with the nursing. She therefore needed to find employment close to home.

From nursing Goitsemang moved on to employment in Gaborone with a former Rhodesian construction company known as Costain during the construction boom that was taking place in Botswana after independence. She was able to find accommodation with her sister, Salalenna, who was back at work by this time as a kitchen maid for a European family. Goitsemang gained promotion from store worker to wage clerk to personnel officer in this company, a position which she held until she left in 1984 in order to return to Molepolole to look after her mother full-time. By this time she had acquired two plots of land in Gaborone. One of them, given to her by the company, provides accommodation for her daughter Eva and her husband, the other, which she bought, is rented out.

Such assets put her in a privileged position compared to many women of her generation. Through employment she was not only able to acquire resources for herself but also assisted her youngest sister, Olebogeng, by nominating Olebogeng for her job when she was transferred to Morupula Colliery, where the company was putting up houses for Anglo American in 1972. Like her sister, Olebogeng experienced stable employment with the company, from that date up until 1989, when it was taken over. She also has a plot of land next to Goitsemang's which she was given by the company.

When Mhudi died in August 1988, Goitsemang became free to look for work but has not done so because she feels the need to look after the household. Apart from the fact that she has reached a stage in the life cycle when women tend to return to the village and concentrate on activities associated with that sphere, she is also reluctant to be away from the household because of a dispute with her brother David (discussed earlier in chapter 2), over its ownership and control.

Goitsemang's younger sisters have followed in her footsteps. Salalenna, who was fifty in 1989, also reached Standard 6 primary school but was too ill to finish the grade. After school she worked as a housemaid for a police officer in Molepolole and moved with him and his family when they went to the Tuli block. She then went to work for a European family in Gaborone. During that time, she had a relationship with a Mokalanga from Francistown. They had two children but never married. Eventually she became too ill to work and returned to live with her mother in Molepolole, where she was living in 1984. She continues to live in the village, although in 1989 she was living in Gaborone with her sister Olebogeng in order to receive medical treatment. Olebogeng, aged forty-five in 1989, completed primary school and worked as a teacher when she left. She then went on to work in Gaborone at the job that Goitsemang acquired for her. She, like her sisters, remains unmarried, although she has children by different fathers.

These profiles have continuity in the next generation. Goitsemang's daughters, Patricia and Eva in generation 4, have acquired an even higher level of education than that of their mother, having reached Form 3 in secondary school (there are 4 forms). After leaving school, Patricia acquired a job as a court clerk at Kgosing in 1980, where she has been working ever since. After 1984 she completed a one-year diploma in local government administration at the University of Botswana. She has been promoted, and in 1989 it looked as though she would be promoted again and be transferred to another government department. She is unusual among women in her generation, not because she is unmarried, but because she has not yet had a child.[24]

Eva, her sister, has however had a child, but this was not until she had left school and was working as a primary school teacher in Gaborone. In 1984, her grandmother Mhudi and aunt Salalenna were looking after her son, Kago, while she went back to work. Since then she has married the father, to whom she is related, as his mother is their cousin. He is the grandson of Kelebale, who was the wife of Radipati's paternal uncle. He also works in Gaborone, being employed by a parastatal organization concerned with surveys and lands, and they live in the house that Goitsemang has built there. In 1989, Kago was back living with his parents and attending primary school in Gaborone, while his sister, Abigail, who was born a year or two ago, is looked after by Goitsemang in Molepolole.

Salalenna also has two daughters. The eldest, Goabone (aged twenty-nine in 1989), completed Form 2 and has worked for a number of years as a teacher at Kealeboga Primary School in Molepolole. Like Patricia, she is unmarried and has no children. Her sister, Maleboga, aged twenty-three in 1989, is still working her way through secondary school in Gaborone and also has no children.

Olebogeng does not have any daughters but has two sons. The eldest, Dominic, was in his third year of a law degree at the University of Botswana in 1989. He can be seen to be following in his uncle David's footsteps. The younger son, Dell, lives with his father in Gaborone and is in Form 2 of secondary school. Unfortunately, no information is available on children born to David and his brothers, Pelonomi and Moses, in nonmarital relationships.

CONTRASTING PERSPECTIVES: DIFFERING FAMILY PROFILES

Within the families of Makokwe and Radipati there is a continuity of experience across generations embracing certain patterns for men and women. The profiles attached to each family present marked differences. On the one hand, Makokwe's family has invested in a basic level of education and focused on agricultural activities and livestock. Employment where it occurs centers on the mines or other low-skilled jobs, which tend to be casual and intermittent or on a contract basis. Such activities are typical of those associated with the peasantariat. Although individuals enter into relationships that are not marital, marriage is still to be found and where it exists often involves parties who are related to one another.

In contrast, Radipati's family operates on another basis. With a high level of education among generations, they are moving away from the peasantariat toward the position of an educated salariat, having experienced stable employment which tends, particularly among the younger generation, to be government based. Employment at the mines has been bypassed (except in one case), and agricultural activities completely neglected by the men in the family. They have no interest in eking out a living this way to obtain the kind of low returns that most people who engage in agriculture from Mosotho kgotla obtain. The field that Radipati's wife brought with her into the marriage is now rented out to others.

There is a marked contrast in the profiles presented by Diane and her children and Radipati's daughters and their children. This is not simply the product of individual circumstance but has its roots in family histories, which draw on different types of activity and have contributed to socially differentiated individuals. This is reflected in the experiences that such individuals have of procreation and marriage.

While almost all adults in Radipati's family have had children, only two relationships have resulted in marriage. However, in contrast with many of the women associated with Mosotho kgotla, especially some-one like Diane, Radipati's three daughters have all had children in rela-tionships which have had greater potential for marriage and reflect a greater degree of choice on the part of the women concerned. For this reason, the women's relationships (except for one) fall within the cate-gory of intermediate relationships rather than, as so many others, within the fleeting and brief categories. In Goitsemang's case, there was poten-tial for a marriage which never materialized, and for this reason the rela-tionship has been classified as intermediate. The families met, agreed to, and discussed marriage on a number of occasions. The man's family provided support for both mother and child and attended the first child's funeral. By the time of the second child's birth, the man's family appeared to lose interest, which was demonstrated by the fact that they did nothing to support this child and did not attend her funeral, a very public sign of their dissociation from the relationship. This relationship provides a typical example of the kind of marital negotiations referred to by Comaroff and Roberts (1977) where the parties start out seriously exploring the potential of the relationship but, over the course of time, one of them withdraws from the process. This is often due to the fact that one of the parties has opted to pursue another relationship instead.

When it came to her second relationship, Goitsemang took a differ-ent approach from that of her family. According to Mhudi,

> After the death of the second child she stayed with us here in Molepo-lole and the family supported her. Her sister Salalenna was working then in Gaborone and could help her. She went to stay with Salalenna in Gaborone and found a job as a clerk. She then met Patrick Kgosidin-tsi, a businessman from Molepolole. He wanted to marry her and came to see us as parents to propose marriage. As he was already married we told him that we are Christians and said that we could not accept a married man marrying our daughter as a second wife. She was in love with him against our will. He visited her here at home without our consent. She had a child. He brought foodstuffs in a truck but we told him to go away and take the foodstuffs with him as we did not want him to marry our daughter. She went back to Gaborone to work and had another child with him.

It is important to be aware that Patrick Kgosidintsi (see fig. 5) is related to the ruling family, being descended from the second house of Sechele I, which makes his family extremely influential in Molepolole. The refer-ence to him as a businessman is not insignificant, because his family, given its position in the elite hierarchy, has opted to develop its spheres of influence through business development and local government.

Victor Kgosidintsi (fig. 5), for example, has been chairman of the Land Board for many years. This relationship had the potential for a customary marriage but was rejected by the family, ostensibly on religious grounds. This may have represented a genuine conflict between values associated with concepts of monogamy and polygyny, but the family's refusal on Christian moral grounds may also be read in the light of political factions within the morafe.[25] While concern for power was never expressly articulated, it may well have been a factor in the family's decision. Conscious of the power of the Kgosidintsis, Goitsemang's family found that Christian marital ideals also provided a diplomatic form of rejection. Her family rejected the foodstuffs and any form of support in order to deny public recognition of the relationship, which they were anxious to avoid.

This relationship brought the older and the younger generation into conflict. However, Goitsemang was able to defy the older members of her family and to remove herself from their control through employment, which brought her into a sphere of activity over which they had no direct influence. She was removed from the kind of pressures that she might have experienced if she had been dependent on domestic and lands activities for her support and the networks associated with them. Through her education and training she had access to alternative means of support. This is not to say that the family network ceased to be important; indeed, Mhudi continued to look after Goitsemang's children, and Goitsemang's ability to pursue this alternative sphere was, at least in the first instance, predicated upon her sister's support.

With her sister, Salalenna, there was the same practice of negotiating marriage as with Goitsemang's first partner, but in this case it was Salalenna herself who lost interest and dropped the relationship. According to Salalenna,

> I left school in 1955 when I was seventeen years old. I went to work as a housemaid for Inspector Townsend, a member of the police force who was working in Molepolole and then in Machaneng and Gaborone. While I was working in Gaborone I met a Mokalanga from Francistown. I became pregnant and told my family. My mother Mhudi and brother David went to see his parents when I was two months pregnant. At the same time the matter was reported to Dr. Merriweather, as we are Christians.[26] We had another child. Up until the birth of the second child I was prepared to marry him, but I changed my mind because he drank a lot. When I first started going out with him I did not know that he was drinking. He was not violent but I felt that as a Christian I should not marry someone who drinks.[27] After the second child was

born I raised a case for support in the magistrate's court in Gaborone on the advice of my employer's wife and of my brother David. The magistrate made an order of support for both children and he supported them up until 1980.

In this case, Salalenna exercised options, first in favor of marriage and then against. The fact that her partner was a Mokalanga may have been significant, because there is a tendency among prominent Tswana merafe, including Bakwena, to view such people as having subordinate status. Within this context the man would not have been seen as an ideal spouse.

Salalenna's younger sister, Olebogeng, never contemplated marriage when she became pregnant. According to Mhudi,

After leaving school Olebogeng went to work in Gaborone as a teacher. She met a man from Francistown and became pregnant. Her brother David went to see the man several times in Gaborone. He asked that we take the matter up with the D.C. [District Commissioner] or magistrate in Gaborone because he was working and did not have time to come to Molepolole. The matter was dealt with by the magistrate and he was ordered to support. He made two payments but the senior magistrate's clerk stole the money. He disappeared after that and could not be traced.

This relationship, unlike the others, was classified as brief on the basis that marriage was never an option and that there was only one child.

Olebogeng's subsequent relationship was more complex in terms of marriage negotiations. Her mother revealed that

Olebogeng then met a Zimbabwean in Gaborone and became pregnant. She told the family and he came and saw us. He told us that the child was his and that he accepted responsibility. The child was born and lived with us here while Olebogeng carried on working in Gaborone as a telephone operator. The father used to visit regularly. After a while the kgotla men sent word to him to ask why he was not visiting so regularly, as he had promised marriage. He came to see us and said that he wanted the child to visit him for a few days. We let him take the child and he has never brought him back. He now lives with his father in Gaborone and goes to school there.

Mhudi was quite distressed about this because an unmarried father has no right to the custody of the child according to Tswana law and custom, but Olebogeng has not done anything about this. Again there are aspects that indicate some attempt at the negotiation of a customary marriage. The man visited regularly and the kgotla men were aware of a marriage promise. However, the man has lost interest in the relationship and has done nothing since he took the child away to live with him.

Men's Unmarried Partnerships with Women

It is not only women who are affected by the negotiation process and ambiguity in relationships. According to his mother, David

> met a girl in Swaziland while at university. The girl's parents drove to Molepolole and introduced themselves to Kgosi Bonewamang.[28] When the issue was discussed it was agreed that they should marry. The girl went back to Swaziland for confinement and then returned to Molepolole with the child. She and David then went to live in Selebi-Pikwe because he had a bar and a bottle store. They had their second child there. As time went on she ran off with someone from Jwaneng [a mining area of Botswana], leaving the children with David, who brought them here. She then came back and took the children with her back to Swaziland. David reported the matter to Kgosi Bonewamang, who advised David not to worry about the mother taking the children because the Swazis were very angry. They claimed that the children belonged to their daughter. The kgosi advised him that the girl's parents no longer wanted him to marry their daughter and that if he went to Swaziland to deal with the matter he would face problems. The girl's parents did not want anything from him; they wanted the children. They did not accept that there was a marriage and had informed Kgosi Bonewamang that they were freeing David and would support the children themselves. That is why the kgosi told him not to pursue the matter.

In this situation, the relationship also had the potential for a customary marriage and was classified as intermediate. The families met and agreed to this, they agreed to the woman living with the man, and the couple had two children. The woman, however, changed her mind and withdrew from the relationship, taking the children with her. It is interesting to note the kgosi's involvement and his advice to David that as there was no prospect of establishing a marriage, he could not seek custody of the children. David's relationship provides an example of the kind of problems that can arise with regard to status. Without marriage a man is not entitled to the custody of the children; on the other hand, without it, there is no duty to support them under the customary system.

David's subsequent relationship with Shelly from Boputhatswana, with whom he had a child, resulted in a civil marriage. However according to Goitsemang in 1989, the marriage had broken down and David had returned to Molepolole, leaving Shelly and the child with her family.

In contrast with David's view of his first relationship, the opinions of his brothers, Pelonomi and Moses, about the status of their relationships was unequivocal. When approached by the women's families, they rejected the prospect of marriage out of hand. In Pelonomi's case, according to his mother, he "met a woman while he was working at the mines in Selebi-Pikwe. He did not want to marry her. David went to see her parents and paid the compensation." Likewise with Moses; he "met a girl from Motlabi's kgotla [part of Basimane ward]." She became pregnant. He denied paternity. Her parents raised a case at the chief's kgotla. He was ordered to pay compensation, which David paid. Both these relationships were classified as brief because in contrast with those in the fleeting category, there was some family interaction and recognition of the relationships, albeit for the purpose of obtaining compensation.

The Younger Generation

Among the members of the younger generation, out of four young adult women only one, Goitsemang's daughter Eva, has had children. Like her mother, she was in a relationship whose nature was the subject of some dissension. According to Mhudi, marriage was never considered; however, according to Eva's younger sister, she was still seeing the father, Shimanyana, Ratsebi's son from Mosotho kgotla (but belonging to Motlabi kgotla), who had promised to marry her. According to Mhudi, "Her uncles [Goitsemang's brothers] went to see his parents and ask for compensation," but this was dropped because they were too poor to pay. Mhudi regarded the purported promise as irrelevant, as he had not taken any of the steps that she considered to be consistent with an approach to marriage. In other words, his actions fell within a private rather than a public domain because no formal steps had been taken to indicate his or his family's intentions. This relationship, on the basis of the sister's information, was classified as current in 1984, and indeed, by 1989 it turned out that Eva and Shimanyana had had another child and married formally with both patlo and registration.

In contrast with Diane and her family, the members of Radipati's family actively engaged in a process of negotiation with regard to their relationships, pursuing and altering their options as circumstances changed. In this process, the women found themselves in relationships which initially had real potential for marriage even though that potential was seldom realized. In some cases it was their decision to put the relationship on another footing, and they were able to have some control over their situation, even if this meant bringing the relationship into the public domain before a third party as a dispute.

The descendants of Koosimile, through the families of Makokwe and Radipati, highlight the different forms that people's lives may take and the implications that this has for individuals, especially women, when it comes to the question of access to resources. For those associated with the peasantariat—whose activities center around subsistence agriculture, livestock, and intermittent employment—experience a different set of options and constraints compared with those among the salariat whose attention is focused on higher education and well-remunerated and stable employment generally within a government-based or -affiliated organization. These life histories mark the varying conditions in which individuals live and the role that these conditions play in shaping their marital perspectives. They also underline the ways in which different responses to gender, procreation, and marriage come back to the issue of power and how it is constituted in all its dimensions.

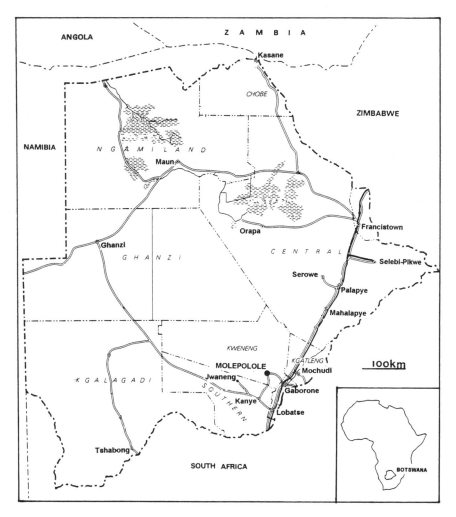

Figure 1 Map of Botswana showing locaons of places mentioned in the text.

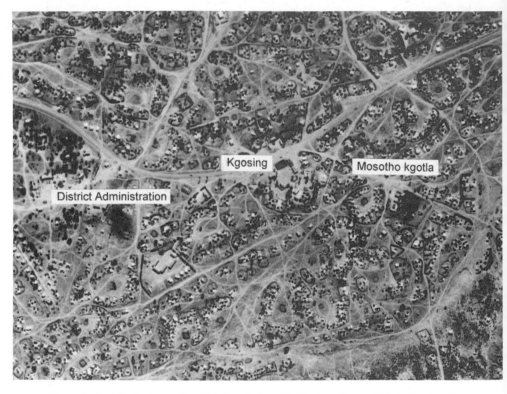

Figure 2 Aerial photograph of Molepolole with the location of Mosotho kgotla, Kgosing, and the District Administration complex in 1984.
(Photo courtesy of the Government of Botswana.)

Figure 3 Mr. Masimega interviewing Ra Tshitoeng Mere in Mosotho kgotla in 1984. (Photo taken by Marianne Enge.)

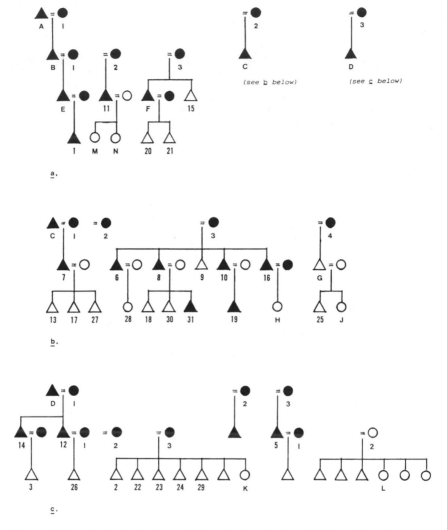

Figure 4 Genealogical relations of Mosotho kgotla households. *a*, Mere's descendants; *b*, Moreri's descendants; *c*, Koosimile's descendants. *A*, Mhiemang; *B*, Mere; *C*, Moreri; *D*, Koosimile; *E*, Ketumile; *F*, Kelatotswe; *G*, Otswataung; *H*, Same; *J*, Wamakhyu; *K*, Olebeng; *L*, Goitsemang; *M*, Mosarwa; *N*, Tsebekgale. Rank order of houses is given by small numerals. Households are identified by large numerals: *1*, Neo Ketumile; *2*, Kemongale; *3*, Koobone; *5*, Radipati; *6*, Keiphe; *7*, Mosotho; *8*, Gasentsima; *9*, Lehubitsa; *10*, Rampole; *11*, Godisaofe; *12*, Makokwe; *13*, Laping; *14*, Phiriyagae; *15*, Tshitoeng; *16*, Robert Moreri; *17*, Basupeng; *18*, Boswanta; *19*, Keitatole; *20*, Macdonald Mere; *21*, Gabriel Mere; *22*, Nkadikang; *23*, Morabane; *24*, Ramojaki; *25*, Modisa; *26*, Motlotlegi; *27*, Tsele; *28*, Diane; *29*, Ntlogelang; *30*, Motlaphele; *31*, Boitlhoko.

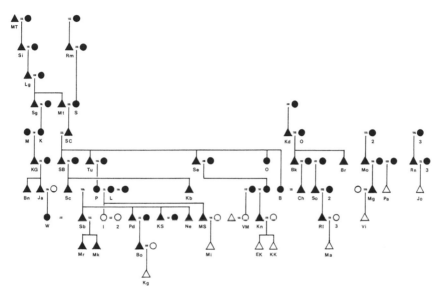

Figure 5 Kwena royal genealogy. Rank order of houses is given by numerals. Designations for persons: *MT,* Motswasele I; *Si,* Seitlhamo; *Rm,* Ramodisa; *Lg,* Legwale; *Mt,* Motswasele II; *S,* Sejelo; *Sg,* Segotlo; *SC,* Sechele; *M,* Mokgokong; *K,* Kebalapile; *Kd,* Kgosidintsi; *KG,* Kgari; *SB,* Sebele I; *Tu,* Tumagole; *Se,* Sebogiso; *O,* Ope (note that this same person appears in two positions); *B,* Bantshang; *Bk,* Bakwena; *Br,* Baruti, *Bn,* Baanami; *Ja,* Jakoba; *Sc,* Sechele II; *P,* Phetogo; *L,* Lena; *Kb,* Kebohula; *Ch,* Chadibitsile; *So,* Seelo; *W,* Senwelo; *Sb,* Sebele II; *Pd,* Padi; *KS,* Kgari Sechele; *Ne,* Neale; *MS,* Mac Sechele; *Kn,* Kenalekgosi; *Mr,* Moruakgomo; *Mk,* Mokgaladi; *Bo,* Bonewamang; *Mi,* Moithale; *EK,* E. K. Sebele; *KK,* K. K. Sebele; *Mo,* Motswakhumo; *Rn,* Ranmossesane; *Mg,* Makgasane; *Pa,* Patrick; *Jo,* Joel; *RI,* Ralengoreng; *Vi,* Victor; *Ma,* Moadisi; *Kg,* Kgari Sechele. *VM* is Mr. Masimega's wife, Virginia.

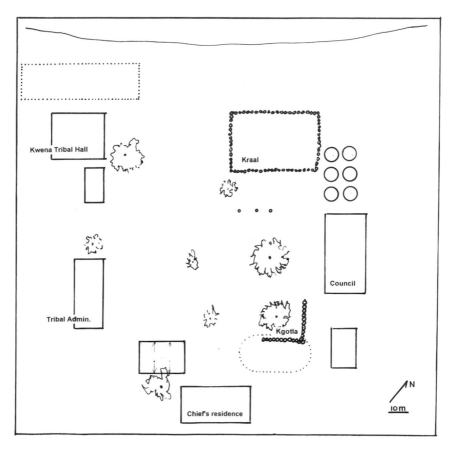

Figure 6 Layout of the chief's kgotla in Molepolole in 1984. The L-shaped tree-trunk stockade that defined the chief's public forum in 1982 (see fig. 7) is shown between the chief's residence and the council building; on this is superimposed the kgotla building erected in 1990 (see figs. 9–11). The vaulted structure used in 1984 (see fig. 8) is above and to the left of the chief's residence. (Drawn by Ed Wilmsen from sketches provided by Ozi Nkabinde.)

Figure 7 The chief's kgotla in session under the trees in 1982. (Photo taken by Victor Cumming.)

Figure 8 A view of the chief's kgotla in 1984. (Photo taken by Marianne Enge.)

Figure 9 A view of the chief's kgotla and chief's residence in 1992. (Photo taken by Ed Wilmsen.)

Figure 10 A view of the cattle kraal and chief's kgotla in 1992. (Photo taken by Ed Wilmsen.)

Figure 11 The chief's kgotla building financed by public subscription at the end of the 1980s. (Photo taken by Ed Wilmsen in 1992.)

Figure 12 Members of the tribal police force talking to Mr. Masimega outside the Bakwena Tribal Hall in the chief's kgotla in 1992. (Photo taken by Ed Wilmsen.)

Figure 13 Inscription for Bakwena Tribal Hall. Note that the spelling of kgotla (khotla) and Sechele (Sechela) uses orthography sometimes used before the independence of Botswana in 1966. (Photo taken by Ed Wilmsen in 1992.)

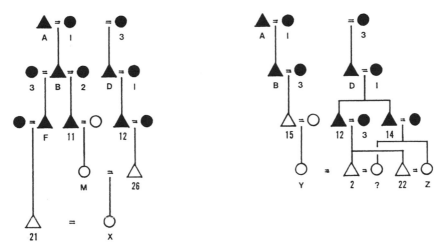

Figure 14 Mosotho kgotla members' relations through marriage. Rank order of houses is given by small numerals. Households are identified by large numerals: *2*, Kemongale; *11*, Godisaofe; *12*, Makokwe; *14*, Phiriyagae; *15*, Tshitoeng; *21*, Gabriel Mcrc; *22*, Nkadikang; *26*, Motlotlegi. Designations for persons: *X*, Gaselefufa; *Y*, Keslibile; *Z*, Phiriyagae's daughter; *?*, Phiriyagae's daughter (not clear if same as *Z*).

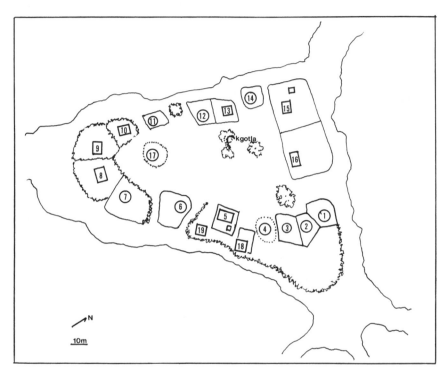

Figure 15 Layout of Mosotho kgotla in 1984. (Drawn by Ed Wilmsen from sketches provided by Ozi Nkabinde.)

Figure 16 Mosotho kgotla as it appeared in 1984. A curved row of tree trunks set into the ground now defines the space; the remains of the original dry-laid, semicircular stone enclosure have been left in place. By 1992, the row of tree trunks had been extended to the tall post seen on the left and most of the stones had been removed. (Photo taken by Marianne Enge.)

Figure 17 Headman Tshenolo's compound, household 1 (original site), in Mosotho kgotla in 1984. (Photo taken by Marianne Enge.)

Figure 18 Women congregating at Gasentsima's compound, household 8 (original site), over daily tasks in 1984. (Photo taken by Marianne Enge.)

Figure 19 Women carrying out domestic duties smearing walls with a plaster of mud and cow dung at household 8 in 1984. (Photo taken by Marianne Enge.)

Figure 20 Radipati's granddaughters outside the front of his house, (household 5; original site), in 1984. (Photo taken by Marianne Enge.)

Figure 21 The back houses which form part of household 5's compound in 1992. (Photo taken by Ed Wilmsen.)

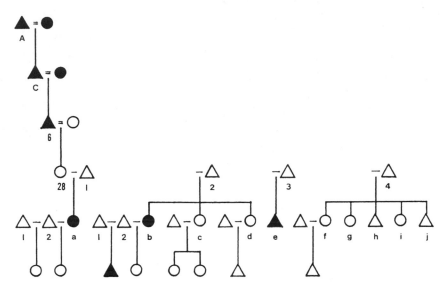

Figure 22 Diane Moreri's family tree. Rank order of households is given by small numerals. Households are identified by large numerals: *6*, Keiphe; *28*, Diane. Designations for persons: *a*, Nametso; *b*, Margaret; *c*, Onneile; *d*, Malutu; *e*, Okhuna; *f*, Khone; *g*, Oaitsi; *h*, Tom; *i*, Manungo; *j*, Issac.

Figure 23 The old buildings of District Administration: the District Commissioner's office and the magistrate's court, in Molepolole in 1982 (now demolished). (Photo taken by Victor Cumming.)

Figure 24 The new complex built in 1986 to house District Administration: the District Commissioner's office, the magistrate's court, and other government offices. (Photo taken by Ed Wilmsen in 1992.)

FOUR

Pregnancy and Marriage: The World of Negotiation and Dispute

So far this book has set the broader context within which women's procreative relationships with men are situated. It has established the economic, political, and social processes which shape family and household networks of which these individuals form part. The detailed analysis of life histories over generations not only demonstrates the crucial role that access to resources (including marriage) occupies in constructing people's lives, but also highlights the gendered world in which women and men live. Thus, women's and men's experiences of procreative relationships and marriage differ. In this world, differing access to resources gives rise to the exercise of different forms of power which affect individuals' abilities to negotiate with one another. These forms of power not only differ on the basis of gender, but also vary between members of the same sex and across generations.

Negotiations in everyday life often involve individuals making various claims on others. Where women are concerned, their claims on men revolve around procreation. For procreation is central to women's lives and takes place in the context of both unmarried and married partnerships which create expectations and obligations among the individuals concerned and their families. Such expectations and obligations often give rise to claims for support, compensation for pregnancy, or rights to property acquired during the course of the relationship. These kinds of claims are a part of the fabric of day-to-day social life, but they also represent an aspect of legal discourse. It is to this discourse that we now turn as we examine these claims in the context of family law in Botswana. The focus here is on the legal dimension of women's pursuit of claims against their male partners and on the role that marital status occupies in this process, which centers on compensation for pregnancy (this chapter), support (chap. 5), and rights to property (chaps. 6 and 7).

The pursuit of such claims involves contact with the formal legal system, which incorporates both common and customary law and the various forums associated with these legal arenas outlined in chapter 1.

106

These include the chief's kgotla, the magistrate's court, and the High Court; the latter two, as part of the formal legal system, fall within the orbit of centralist legal discourse. But the analysis of law that is presented in this and the subsequent three chapters is one that completely undermines any attempt to uphold a legal centralist model of law. Although it is constituted within the framework of the state and draws on certain key elements such as statutes, cases, and formal legal institutions that are associated with a centralist model of law, my analysis is one that establishes another perspective on law. This arises through an analysis that is based on the ways in which those elements associated with legal centralism are integrated into social life.

What is central to my account of law, as set out in chapter 1, are the points of connection that link social and legal domains. This is particularly important with respect to women's access to, and use of, law. For those factors which inform social processes of negotiation, such as access to resources, status, power, and gender continue to have an impact upon legal process. Not only do such factors operate to constrain or facilitate access to legal process, but they also have an impact on the legal process itself, regardless of whether the legal arena is a customary or a common law forum. My approach defeats any analysis of law which conceives of these forums as representing separate and autonomous legal systems embedded in the dual systems theory of law endorsed by Hooker (1975) and others.

In Molepolole, those arenas designated as legal forums by the state are the chief's kgotla and the magistrate's court. The latter, which is located in the kgosi's ward, Kgosing, not only functions as the central institution in the morafe's affairs, but also operates as part of a system of local administration which includes formal legal regulation. This system was established by the British when they created "tribal administration," now represents one of the four types of local authorities that exist in the country, which also include District Administration, land boards, and district and urban councils (figs. 23, 24).[1] In contrast with other civil servants, those presiding over tribal administration are appointed on the basis of their primary affiliation with the morafe. Among Bakwena, these officers, who are officially designated the chief (who during my research was represented by the chief regent),[2] the deputy chief, and the senior chief's representative, are appointed on the basis of their links with Kwena ruling elites descended from Sechele I (1833–92). As is often the case with succession to office, there has been much infighting and genealogical manipulation surrounding these appointments (Ramsay 1991:

409–13). Such officers are not required to have a formal legal training, because they are deemed, through their position within the morafe, to have the knowledge that is necessary to uphold customary law and to be able to learn what is necessary for the application of common law in office.

In contrast, magistrates, their clerks, and those in charge of District Administration, headed by the District Commissioner, are usually drawn from other merafe. In their case, it is government policy to bring in civil servants from other areas where possible and to rotate them on a regular basis. In addition, their appointment and career development depends on attaining a certain level of education (in the case of magistrates this also includes a formal legal training), which does not apply to chiefly office.

Such differences appear, initially, to support a view that upholds a separation between national and local or regional forms of regulation (embodied in common and customary law) through their disparate affiliations and orientation. But ethnographic analysis highlights the fact that those working within these institutions perceive of their roles, and those of their institutions, as forming part of an overall system of governance and legal regulation. This is illustrated by the fact that, in Molepolole, the relationship between senior personnel from the chief's kgotla and the District Commissioner and his staff has tended to be a cooperative one based on mutual respect and regular communication.[3] Where distinctions are drawn between the jurisdiction of the chief's kgotla and the magistrate's court (as, for example, in the case of compensation for pregnancy and maintenance, which will be discussed shortly), this is done with a sense of the overall context in which the legal system operates. Inevitably there are also tensions in this working relationship between personnel and institutions but these represent negotiations over power and authority as it is constituted within the larger domain to which they belong. Thus, no notion of separate and autonomous systems of law, as perceived by Hooker (1975) and other juristic pluralists, can be sustained.

In this chapter, these issues will be addressed in the context of procreation and how this is accommodated within social life. As pregnancy is something which affects women of all ages, the issue is how they, their families, and their partners' families respond to this situation. As the subsequent narratives will show, negotiations are entered into where possible by all those concerned in order to establish whether the relationship has the potential for marriage, or whether it gives rise to a claim for compensation. In many cases agreement is reached, although often not acted upon, but even where this is not so, conflict does not necessarily arise between those who are involved. In some cases, however, the individuals concerned take their claims to one of the dispute forums that is acknowledged by the state as a legal institution. In such a setting, claims to compensation for pregnancy are assessed in the light of the status that is attributed to the relationship in question and certain other factors which derive from a social framework that informs everyday social life.

NEGOTIATIONS OVER PREGNANCY AND MARRIAGE

One of the recurring aspects of family life is procreation. The contexts within which procreation and marriage are negotiated are various, as the life histories from the previous chapter show, although marriage—even if rejected—plays a role in all of them as a standard against which relationships are assessed. In Mosotho kgotla, in well over half the cases where pregnancy occurred, steps were taken by the families to discuss the situation.[4] When there were no meetings this was usually for good reasons. When a meeting was sought, it was to explore the options of marriage or compensation. Makokwe's son, Ramojaki, speaks for many when he states that when the first of his daughters became pregnant, "we went to see his [the man's] family with a view to compensation or marriage." Schapera (1938:133) remarked on this process of negotiation over pregnancy in the 1930s. He also observed that the option of compensation or marriage was only good for the woman's first pregnancy. In such a case, a woman's family was entitled to pursue marriage, or if that could not be arranged "to receive compensation in cattle, for the girl had been spoiled (o senyegile) and her prospects of marriage greatly decreased" (1938:266). There was no claim thereafter, as it was "necessary to prevent some parents from deliberately encouraging their daughters to lead a loose life, in effect prostituting them, for the sake of cattle which could then be claimed whenever pregnancy ensued" (Schapera 1938:267).

Schapera's references are to Bakgatla, another Tswana morafe, but Bakwena also follow this rule, allowing eight head of cattle for compensation rather than the six awarded by Bakgatla. Among both groups, it is now accepted that compensation may be paid by installments and in money instead of cattle, which among Bakwena amounts to the sum of 640 pula. Views about the nature and purpose of this compensation vary among those living in Molepolole today. Some say that it is paid to the father because, given his daughter's diminished prospects of marriage, he will remain responsible for supporting both her and her child. They adopt Schapera's view (Schapera 1938:266). Others, in the wake of knowledge regarding maintenance payments from the magistrate's court, view such compensation as a payment made to the mother for the support of the child. As attitudes shift between compensation for lack of marriage prospects toward support, the distinction between the two becomes blurred, especially among the younger generation.

When families in Mosotho kgotla met for discussion, over half deliberated on and agreed to marriage.[5] In some cases, these marriages have been formalized,[6] while in others the relationship continues on an informal basis; but the majority of relationships have ended.[7] Some of these liaisons had marks associated with the preliminary stages of a customary marriage, while in others it was clear from the start that agreement to marriage was just a strategy to avoid paying compensation and was never really intended, as in Lebalang's case. Her first liaison was with a miner from Thamaga, whose parents did nothing beyond agreeing to marriage when she became pregnant. They did not visit Lebalang's family or provide support of any kind, signs that they did not take the relationship seriously. Such was the experience of Diane's daughters Margaret and Malutu, along with their sister Nametso in her second relationship.

There were several cases where compensation and not marriage was the focus of discussion;[8] most of these involved first relationships.[9] In some cases the woman's family did not seek marriage, but decided to settle for compensation. In others, there was not even the semblance of agreement due to avoidance or denial of responsibility. In Flora's case, her mother, Setswamosimeng, observed that she "met the father at school in Moshupa. We wrote to the boy's father and he replied but dodged meetings. I tried to see the boy's parents several times with my sister Mosarwa's eldest son, Gaethuse, but they kept saying that they were at Orapa. They were just avoiding the issue." The matter was not pursued because "the boy's father was a crook and [I] was afraid that if the matter was pushed regarding marriage he might hurt my daughter. I did not trust him over marriage or compensation." As an elderly widow, Setswamosimeng had to rely on her sister's son to act as the family's male representative. With no sons of her own and living at a subsistence level, unable to plow for lack of resources and with no livestock, she fits the profile for many female-headed households. In such a position, neither she nor her daughter had any power whatsoever to negotiate.

Negotiation is also inhibited where a man denies that he is responsible for the pregnancy, as in Nametso's case. Her mother Diane recalled, "Nametso was at secondary school in Mahalapye when she first became pregnant. My brother went and spoke to the man, who was by that time working in Gaborone. He denied emphatically that he was the father, and we gave up." Where there was no contact between families, it was usually for good reason. In over one-third of cases this was because the families knew that they had no claim on the man.[10] The woman had already had children in a previous relationship. That was the position of Baikgodisi, who is in her late forties and whose family left her second partner alone "because I already had too many children with the first man." By then she had already had eight children. The same was true for Mmanchibidu, whose mother stated that the family did nothing about her second liaison "because she had a child with a man years before."

People know the social framework they operate within and act accordingly. Nothing is to be gained in pursuing the issue of a second pregnancy, because no formal claim lies, although a few families do so and some fathers respond. Others leave well alone and are grateful for whatever support the man may contribute, as in Neo's case, where no action was contemplated by her family "because the man was supporting the children and we were reluctant to upset him."

This attitude is not uncommon. Tobo's mother reported that no action was taken against her son when his partner became pregnant because "the child was looked after from confinement onwards and is still being supported." In a few cases, it was for this reason that there was no formal familial contact. Where some support is provided it is wiser to leave well alone and allow the relationship to develop of its own accord, especially where one of the parties has far greater social standing than the other. In the case of a Kgalagadi woman, like the one involved with Motlaphele's son, Ramaijo, her family is unlikely to initiate any contact with the man's family. This is because of the low status that many Batswana still accord to Bakgalagadi, who were serfs in the past. Given their position, the woman's family has little power to negotiate, and as their status often coincides with an extremely vulnerable economic situation, it is more prudent to accept whatever is on offer.[11]

In some cases there was no contact because the women would not reveal the father's identity.[12] Very often this was due to fear, shame, or embarrassment, particularly where it was a first pregnancy and the girl was at school (as in most of these cases).[13] Women are more vulnerable at this stage in their life cycle and susceptible to the pressure that men exert to keep quiet about their identity. Several women said nothing because the man had secretly promised to marry them, or because of the man's social standing as a teacher or a government employee. In these circumstances women become silenced by the perceived and actual power of these men. There were only two cases where women mature enough to genuinely opt for nondisclosure remained silent. Both cases involved a second pregnancy.

Most of the reasons for noncontact are attributable to pragmatic considerations, like the man's disappearance or location miles away. But in a few cases this was not so. Some families simply considered the matter irrelevant. Recall Makokwe's daughter, Olebeng. Consider Setswamosimeng, who stated that while she was married to Nitko from Molepolole "he neglected me and lived with other women and I had a child with a friend." She never contemplated any action "because I wanted the child." Setswamosimeng's comment is important. It stresses an aspect that must not be ignored, which is that Bakwena regard the birth of children as natural and generally to be welcomed. Children always have a place. Should they find that they are not affiliated with their father's family, because their mother is not married to their father and his family has taken no steps to recognize them, they will remain attached to their mother's family. The concept of illegitimacy as such has no currency among Batswana and other African societies (Roberts 1977b:7; Daniels 1975:159–68). It is true that children who remain affiliated with their mother's family may be treated somewhat differently from offspring of their uncles' marriages when it comes to inheritance, but their position is not adequately characterized by use of the Western term "illegitimate."

Although the experience of pregnancy is a personal matter which evokes a range of emotions and responses, it does occur within a social framework which both informs and is receptive to people's actions. The overall picture that emerges from these accounts of pregnancy is one in which individuals and/or their families followed a familiar course, that is, they did seek to negotiate marriage or compensation. Where they did not do so, this was often in keeping with knowledge that such claims were no longer viable for the pragmatic reasons outlined above.

The Social and Legal Dimensions of Procreation

The life histories and narratives show how procreation, which is an integral part of social life, is accommodated within peoples' lives. Pregnancy is a normal event for a woman, often occurring at an early stage in her life cycle. How it is dealt with varies, but where possible the families enter into some form of negotiation. Such negotiations are essential for initiating and pursuing the processes that may lead to a customary marriage and, as such, form part of a broader social domain which does not necessarily depend on conflict for its construction. Whatever the outcome of these negotiations, they form an inherent part of social discourse which is not, initially, predicated on conflict or dispute. In some cases, parties happily reach agreement regarding compensation or marriage. In others, they do not but parties may not feel obliged to pursue the matter as a dispute. For many the end is neither consensus nor conflict, but an indeterminate state where the matter is left hanging, or silently slips into abeyance while individuals and their families turn elsewhere to explore another relationship's potential.

Nevertheless, these processes may provide the basis on which a dispute may develop, where one side is dissatisfied and wishes to take the matter further. This happens where negotiations move beyond the families concerned, into a more public arena, engaging the participation of a third party who is a public figure. Such a figure may be the headman of a family's kgotla, or the wardhead, or an official associated with the chief's kgotla or the magistrate's court. Ideally, the dispute should pass through the hierarchy of the kgotla system before it reaches the chief's kgotla or magistrate's court. It is not considered appropriate to raise the dispute directly in the magistrate's court without first having attempted some form of family or kgotla mediation, although it is increasingly done. Women, however, can and do go straight to the magistrate's court for a number of reasons. Some do so because they consider that they will not receive a fair hearing in the kgotla due to the man's status and local connections, which will operate in his favor to place him in a more powerful position than the woman and so put her at a disadvantage. On the other hand a desire to circumvent nepotism is not the only reason why women go to the court. There may be pragmatic considerations, such as avoiding the kind of delay that ensues in the kgotla because proceedings cannot take place until all the relevant family members are present. Assembling all such members is time consuming, particularly where they are living and working in other parts of Botswana or even outside the country. Or women may simply wish to deal with the matter themselves, free from intervention by family or kin. This is especially the case where their relationship with the man is a tenuous one.

Whatever the position, so far as those within the local kgotla system are concerned, to establish a legal boundary (as the formal legal system does) at a level designated "customary court" is artificial. Local headmen and subwardheads as well as wardheads regard themselves as part of a system in which they apply mekgwa le melao to those who come before them. As the subsequent discussions demonstrate, this Tswana law is viewed as an integral part of Kwena society, permeating all the institutions on which it is built and out of which it grows. This includes kgotlas and wards, which are perceived to be very much engaged in dealing with law. In this sense, for Bakwena, law is not reserved as it is in the formal legal system for specialist institutions or personnel, but belongs to the community in general and operates at every level of society.

For this reason what amounts to law in Botswana is a complex question. For law derives from multiple sources and sites which draw on written texts, institutions, and broader social frames of reference contained within the unwritten customary law, mekgwa le melao ya Setswana. Perceptions of what amounts to law vary according to the terms of reference that are applied. So, as other scholars (Woodman 1988; Rwezaura n.d.) have noted, customary law as lived in everyday life, often referred to as "living law" (Ehrlich 1936), may differ from that which is applied by local customary courts, which may vary yet again from what is interpreted as customary law in the most senior courts that form part of a national legal system. These observations raise questions about how law is to be perceived that extend beyond an African context. It is these questions that the new or strong form of legal pluralism (J. Griffiths 1986) pursued in Europe and North America seeks to address.

Local Perspectives: Ward Members

At the start of my research in Molepolole in 1982 I met with members of the six major wards. We discussed family life and the issues that it raises for handling daily life. Invariably, what was stressed as the major concern was women demanding compensation for pregnancy. All wards agreed that the number of these cases had dramatically increased.[14] Members of Kgosing ward commented that these cases seldom arose "in the past [because they were] dealt with by the parents. Now such cases are common." But they acknowledged that as early as the 1930s Kgosi Kgari Sechele instituted the practice of awarding eight head of cattle as compensation for unmarried women to try to control the situation.[15] It is not a new phenomenon, but has existed as part of Kwena society, if not Tswana society generally, for over fifty years.

Tshosa ward members felt strongly that the number of these pregnancies "has created tension amongst us as a people" brought about by demands for support at the kgotla. This "gives us a headache because we have to trace back to find out how and when they married"—a statement that upholds the importance of marriage and how it is used as a paradigm for ordering relationships.

The difficulty stems from the ambiguity of Tswana marriage processes discussed earlier and highlighted by Teko and Nyana's disputes at the end of this chapter. Mosotho data show how most relationships lack the hallmark of a formal marriage, which leaves them open to endless reinterpretation. A claim for eight head of cattle or 640 pula can only be made if the woman is unmarried, so it fails if the relationship is classed as a marriage. Even where it is clearly accepted that the relationship is not a marriage, which is often the case in such disputes, there are other hurdles to be overcome.

Some wards state that no claim lies if nothing was done by the woman's family before or immediately after the birth of the child. A Kgosing member explains,

> The Tswana law goes this way. Normally the girl's parents are expected to report [the matter] to the boy's parents [so] that they [the boy's parents] can stop their boy spending time with the [girl's] family. If the boy's parents have been told that they should stop their boy spending late hours and they did not take any action, they would be told that they should have done something. The girl's parents would have the latitude to sue for seduction. But if the girl's parents don't say anything until the child is born or there are two children there is not much latitude to sue for seduction [on which a claim for compensation is based].

Another member observed that "Tswana law is reluctant to support parents who do not report" at the appropriate time, just before or after the birth of the first child. Such views articulate the classic approach to pregnancy recorded by Schapera in the 1930s, where the claim is based on the woman's impaired marriage prospects. According to this view, a woman's family is entitled to claim for impaired marriage prospects only where they can establish that they had no knowledge of the actual relationship or, alternatively, that they did all they could to steer the liaison into an appropriate form, for example, by ordering the man to keep away from their daughter at night or by reporting his behavior to his family. Failure to report to the man's family, especially after the birth of the child, gives rise to the presumption that the woman's family has acquiesced in the relationship (which is often the case where economic support for the woman's family is provided by the man). Knowledge on the part of the woman's family is crucial. Along with inaction it implies an acquiescence in what is happening. This in turn implies acceptance of whatever benefits accrue from the relationship while it lasts. Such acceptance rules out any claim for compensation.

Where a woman's family can establish that they had no knowledge of their daughter's relationship with a man they can claim compensation for pregnancy, but only where such a pregnancy represents the birth of her first child. In all cases of a second or subsequent pregnancy the claim will fail. In such cases, Ntloedibe ward members considered that the relationship had become "one of concubinage," which is distinguished from a marital relationship. Although a socially recognized form of relationship, concubinage lacks enforceable obligations of support within the kgotla structure. However, "if the boy's parents pay one kgomo [cow] he may take the children and they will be regarded as belonging to his kgotla," if not, the children "stay with the woman" and remain affiliated with her family.

Other wards are more flexible in their approach to such relationships. Members of Borakalalo ward expressed the view that they would allow a woman compensation even if she had two children with a man because "even if several children are born, it is treated as seduction, the future of the young woman has been frustrated by such action." In other words, it is the relationship itself rather than the number of pregnancies that count. This position accommodates the ambiguities that may beset a relationship due to the nature of customary marriage. It allows for a claim where such marriage never materializes. For this reason Mr. Kgosiensho (former deputy chief) was prepared to make a compensation order where it was the woman's first relationship and she had more than one child, provided all the children had the same father.

There is some support for this among certain members of Kgosing, who believe "it does not matter how many children are born, what matters is the first child that is born" (i.e., that all the children have the same father and the action is raised in respect of the first child). However, all wards unanimously agreed that compensation could not be awarded where a woman had children by two different fathers, although some expressed the view that there was a moral obligation to provide "some maintenance for the children."

These views at ward meetings were mainly articulated by older men, as young men were often away working. While women were present and did participate (especially when asked to comment), the kgotla is very much perceived of as a male space. Men tend the kgotla fire and carry out the religious and ceremonial rites associated with it, and they are expected to attend regularly when in the village. Although it is a public space for all kinds of activities, the kgotla's most common role is that of a men's talking place. Given the ways in which the kgotla is identified with male interests (for political and social purposes), women take care over the kinds of interventions that they make and the disputes that they raise, as well as the terms upon which they present them.

However, while women proceed with caution in this arena, the older male perception of the kgotla's role today is one of diminished authority and control. Men talk of a lack of respect, which they attribute to people's beliefs "that they are self-governing, that is, free from authority." This means that "they go [straight] to Kgosing instead of going to the traditional headman." This kind of belief and behavior is especially attributed to those labeled "intellectuals," who are defined as people with an education employed in the civil service, such as teachers, and urban workers with highly paid jobs. In contrast, mine workers were characterized as the kind of people who support the kgotla system, although my research on disputes provided no evidence of this.

Tshosa ward members particularly expressed concern about people acting on their own and ignoring parental or kgotla controls. Women were cast as the main culprits in this respect. "In this village there are too many harlots. Some girls go around looking for boys and when they are seduced they go to the D.C. [meaning the magistrate's court] without coming to the kgotla." Such women have put themselves beyond the kgotla's authority and thus its control. They are seen as actively pursuing procreative relationships and entrapping men. Their freedom to do so is blamed on the fact that "people are from different places and people come to stay here leaving parents outside Molepolole and become independent. A young girl comes to work in the kitchen, for example, a young man gets land, they live together and when he neglects her she goes straight to the D.C. [meaning the magistrate] for maintenance."

This scenario is a common one, as borne out by the Mosotho and other narratives. However, it is not the whole story. Such situations, which usually reflect liaisons that are informal due to lack of consultation between the families concerned, also occur where both parties are from Molepolole. In this context, parents may know about the affair but do nothing because they rely on whatever support is forthcoming from their daughter's partner. The tacit role of economics here is something that the older generation, notably men, are reluctant to acknowledge. The idea that informal liaisons are more prevalent where parties come from different areas is not supported by my research findings. These show that unions need not become marriages, last longer, or have greater social recognition where the parties are from the village (A. Griffiths 1988b). Location may free parties from familial constraints, but it is only one of many factors that may be manipulated in the negotiation process.

Engaging with the Formal Legal System

Outside of familial negotiations, most people know the options that are open to them and act on them or let the matter rest. Knowledge may preclude action: Diane "knew after the first child I could not use the customary court." She was unable to use the magistrate's court because "at that time there was no provision for support" (i.e., there was no Affiliation Act in force). She acknowledged that even if such a provision had been in force she would not have made use of it because "I felt it was useless to do anything when a man turned away from his promises." This attitude is not uncommon. The woman's family may act initially to test a liaison's potential but on discovering the other party's lack of commitment let the matter drop. Where they can support the mother and child without the father's assistance, as in Olibile's case (G.2), they let things lie.

Mmanchibidu (G.3) knew that she could go to Kgosing with her first pregnancy and to the magistrate's court for support for her other children. She did neither, because her first child died, a bad omen, and "because I had children before the support law was in operation. When it came into force I was able to support the children and did not use it. I was well supported by my family, mainly my father and my brothers." Similarly, Seiphimolo (G.3), who is one of the few women making a living from running a shebeen,[16] never took action because "my father, Rampole, and my brothers helped me with the children's school fees when they could. I knew that I could go to the magistrate but did not because I was managing. I was quite able to support the children." She commented that "if I had had a problem with support I would have gone to the magistrate." She knew Kgosing would not pay compensation for the second child and observed that "even with the first child they like to refer the case back to parents to settle."

Women often ignore their first pregnancy especially when they are at a young, vulnerable age. As Oailse Timpa explained, she did not act on her first pregnancy because "I was still young then [nineteen or twenty] and did not know that I could go to the D.C. [the magistrate] I didn't even know that nursing a child was troublesome." However, Oailse had learned from other friends' experiences that she could go to the magistrate's court, and with her second pregnancy "I had by then realized the problems of nursing a baby. A baby needs washing, feeding, and clothing and friends advised me to go. I am very discouraged because every time I go to the D.C.'s office I am asked why I had a child and why I worry about it." Many women learn about the magistrate's court through other women, especially from friends or relatives. In some cases, their attention is directed toward the court by employers who advise them to raise maintenance claims, or by kgotla officials who, in turning them away from the kgotla, advise them to pursue their action for support in the magistrate's court.

Sometimes generations approach the issue differently. Setswamosimeng's daughter, Flora (G.4), went to the magistrate's court on her own initiative after her second pregnancy. According to Setswamosimeng, Flora is a "young woman of today and must have seen what was going on there. Young people today know what is going on by practice. They observe what is going on. They make choices themselves." In going to the magistrate Flora acted without any family consultation. This was not something her mother would have done. Setswamosimeng (G.3) "would have gone to Kgosing[17] because we older people have not known before of going to the magistrate."

However, within Setswamosimengs's generation there are those who have used the magistrate's court. Recall Radipati's daughters, Salalenna and Olebogeng, who both went to the magistrate's court for maintenance. Salalenna observed, "I did not go for cattle compensation originally because it was easier to raise the matter before the magistrate where I was living in Gaborone." While marriage was being contemplated, no action was taken, but once it was rejected Salalenna and her family felt free to seek support. There was no question of marriage for Olebogeng. This option was rejected from the start when her mother and her brother raised the matter with the magistrate in Gaborone.

In both these cases, the fathers came from Francistown, which is in the eastern part of Botswana, a long way away from Molepolole. The parties met in Gaborone, where they were working. The scenario fits the one, depicted by members of wards earlier, of parties from different areas coming together in a location due to the exigencies of employment, but without cutting family ties. For both Salalenna and Olebogeng residence in Gaborone made it more convenient to deal with the man before a magistrate than to mobilize the kgotla system, which would have required assembling a whole array of family members from diverse locales. The difficulties inherent in using the kgotla system make the magistrate's court a more viable option for some (A. Griffiths 1984:9–10). This is especially true where families prove uncooperative or where women, like Flora, seek to act independently, freed from the constraints of customary institutions.

Family Histories, Networks, and Access to Law

Parties' attitudes and actions are to some extent shaped by the activities that inform their lives. Given Radipati's family profile, highly educated, with women as well as men in employment and linked to the salariat, it is not surprising that the magistrate's court formed part of their sphere of operations. Contrast them with Makokwe's son, Ramojaki, who takes a different approach. Ramojaki belongs to a family that has invested in activities associated with the peasantariat. Most women in his family group, unlike those in Radipati's household, have focused their energies on the agricultural and domestic sphere, with only a few of the younger generation experiencing any kind of formal employment.

Laping is of the same generation as Ramojaki. He comes from the same family tradition with the same interests. He has little formal education and works as a miner. Both men feel very strongly tied to the kgotla system, with its emphasis on indigenous links and local connections. When Laping's eldest daughter, Sebena, became pregnant, the matter was discussed with the man's family, which agreed to marriage. However, the man's family did nothing, and after the birth of the second child, the father disappeared. When Laping pursued the issue, he was told that the man, Dikang, was still at the mines and that he would make arrangements for marriage on his return. Dissatisfied with this, Laping went to report the matter at Kgosing, and arrangements were made to have a hearing on Dikang's return. But when Dikang returned, he came home with a wife and it was too late for action.

According to Laping, with Sebena's first pregnancy "we never considered going to the magistrate's court." This is understandable given that the relationship appeared to have potential for marriage. When it failed to progress they still did not opt for the magistrate's court because "we felt the right thing to do was to go to Kgosing as this is the proper channel for such problems." Ramojaki shares this view. He accepts that in negotiations over his seventeen-year-old daughter Okahune's pregnancy "if they agree to pay eight head of cattle that is sufficient." Although a claim may lie for both compensation and maintenance,[18] and both have been awarded in Molepolole on occasion,[19] most people consider that this is unjust and that a choice must be made.[20] In Ramojaki's case, "if the man's family do not pay up we will to Kgosing." He opts for Kgosing over the magistrate's court because "we Batswana know our procedure and are inclined to report to Kgosing even although we know we can go to the D.C.'s [magistrate's] court. It is only children who go to the D.C.'s court. In a situation like this [a first child] we would go to Kgosing."

Individuals may be predisposed toward certain attitudes through the activities and networks they participate in, but they are not bound by them. People shop around to obtain what they want. Those linked to the peasantariat's sphere of activities often have a tendency to favor Kgosing over the magistrate's court, but when this fails to provide the remedy they seek they will go elsewhere. Such forum shopping works both ways, so that a claim initially taken to the magistrate's court may at a later stage be transferred to the chief's kgotla (for more information on this see A. Griffiths 1984).

Such transfers usually occur where women fail to find satisfaction in one forum and seek to rectify the situation by trying another. Some women opt for the chief's kgotla in the first instance where pregnancy is concerned, because they favor a lump sum, a once-and-for-all payment, over a smaller periodical payment made at regular intervals. However, when they experience the kinds of delays that can take place before a case is heard, they become disillusioned by the lack of action and transfer the matter to the magistrate's court. On the other hand, there are women who initiate proceeding in the magistrate's court precisely because they prefer a smaller but regular set of income payments that will support the child until he or she reaches the age of sixteen. However, they may change their minds and transfer their case to the chief's kgotla because of the backlog of cases that the magistrate's court has to deal with (due to the low priority attributed to maintenance cases) and, in some instances, due to the attitude of the officials they encounter.

These accounts mark the importance of social factors in determining the legal options that people pursue. Those who use the chief's kgotla must meet certain requirements, which are portrayed in the hearings described below. The hearings underline the kinds of arguments presented there and the central role that marriage plays in the construction of relationships as parties dispute whether their liaison amounted to some other type of relationship. The texts depict what occurs when pregnancy and marriage issues move beyond the family compound and become public through the use of forums, like the kgotla or magistrate's court, and exposure to third parties.

TEKO MERE'S DISPUTE

Family History and Network

Teko Mere is a part of the network associated with Makokwe's family. She is the daughter of Keselibile, who has had a long-standing relationship with Makokwe's son Kemongale (fig. 4c). Like her aunt Olebeng, Makokwe's daughter, she attended school but has never had formal employment and has had several children in different relationships. Both she and her immediate family form part of a network whose connections revolve around lands, cattle, mining, and domestic activities, which associate them with the peasantariat. Their political links are with those who run Kgosing. Teko's grandfather, Tshitoeng Mere, who appears with her in the case, was a favorite of the late Kgosi Kgari Sechele II; Tshitoeng was a member of the tribal police and sat regularly with the elders in the chief's kgotla. Due to his connections he has been registered at Kgosing as the headman of Mosotho kgotla, although the late Kgosi Bonewamang (1971–78) endorsed another man's (Tshenolo's) claim to the position.

Given this background, it is not surprising that the issue of pregnancy was pursued in the chief's kgotla. In addition, Teko did not have to outlay expenses, as access to this forum is free. There are no court costs, except in the case of appeals from the chief's kgotla to the magistrate's court, in which case there is an administrative charge of four pula, which was about $2.40 in 1989. No legal representation is required; indeed, it is expressly excluded from this arena. Proceedings are conducted in the local language, Setswana (as they are throughout the kgotla system), rather than English, although both languages have official status in Botswana.

According to Teko, when her partner failed to support her and the children despite several meetings, she decided to raise a case at Kgosing herself. This was because she was angry and desired some public recognition of wrong. She raised the case with his parents' consent because "he deceived me, he told me that he was going to marry me. We were together eight years and then he stopped supporting me and the children. I knew to go to Kgosing through other friends who had been there."

Ruling

The third party hearing the case was the deputy chief, Mr. Kgosiensho. An abridged account of the hearing which Mr. Masimega and I attended in 1982 is presented in appendix B. The deputy chief ruled in Rankolwane's favor on the grounds that Teko had two previous children with another man and that her family had failed to follow proper Tswana procedure. The parties were notified of a right to appeal within thirty days. Teko lodged a written request for appeal on the grounds that Rankolwane was the father of all three children, that he neglected to support her and the children, and that Mr. Kgosiensho was biased because he "wandered in and out of the case" and "had already made his decision without giving me a proper hearing."

Competing Perspectives

When the District Commissioner examined Teko's appeal he ordered the case to be retried. This had nothing to do with Teko's allegations concerning Mr. Kgosiensho but concerned her grandfather's participation in the dispute. The District Commissioner wrote, "The reason is simple and single. Tshitoeng Mere appears as the complainant's witness and also as a court member. This has never happened anywhere. One cannot testify against a defendant and later ask him questions as a member." Here a conflict of values arises in the approach taken by the District Commissioner and that adopted by Mr. Kgosiensho. The District Commissioner, a Motswana, espouses a European concept of justice in his view that a person cannot appear in a public forum in two capacities, as a court member and as a complainant's supporter. Mr. Kgosiensho, who had discussed the matter at length with the District Commissioner over the phone, nevertheless permitted Tshitoeng to speak "because I considered him as the parent of the child who normally is the person to claim eight head of cattle in accordance with Tswana practice. I felt there was nothing wrong with him participating in the case and being a court councillor." Councillor is an honorary title given to those of the kgosi's inner circle whose views are consulted during a case. The District Commissioner considered Tshitoeng's presence as such prejudiced the case. Mr. Kgosiensho disagreed. In his view the hearing was not prejudiced despite Tshitoeng's evidence because "a court councillor has to follow proper procedure and will do this regardless of whether it is his own child or not [that is involved]."

The case was retried on 11 January 1984.[21] This time it was heard by the chief regent, Mr. Mac Sechele. It pursued the same arguments presented in the initial hearing, with Teko stressing agreement to marriage and recognition of the union through support provided during confinement. But she added a new element, a gift of herbs from the man's family after the child's birth. This implied a form of recognition, as it is Tswana practice for married couples to use herbs after a child's birth before they resume sexual relations. By making this claim, Teko underlined that her relationship with Rankolwane was a marriage-type relationship. She ended once again by stating that she had reported to his parents, who had given up and told her to go to Kgosing. This time the chief regent reached a different decision from that of Mr. Kgosiensho. His reasoning was that "the complainant told the court that the defendant was supporting two children and she even explained that the defendant's father Keboletse was curing them with traditional medicine to unite them according to Tswana custom. This proves that he impregnated Teko. If Keboletse had not used that Tswana custom there could be no evidence of impregnation, and you [the man] do not deny the third child is yours. The court will order you to pay for the third child." The order was to pay eight head of cattle or the monetary equivalent (640 pula). As before, rights of appeal were noted.

Why were there differing judgments? When questioned, Mr. Kgosiensho claimed a different view of Tswana law and custom from that of the chief regent. In his view, "According to Tswana custom the woman had two children by another man so there was no room for compensation for the third child." He did say, however, that if Rankolwane had been the first child's father he would have awarded compensation although Teko waited until after the third child's birth to bring a case. I queried this in light of womens' experiences at Kgosing. If they have children, they are usually dismissed without any discussion of their situation or of whether such grounds apply. This is borne out by a recorded case (MO 44/80) where a woman came to Kgosing pregnant with her third child. She alleged neglect but was turned away with the ruling

"There is no law governing concubinage. Therefore this woman is to report this case to the D.C. [magistrate] for maintenance."

Asked to comment on the chief regent's decision in Teko's case, Mr. Kgosiensho and another kgotla man stated that it had been reached on the basis of nepotism toward Tshitoeng. While Teko referred to marriage negotiations and Tshitoeng stressed this aspect of the dispute (which was upheld by the chief regent), the prevailing community view rejected compensation here. Even if the claim was based on breach of promise to marry instead of on seduction, it failed because Teko already had children from a liaison prior to the one that gave rise to the dispute. In our discussions Teko openly revealed that the father of her first child was a man whom she had met at the Molepolole Agricultural Fair and had never seen since.

Teko's Dilemma

Rankolwane appealed to the magistrate's court on 16 January 1984, arguing that he was not liable for compensation because Teko already had two children. According to Teko in 1984, she heard the magistrate's clerk tell Rankolwane that there was no case and he need not provide support, although the case had not yet been formally processed by the magistrate's court. This informal appraisal failed to take account of rights to maintenance under the Affiliation Proceedings Act. However, when Teko made inquiries, she was informed that the case was still pending. She was not optimistic about the outcome and felt "compelled to leave the matter there."

Rankolwane died later in 1984. Teko now has a relationship with Alfred from Mochudi with whom she has two children. There has been no further contact with Rankolwane's family. Teko continues to look after her children and Tshitoeng, who is now blind. She would like to be employed, but it is hard in her situation, as "it is difficult to make a living when you are not married and not working." Her family does not assist her, although her brothers are employed. She manages because Alfred, who works in construction, provides some support for her and the children.

In Teko's case she was caught between conflicting Tswana notions of propriety. In her environment the chief's kgotla was the natural place for her to bring her claim. Living as she does, given her family's activities, it was the appropriate forum for her to make a public statement about the end of her relationship as well as the place for her to seek support. Indeed, her grandfather's relationship with those in authority was to her advantage in the second hearing, an advantage which was only displaced by Rankolwane's insistence on appealing to the magistrate's court. But though one set of factors predisposed her toward the kgotla, another set operated against her. The latter centered on the rule that a woman is not entitled to compensation if she has more than one child, especially where a second partner is involved. The chief regent's decision on this matter was regarded as inappropriate by many in the community.

Implications for Women

Teko's position is common. It reflects a social reality, that there are a significant number of unmarried women who have several children with different fathers.[22] These women and their families are excluded from a remedy under the customary system. They are well aware of this, and in many cases where they failed to negotiate outside dispute forums this was because a second or further pregnancy was involved. In this area Bakwena ignore social reality, unlike neighboring Bakgatla, who now allow compensation for each pregnancy.

As women like Teko age, problems with support intensify. Without an income from informal sources, employment, or family members, they are more than ever dependent on their male partners. Having had a number of liaisons, they are not regarded by Bakwena as prime marriage partners. In addition to age, they have to contend with demographic constraints and the fact that men prefer women younger than themselves by as much as ten years or more. Older women have less power to negotiate procreative relationships with men and may have to accept whatever type of union is offered in order to acquire some support, however temporary.

Although women can opt to use the magistrate's court, which is available to them regardless of the number of children involved, there are problems with access. In the past, access was restricted in that the court only met once a week and gave priority to criminal cases. The result was a backlog of civil, chiefly maintenance, cases. To quote Oailse Timpa (twenty-six), "I went to report the case to the D.C. [the magistrate]. This was in November 1977. It took a long time before they were able to call us together. Our case was heard in August 1978." She was more fortunate than others, some of whom have had to wait several years for a hearing and are still waiting. Since 1989 there has been a resident magistrate in Molepolole but he recognizes that this is still a problem. The sheer volume of work means it is hard to reserve one day a week to deal with the backlog as well as the current maintenance cases.

Access is not the only problem. While parties do not need legal representation or to pay a fee (except on appeal from the chief's kgotla), proceedings in this forum are conducted in English, with which parties may have less familiarity than Setswana. For those who are unable to follow the proceedings an interpreter is provided, but this changes the dynamics of the process as another layer is added. An even more important consideration is that those unmarried women who are claiming maintenance have to meet the conditions of the Affiliation Proceedings Act 1970 [Cap.28:02] with which they are unfamiliar. The crucial provisions are those concerning proof of paternity and the time limit for raising an action. Under the act a woman's allegations of paternity must be "corroborated in some material particular by other evidence to the court's satisfaction" [s.6 (2)]. The problem is that most parties to maintenance cases in Molepolole are not legally represented and appear alone before a magistrate. This was certainly so in 1982 and 1984, though there were some signs of representation in 1989, when a lawyer's office opened in village. Prior to this parties desiring legal advice and representation had to travel to Gaborone, the capital, to acquire it. But for the most part, in these cases there is no such representation, and where there are no witnesses or letters to establish the nature of the liaison, it is one person's word against another. Under such circumstances it is difficult to meet the requirement for corroboration.

Most magistrates are aware of this, and many of them, not just in Molepolole but in Gaborone and Lobatse,[23] handle this by seeing if the man admits to having had sexual intercourse around the time the woman conceived. If he does they treat this as a form of corroboration, giving rise to a presumption of paternity.[24] If not, there is little they can do. They do not believe in pressuring the man to have a blood test. Their attitude contrasts with that of officials in the chief's kgotla in Molepolole, notably the chief regent, Mr. Mac Sechele. He claimed he was happy to apply such pressure where a man denied paternity for a first pregnancy. I never witnessed this, as the man usually admitted paternity when pressed. This was because of the kgotla's predisposition to back the woman's account in such a case. In this instance, the onus is on the man to prove otherwise.

It is not only lack of knowledge about the magistrate's court that causes women problems. They may also be in danger of being misled by a man's promise of marriage so that they are unable to provide the necessary corroboration for their story when the time comes. This experience is a common one among young women. It leads to the second problem, that of the time limit that women face. Under the act they must raise an action within twelve months from the date of the child's birth, or "at any subsequent time" provided the man alleged to be the father "has within twelve months next after the birth paid money or supplied food, clothing or other necessaries for its maintenance" [S.4 (a) and (b)]. The latter provision is there to take into account that men may promise marriage and then disappear, as well the ambiguities surrounding the negotiation of a customary marriage. But by the time it is clear that a relationship will not become such a marriage the time limit has often expired and evidence of support may be hard to produce in court. While the 1970 act was amended in 1977,[25] this simply raised the ceiling on amounts payable under the act and did not alter the time limit. Aware of this, a number of magistrates admit that they simply ignore the time limit.[26] However, if the case is appealed to the High Court, which is unusual, it will be dismissed.[27]

The problems women experience in Molepolole are duplicated elsewhere. For a detailed account of the difficulties women face in these circumstances the reader may refer to the work of Molokomme (1991) and the Women and Law in Southern Africa Trust (1992). My earlier research suggested that it was mainly educated women and government employees who used the magistrate's court in Molepolole, but this impression was dispelled as the research progressed and it became clear that the court was used by women from all sections of the community. Molokomme's research (1991:183) among Bangwaketse suggests a link between women's education (but not formal employment) and their use of the magistrate's court. In Molepolole, however, the court has a broader clientele, and the resident magistrate in 1989 observed that in his experience, women who use the court are generally uneducated and poor. They are usually unemployed or living on very low incomes.

While it is true that some parties appear to make choices and engage in forum shopping, it does seem that for many women the magistrate's court is the last resort, where they go in desperation when all else has failed. When it comes to payment, however, neither the chief's kgotla nor the magistrate's court in Molepolole has a good track record as an effective enforcement agency. This is in keeping with findings elsewhere (Brown 1985; Molokomme 1991:231).

In Teko's case, the parties presented their claims by manipulating certain facts. These included arguments over reporting, knowledge of pregnancy, and meetings between the families. Such elements are essential to establishing the validity of a claim. Among Bakwena, those who have a genuine grievance show this by initiating action, by being the first to report to the their own as well as their partner's family.

In successful compensation claims based on recognition of the man's responsibility or on the failure of marriage negotiations, a party must demonstrate that the other family was aware of the situation and participated in the negotiation process. While Teko was unsuccessful in her manipulation of these norms (except in the second hearing, which has been ignored), Nyana, whose case follows, was able to manipulate them to her advantage.

NYANA SEGETHSHO'S DISPUTE

Nyana made a claim against her partner, Mokwaledi, in the chief's kgotla in a dispute that Mr. Masimega and I attended in 1982. An abridged account of the hearing is presented in appendix C. Nyana, like Teko, stressed her desire for compensation and separation, saying, "The defendant has caused me to bear a child and does not support me. Now that he is not supporting me I want him to compensate me and we part." Mr. Kgosiensho, hearing the case, encouraged her to go on. Nyana continued, "There was an engagement reached at the time. The arrangement was made between my parents and his parents. Then I don't know what happened." Mokwaledi was allowed to question her but declined.

After lengthy questioning, Mr. Kgosiensho brought the proceedings to an end. He told Mokwaledi, "I look upon you as a person who does not know Tswana law and custom because you were given special permission to live with the girl you were engaged to and then you abandoned her. You did not tell anybody, either your parents or her parents; that shows that you do not know anything about Tswana law." He then turned to Nyana to ask about her final wishes. She stressed once again, "All I can say is that he compensates me and that we part." Mokwaledi was then asked to make a final comment, which was, "My last words are I want to marry her." After this Mr. Kgosiensho summarized the evidence presented and his response to it. His summing up is quoted at length here because it articulates the factors that form part of mekgwa le melao that, in Mr. Kgosiensho's view, underlie a Tswana marriage. He began,

The complainant has explained to this court that the defender fell in love with her and that they consulted their parents on both sides about marriage. The parents on both sides acted accordingly by presenting the articles which are in accordance with Tswana procedure in marriage called peelela. They finally gave special permission for the two lovers to live together with a pending arrangement for marriage. The marriage was to take place immediately after the plowing season in January 1978. No action was ever taken until they had a child. In this case the child was born outside the procedure in terms of Tswana law. The complainant has told this court that her father has many a time been in contact with the defender's parents finding out about the proposed marriage. Nothing was then done, no action was taken until the case was brought here.[28]

In his defense the defendant states that what the complainant says is the truth. He states that he went away from her because at one time when he visited her she threw away his personal effects. This is just a clumsy excuse because if he knew anything about the law of marriage according to Tswana custom there would not be a case like this. He never took any trouble to report to his "wife's" parents what his complaint was at the time. There is no marriage under Tswana custom where a husband will leave his wife and child for one year without any communication.

In other words, such behavior does not signify a marriage.

The case was adjourned for a few minutes. When he returned, Mr. Kgosiensho concluded

According to Tswana custom there is no engagement that would last for four years.[29] With regard to what you wish as defendant this court cannot prevent you from marrying Nyana if you so wish. Now this is the court order. You are going to bring out eight head of cattle to compensate Nyana for having given her a child.

The parties had different strategies for manipulating their claims. Nyana emphasized that this was her first child and that she was claiming compensation, but the man tried to refute her claim by arguing they were married. While the man in Teko's dispute argued that she was simply a nyatsi and matched this image by referring to all the children she had when she raised the case, Nyana's partner adopted a completely different approach. He knew that where a woman comes to the kgotla with her first child and alleges that a certain man is the father she is usually believed. Her word is sufficient. The man has to meet more stringent requirements for his denial of paternity to be accepted. Though women are powerless to pursue claims if they have several children, for that brief period with their first child they acquire a superior bargaining position over men.

Unlike Teko's case, which was initiated at Kgosing, Nyana's case came through the ranks, from the parties' own subward, Bobadidi, via Kgaimena kgotla to Maunatlala senior ward until it finally reached Kgosing. The whole process from start to finish took four years, with the man and his family failing to attend any kgotla meetings until the one at Kgosing. Compared with Teko, Nyana and her family did not let the matter lapse for years but actively pursued it through various dispute forums until it reached Kgosing. In the interim, she had no further children. After the case, Nyana disclosed knowledge of her right to use the magistrate's court, which she rejected as a forum because "I did not like the method of support and I wanted to settle up once and for all."

Such experiences accentuate women's position within society. But while childbirth is something that all women have in common, their actual experiences vary greatly. This is something which law fails to acknowledge because its focus on procreation as their common mark of identity ignores the differing contexts in which procreation is experienced and which account in large measure for women's dependence on men in a variety of arrangements. For in reality, women's situations differ according to the type of activities that they and their family pursue. There are those like Makokwe's daughter, Olebeng, and Teko, whose sphere is restricted to the world of domestic tasks and subsistence agriculture associated with the peasantariat. The diminishing returns in this sphere, caused in part by drought but also by a general decline in informal sector productivity, have perpetuated the dependence of these women on men, so that they rely on their fathers, brothers, or partners for support.

In contrast, there are women such as Radipati's daughter Goitsemang and her sisters whose sphere includes education and formal employment, both of which link them to the salariat. While they too have relied on men for support, their reliance has been limited to short periods preceding and following their giving birth and has not been so extensive or all encompassing. Through their direct access to money as primary wage earners, these women have acquired a greater degree of independence, as evidenced by Goitsemang, who has built her own house in the capital city, Gaborone.

It is within such contexts that pregnancy negotiations take place. They form part of the basic fabric of social life which occurs, for the most part, outside formal institutions such as dispute forums. In this process, various factors operate to structure outcomes according to procedures for reporting, family meetings, and the number of pregnancies involved. These factors affect the formal legal sphere where negotiations are pursued in various forums. The different ways in which they do so and how parties manipulate them are marked by Teko and Nyana's disputes.

In Teko's case, though her background predisposed her toward the chief's kgotla, she failed to establish her claim because she had several children by two different fathers. This contravened the view that compensation is only due for the first child's birth.[30] As a result, her partner's argument, that she was simply a nyatsi and as such not entitled to support, was the one that the community upheld. In contrast, Nyana was successful in her claim. She met the ideal condition of having only one child with one man, while her partner failed to establish the marriage that would have thwarted her compensation claim. Nyana depicts the power women may wield with their first pregnancy, a power lost, as in Teko's case, with subsequent pregnancies.

As the pattern for women in Mosotho kgotla is to have several children during their lifetimes, they only briefly experience a superior bargaining position over men. They may turn to the magistrate's court for help, but this presents problems given the realities of access, proof of paternity, and enforced time limits that they face. This does not necessarily improve with a change of location. Those who have gone to a magistrate's court elsewhere—for example, in Gaborone—have also encountered similar difficulties.

Teko's and Nyana's disputes highlight the kinds of factors that determine how women's claims to compensation for pregnancy will be received. As such they form part of a broader dimension which is concerned with the framework of social relations into which women's procreative relationships with men must be placed. This enterprise is not confined to situations of conflict or dispute, but forms part of social life in general. In this context, marriage plays a key role, for it is used as the marker (though an often unarticulated marker) in terms of which all relationships acquire their identity, whether as marital, potentially marital, or nonmarital liaisons. This is so even although the construction of identity may vary over the course of time as individuals seek to recast the nature of their relationships.

In this process, women's narratives reveal the extent to which women's power to negotiate their partnerships with men depends upon their position in the social order and the stage that they have reached in their life cycle with respect to the number of children they have. Faced with the proposition that procreation is a fact of life, women must nonetheless accommodate such childbearing within socially sanctioned parameters that dictate the terms for recognition of a relationship and the types of obligation that are assigned to it wherever marriage is discounted.

This creates problems for women, not only because of the ambiguity surrounding the creation of a customary marriage, but also because of the social pressure they experience to bear children. Being a mother not only marks the transition from being a girl to a woman but gives the father an enhanced status among his peers, as proof of his masculinity (regardless of the actual status of the relationship). A woman must balance the social expectation that she will have children with an assessment of the circumstances surrounding her partnership with a man. There is no doubt that having children with a man places the relationship on another footing, which may enhance its credibility, but should that relationship break down, the woman and children may find themselves left in a vulnerable position because of the difficulties they face in establishing grounds for support or compensation or enforcing their claims.

The difficulties that women encounter in this situation are reinforced by their experiences of courts and the legal system, which uphold the social basis upon which women's partnerships with men are constructed and interpreted. The narratives presented in this chapter underline the extent to which social understandings, expectations, and values permeate law, regardless of whether law is located within a customary or Western-type setting. This is illustrated by the ways in which procreative relationships are viewed and handled in the ordinary world of everyday life as well as in state legal forums. Where pregnancy is concerned, there is a set of social practices which frame negotiations between individuals and their families and which inform legal debate. Thus, the kinds of claims made by a legal centralist model of law with respect to autonomy and immunity from ordinary social processes cannot be sustained. Nor can such a model's view of legal pluralism, as endorsing separate and parallel spheres of law (in terms of common and customary law), be upheld. Ethnographic research demonstrates the extent to which such systems become interconnected through people's (including legal personnel's) perceptions and use of law overall, in relation to the social processes of which it forms part.

FIVE

The Gendered World of Marriage: Claims of Desertion and Neglect

Marriage forms part of the social processes referred to in the last chapter. Indeed, it provides a focal point for assessing the types of partnership that a woman has with a man and the obligations that ensue when an issue arises between the parties. In this chapter the focus shifts away from the ambiguities surrounding the status of relationships to center on those that are acknowledged as marriages. It depicts individuals disputing as husbands and wives and the kinds of claims they make with respect to one another in this context, a context derived from common understandings about the nature of their spousal roles and the social behavior associated with them. Once again, as in the previous chapter, the social world impinges on marital relations to define their characteristics. What is at stake in the process of marital negotiations and disputes is the way in which the roles of husband and wife are configured and how women and men vie with one another to establish conformity with the social expectations attached to their particular spousal roles (while discrediting such claims from their partners). The tensions that surface in unions between the sexes, as portrayed in chapter 4, are also present in some formal or socially recognized marriages. But they are articulated differently when presented in the context of marital obligations. In these cases emphasis is placed on marital conduct and the roles assigned to spouses. Such roles, which have a social base and derive from social expectations of marriage, are reenacted in a legal arena and used as central reference points for the handling of disputes. Thus, social and legal worlds intersect, not (as in chapter 4) to deny the status of marriage, but to reaffirm it. Yet again, the legal centralist model of law as divorced from social life is discredited.

The social world that gives rise to the spousal roles of husband and wife is a gendered one. Where marriage is concerned, men and women find themselves differentially situated regarding the kinds of claims they can make on one another as spouses. Thus, a man may directly address his wife's infidelity in the kgotla, but to directly address a husband in this way is considered inappropriate conduct for a wife. Not only does she have to raise the issue more indirectly, through claims of neglect and lack of support, but there is no question of her being entitled to compensation from her spouse's lover (in contrast with her husband, who is so entitled). Such asymmetry exists because what is regarded as socially acceptable behavior for spouses varies according to different sets of expectations that arise in relation to the conduct of spouses derived from an ideal model that is embodied in the concepts of the good husband and the good wife. While such a model is often at odds with real life, and members of the younger generation dispute its terms, nonetheless, it continues to operate as a powerful paradigm in the management of marital disputes described in this and the subsequent two chapters. However individuals perceive the true nature of marital relations, they revert to this paradigm when it comes to asserting claims in disputes

In terms of this model, certain characteristics are attributed to a "good" wife. Such a woman always attends to her man regardless of when he returns home and where he has been. She is always prepared to cook for him, to wash his clothes, and to work hard to develop their household. She only complains about his affairs with other women if he neglects her or the children. She does not have affairs herself, or gossip about her husband, or bring his name into disrepute. Nor does she criticize him to his children or set them against him. Where real problems arise in their relationship, she acts by reporting them to both families and enlisting their assistance as mediators. Where this is unsuccessful, the help of the local headman is enlisted. For his part, a "good" husband may have affairs but he does not ill treat, neglect, or fail to support his family. He does not leave his wife, or live apart from her without cause, and he does not use her household property to support another woman. It is also his duty to report any marital difficulties where they arise.

These standards are manipulated and exploited in disputes representing unions not yet at the stage of formal or public dissolution. In these disputes, where the union has run into problems but is still ongoing (or the fiction is maintained that this is so), what is at stake for most women and their families is their property rights. These must be protected against encroachment through the present and future actions of their spouses. What lies behind these disputes is concern for the future rather than (as in Teko and Nyana's cases) an appraisal of the past.

Where a relationship is problematic, a dispute is made public in order to protect a woman and her children's property rights. This is achieved in a number of ways. It may, in the most immediate sense, be

used to exert pressure on a man to stop using accumulated family resources to provide for another women. This is a common complaint in
marital disputes, including those examined in this chapter.

But a public discussion may also be initiated for other reasons. These
may have less to do with the immediate and concrete return of property
than with an individual's or family's need to make a public statement
about the relationship, to put their position on record. Women often
use this means to vindicate their position by publicly censuring the
man and his family. They do not expect the issues raised to be dealt with
as a result of the case, so that support for them and their children
will follow or appropriation of their household property will cease. They
will, however, have had a chance to vent their frustrations, to enlist
social support, and to expose the man to some form of public humiliation by subjecting their union to public scrutiny.

The fact that problems cannot be accommodated through normal
family channels (by relatives meeting on both sides) reflects badly on
everyone, especially the man. As head of the household he has failed to
maintain his authority in the family domain. Women here have little to
lose, so they can play on their weaker position to make the man lose
face. It is well known that Batswana love to display their oratorical skills
through the medium of disputes, but marital disputes are regarded in a
different light, as matters which should not, where possible, be aired
in public.

When these disputes do occur, however, they can be used to establish future credibility and as a bargaining chip in a relationship potentially facing dissolution. As chapter 7 will demonstrate, when unions are
formally dissolved and property rights are at stake, the issue of conduct
and fault (in terms of failing to adhere to marital codes) is central among
Bakwena. So, by preempting the other spouse, by constructing an image
of the aggrieved party who has tried all the normal channels, prospective
credibility may be established, which can be mobilized if the relationship finally collapses and a redistribution of property takes place.

This is how the disputes dissected in this chapter must be read, as
part of ongoing social relationships—neither privileged as central reference points out of which social relations are constructed nor treated as
end points of discussion. In the following chapters, disputes are shown
to function as part of continuing relations between individuals and their
families which I trace over numbers of years. They form part of an extended study, in which moments of dispute in the kgotla are balanced
by reference to social responses and what happens over the longer term.

Far from taking dispute as the starting point, I begin with the social processes that may or may not promote the kinds of disputes examined.

THE KGOSIDINTSIS

The Kgosidintsis, whose relationship gave rise to dispute, have firm ties with Molepolole. Manaka, the wife, and her family belong to Maribana ward; her husband, Joel, belongs to Mokgalo ward and is well connected in terms of village politics. He is part of the Kgosidintsi family which is descended from the royal family's second house through Motswasele I (fig. 5). He is also directly related to the headman of Mokgalo ward, one of the six major wards in Molepolole. However, Manaka claims "he is the son of a poor man who married a widow when he was a boy. He never had any estate." But, unlike many men of his generation, he did acquire an education, and in 1954 after primary school he trained as a teacher at Kimberley in South Africa.[1] He was a teacher when he met Manaka, who was in his class at school. When Manaka left school to pursue a relationship with him, she had completed Standard 6 of primary school. This was in the 1950s. The relationship persisted until the start of the 1980s when conflict erupted (in her view) because Joel took their family property and went to live with another woman. By then they had had nine children, several of whom were adults.

When handled in a public forum the relationship was treated as a marriage, although Mr. Bakwena, headman of Mokgalo, had his doubts because "patlo had not been made when Manaka fell in love with Joel. They married without their parents' agreement." He recalled that when conflict arose, kgotla members "wished to bring the case to a final settlement by putting patlo into effect because the couple already had children." Here is an example of attempts by ward members to model a relationship on marriage, which will be discussed in chapter 7.

For Manaka their relationship was a marriage because "consultation was made with my parents [by Joel and his relatives] and it was agreed that marriage would be registered in due course. That was in 1957. However, he delayed. His headman and my parents wanted us to marry but he delayed until misunderstanding arose."

The relationship's status was never in fact questioned in the hearings, but accorded social recognition as a marriage. This was due to prolonged family consultations well known to kgotla members, along with Manaka's long-standing residence in Joel's kgotla and the many children they had together. At the beginning Joel had nothing, but Manaka claimed to have brought some cattle with her, which had been built up into a herd over the years. They initially plowed his mother's lands for four years before reverting to Manaka's family lands at Sekhukhwane "because he refused to marry me according to law, that is why I went back to my mother's lands." This is not unusual. It is done to pressure a man, particularly where there are children, because it reaffirms links with the woman's family which could potentially bar a man's claims to his children.

Hearing in the Chief's Kgotla

Manaka's account. The first hearing Mr. Masimega and I attended was at Kgosing on 16 June 1982 with Mr. Kgosiensho presiding. An abridged account of the hearing is provided in appendix D. In her opening remarks Manaka tried to safeguard the family property which she alleged Joel (fifty-four) appropriated to support another woman's family. In her claim she presented Joel in a bad light, as a bad husband, by highlighting behavior which is unacceptable in both a marital and social context. She stressed that he deserted her. She did not directly challenge his affair with the other woman, but raised it through his lack of support, adroitly avoiding confrontation with male sexual mores but playing on the prevailing view that a man having an affair must not neglect his family.

In addition to neglect she alleged that Joel had used household property to support another woman. This is contrary to Bakwena and other Tswana merafe's rules relating to property. These require a man to establish separate households with their own resources for each wife. The huts, fields, cattle, and so forth, associated with one household may not be appropriated by another. The theory is that in this way the children from each household will be guaranteed some form of inheritance.

Manaka also raised more serious allegations about Joel having sex with a widow who had not been ritually cleansed. This is forbidden. Among Bakwena, a widow must abstain from sex for twelve months after her husband's death. During that time, especially two to three months after the death, she takes traditional medicines mixed in with her food. After that any man wishing to have sex with her must use certain herbs. Where individuals flout these rules, there is a belief that they will sicken and may die. In juxtaposing Joel's meetings with the widow with his ensuing sickness Manaka sets up an image of an illicit relationship breaking the bounds of social convention. By presenting Joel as someone who defies convention and the spirit world, Manaka makes a very serious allegation which she knows will have an impact on all present at the dispute. Such behavior is considered to have ramifications which extend beyond the individuals concerned into the community at large.[2]

At the end of Manaka's account it was late in the afternoon, and the case was adjourned until the next day.

Joel's account. The next morning Joel set about discrediting Manaka in his alternative version of events. He began by undermining her credibility by arguing that, far from acting appropriately, she prematurely came to the kgotla without having pursued the matter through the normal channels. In addition he presented her as a brazen woman who did not act as a wife should: "My wife is not ashamed of scandalizing my name and saying anything undesirable to my feelings in public, like she is doing now." Not only that, but to make matter worse, she is a liar: "Even the statement she gave yesterday about me is a false statement. My wife knows very well that I respect her. Even the local people where we stay know so." He attempts to shift the blame for what has occurred onto her: "She has suddenly changed this year. Her excuse is that I am married to a widow woman who she mentioned yesterday. It is false that my wife says that I moved my livestock property to the kraal of the widow in question and also that I spend my earnings with that women." He presents Manaka as an unreliable person who is a dangerous woman because she engages in physical violence. He uses this to justify why he no longer lives with her: "At the beginning of the Easter holidays, on a Sunday afternoon, my wife assaulted me inside the kitchen when we were together. She closed the door, which I did not notice. Then she picked up an iron store opener [a crowbar; he then held this up for kgotla members to see] and hit me on the head. I can still feel the wound; it has not healed properly [and he pointed to a scar on his forehead]. I think that at that moment she intended to kill me. It was then, after all these incidents, that I told my wife that I was not willing to stay with her when she behaves like a beast, just like a lion." He ends his statement by placing the ball in his wife's court: "I don't know what my wife wants me to do now because at the beginning of this year she told me that I will never have conjugal rights with her and saying that she is doing away with me altogether [i.e., divorcing him]."

Manaka then tried to refute these allegations and to explain her assault on him in terms of self-defense. Kgotla members then questioned Joel about his allegations to test their veracity. At the end of this process the kgotla found as follows:

Mr. Kgosiensho's summation and ruling

Manaka has told this kgotla that she has a very important complaint which has taken [i.e., been going on for] a very long time. It was about a disagreement with her husband which she often reported to her husband's parents. It would appear that her husband's parents never took any action. The complainant [Manaka] states that her husband is in love with a woman called Bogadinyana. She states that whenever they talk about the matter there is a great deal of disagreement. She states that her husband has taken some of the property to the place of the woman with whom he is in love. This resulted in a fight taking place between her and her husband. Her husband also admits that this the cause of the trouble between them. He says that his wife says that he is in love with Bogadinyana when he is not. He says he began to fall in love with Bogadinyana because his wife was falsely accusing him of being in love. He has also told this kgotla that he reported the matter to his wife's parents and no action was taken.

In examining this case, this kgotla finds that when the complainant told the defendant that she did not like him to continue his love affair with Bogadinyana, the defendant disagreed and felt that as a man he had the right to do so against his wife's will. That is the main source of disorder in their life and caused quarrels and fighting. Had the defendant listened to his wife's advice there would not be such a case as we are listening to here today.

This is the order of the kgotla. The law is never disturbed in any part of its course. Mr. Kgosidintsi has interfered with the peace within his family by falling in love with Bogadinyana. This kgotla orders the defendant Mr. Kgosidintsi to go from here and settle in peace and harmony with his wife. He is going to restore the articles he removed from his wife's house back to their home and settle in peace with her. It is very shameful for a man of his status, an educated respectable man in his position of employment, that he allows himself to be exposed to a dispute of this nature which is a sheer matter of concubinage. Nowadays a man of his status is looked upon as an example to the public in matters of this nature.

And you, Manaka, the defendant's wife, you must bear in mind that a man is treated as delicately as a breakable article like glass. That means if your husband does something careless, if you storm against him so vigorously without any respect, he may lose interest in you and then divorce you straightaway. You are therefore returning to your house to live with your husband in peace, realizing that he is your husband and you must obey him in as much as he obeys you. If he does not listen to you, it is best to take action by prosecuting him rather than hitting and beating him as he has shown us [with an iron crowbar]. That is all.

Law in the Social Context: The Gender Dimension

This ruling, that both parties should go and "live together in peace and harmony," is very common in such disputes. It is something of a set text along the lines of a preordained homily. The social pressures of the kgotla are mobilized, but at the end of the day it is left to the parties themselves to make the relationship work. In going public, Manaka undermined Joel's authority as a husband because he could not contain the domestic situation. Just as women know that they should not raise the issue of their husband's infidelity directly (without reference to neglect), when they do so, the accusation reflects badly on the man as someone who has lost control and whose actions have exceeded the bounds of propriety.

Joel's failure to keep the matter out of the public domain undermined his authority not only as a husband, but also as a man. This was vividly reinforced by the fact that Manaka also severely assaulted him, yet further proof that he could not contain his unruly wife. In raising the dispute, Manaka subjected Joel to public humiliation, which was reinforced in Mr. Kgosiensho's final admonition to Joel, that it was shameful for a man of his status to have allowed himself to be exposed to such a dispute.

This statement is ambiguous. On the face of it, it censures Joel's actual behavior. But it can also be interpreted to mean that Joel should never have lost control of the situation to such an extent that his wife would raise a dispute about "a sheer matter of concubinage." Women are powerless to prevent man entering another relationship (regardless of Mr. Kgosiensho's rhetoric about consent), but they can make it uncomfortable for the man to persist in his behavior. This often takes the form of refusing to cook for him, or to do his washing, or locking him out of the family compound. The most extreme form is to raise a case.

But though Manaka succeeded in exposing Joel to public humiliation, her success was brief. Little was achieved with regard to property, on which the dispute was based. Their relationship continued to deteriorate. When interviewed in 1984, Manaka stated that nothing had altered. In the interim she had had to report to her husband's relatives yet again and to consult her maternal uncle Mokgothuotsile (as her father was dead). As a result another dispute took place in Kgosing kgotla in 1984 (MO 247/84).[3] On this occasion Manaka was accompanied by her brother, Rapelang, her paternal uncle, Setlhabi, her maternal uncle, and her mother's older brother, Shankomorwaeng. The subwardhead of Mokgalo was also present. This indicated strong familial support for her case.

The dispute covered the same issues and followed the same form as in 1982. The outcome was the same. The parties were ordered to go and live in peace and Joel was told to restore the property that he had given to the other woman, Bogadinyana. On this occasion, the cattle forming part of the dispute were placed in the kraal at Kgosing. After it was over they were returned to their original kraal. This accomplished nothing, according to Manaka, as Joel promptly removed them again. Their relationship was beyond repair, and by 1989 Manaka stated that they were divorced.

Access to Resources: Division of Property

A somewhat different account is presented by Mr. Bakwena, the headman of Mokgalo ward. He commented that after 1984 Manaka and Joel continued to fight and "the matter was referred from Kgosing back to Mokgalo. This was in 1985." They tried to settle the matter in the kgotla throughout 1985–86, "but the case could not be settled because Manaka's relatives would not respond to the call to talk to Joel's relatives. The situation was left as it was. Joel went to live separately, leaving the house property and children with Manaka, and the situation remains like that."

Manaka told another story. She claimed that after 1984 they were finally divorced. A division of property was made at Kgosing. By that time she and Joel had built up a herd of sixty-nine cattle and thirty-six goats. However, when it came to bringing the livestock to Kgosing, Joel "ate" them (caused them to disappear) so that there were only ten head left, which the kgotla awarded to her. This underlines the vulnerable position of women where access to and control over cattle is systematically regulated by men. As Joel had no grounds for divorce she was also allowed to retain the premises in Mokgalo ward. When interrogated by the kgotla, he wanted to leave her with nothing "because he had the right to do so," but the kgotla insisted that their property must be shared.

Although Manaka did not get what she felt she was due, the fact she had raised prior cases with some family support may have effected the outcome and bolstered her award. Nothing was said about the huts or the children. "They [kgotla men] just left things as they were." At this point Manaka intended to develop the premises at Mokgalo, but "Joel chased me away." His intimidation continued. He came and threw all her household utensils into the yard. When she found the kgotla would do nothing she turned elsewhere and applied to the Land Board in 1985–86 for a site to build her own home. She had to do this because the kgosi "doesn't even care, he was not interested in me retaining my home." As for the cattle, these have long since disappeared. After the ten were placed in her custody at Kgosing, "Joel came and stole them from the cattlepost." She reported this, and they were returned, but Joel stole them again and sold them all. This time the people at Kgosing did not act.

Access to Law: The Problems of Enforcement

Manaka was disheartened by her encounter with kgotla officials. When she went to complain to Victor Kgosidintsi (fig. 5), the former headman of her husband's kgotla, he was "no use because he is related to Joel. He is Joel's paternal uncle." He did nothing. As for the others she felt that "the judicial officers at Kgosing are not honest." What she meant was when she spoke to them "face to face, they would do nothing." She gave up seeing Mr. Sebele, the senior chief's representative at that time, and Mr. Kgosiensho, the deputy chief. Indeed, Mr. Sebele made it clear that the chief's kgotla could do no more. He explained that an impasse had been reached. If her husband would not return there was nothing he could do; he could not forcibly bring him back.

When asked if kgotla officials acted this way because she was a woman, Manaka disagreed. In her opinion they acted as they did out of respect for her husband's birthright, because "he is almost their equal and they recognize his high rank and respect the fact that he is an educated man." In 1989, Manaka was extremely bitter about her experiences. She resented the loss of all she had worked for, and that in middle age she had to start all over again. Her children, some of whom are working, provide what they can, but as they have just started to be employed, "they do not give much." She still has children in primary school, who require support. Like many women she does what she can through the informal sector, and "one way I can support myself is to make dresses and knit woolen hats for sale."

In addition, she has problems due to accumulated debts on a bottle store she established with an eight-thousand-pula loan from the National Development Bank. She maintains these debts arose because Joel appropriated all the stock in 1985 with the result that the business had to close. It reopened in 1987 but "is not doing well. It just sits there doing nothing. The stock is going very slowly." She considers Joel should share responsibility for repayment of the loan since he took away her earmarked cattle "leaving me with nothing." In this situation she is powerless, and her attempts to diversify her efforts beyond lands and cattle activities have come to nothing. This galls her because when they began living together Joel had no cattle. It was she who built up their herd by investing in livestock from the produce she acquired from her plowfields. It was this livestock that backed the application for a license to open the bottle store and provided security for the loan. In the kgotla her claims for more than ten head of cattle on these grounds were ignored, although she repeatedly raised the issue.[4]

THE MARITAL CYCLE OF DISPUTE

The dispute arising out of Joel and Manaka's relationship not only depicts how marital discord is handled, but also represents a stage attached to the processing of all such disputes. At this stage, whatever the reality, the parties' relationship is treated as an ongoing concern. Unlike the parties to the disputes in chapter 4, who all (except one) publicly acknowledged that their relationships had ended, Joel and Manaka never publicly acknowledged this and the fiction of an ongoing relationship was endorsed by the kgotla.

Having passed through this stage, a marriage may eventually be publicly dissolved by divorce or division of property. However, given the consequences attached to such dissolution (particularly with regard to property), individuals and their families seek divorce only as a last resort. There are advantages for both spouses in maintaining a marriage when their personal relationship is in fact over. So, in Joel and Manaka's case, while the marriage subsisted, Joel maintained control over the family property and was not required to cede any of it to Manaka, as he would have had to do on divorce. From Manaka's perspective, despite these circumstances, she was better off as a wife because, despite Joel's misappropriations, she had access to a greater range of resources than she would have had on divorce (even if such access was difficult to enforce).

Parties must assess their actual and their potential circumstances. For Joel, the equation would demand setting de facto control over family assets against potential encroachment through any property award that might be made to Manaka on divorce. For Manaka, it would involve assessing current disadvantages with respect to property (which might be circumvented if male support could be recruited, for example, at the cattlepost), as measured against the unpredictability of a property award on divorce, which would certainly reflect only a fraction of the family assets.

Ultimately Joel and Manaka's marriage was publicly dissolved. However, not all marriages that become disputes in the courts end in this way. Eva and Patrick Makoka raised two marital disputes at Kgosing in 1982 and 1983, but they were able to reconcile their differences. In 1989 they were still living together, with Eva commenting that "he is now a husband to me, just like when we got married."

THE MAKOKAS

Like many families in Botswana, the Makokas have close links with relatives in South Africa. Eva's family come from Johannesburg, although Eva's mother was born in Botswana. Eva herself was born in Pretoria in 1933 but came to live with her grandmother in Botswana in 1939. She met Patrick while they were at school in Mochudi from 1943–49. In 1949 she went back to live with her mother in Johannesburg and continued her education up to Form 2 in secondary school there. She met Patrick several years later when he came to work for the Native Council in Johannesburg. According to Eva, "In 1959 we spoke of marriage. My father had died in 1953 but Patrick's family spoke with my mother and with my father's relatives from Molepolole who came to Johannesburg to discuss the marriage. We married in 1960 and bogadi was paid."

Patrick's family is from South Africa and he has important political connections. He was born in 1936. His father was a headman in Rustenburg, but his family moved to Molepolole in 1952 when "they had a misunderstanding with the government." They were living then on a mission farm in the Transvaal. Compelled to move because of the enforcement of the Group Areas Act, they refused to resettle on the land allocated to them because the land was too poor for farming. As the Makokas are related to Bakwena, representing a branch who split off from the group during the Matebele wars, they asked Kgari Sechele II for permission to settle among Bakwena in Molepolole. This was granted, and Patrick Makoka's brother is now head of Phalane, a subward of Kgosing.

Eva and Patrick had three children, all of whom died. While in South Africa, Eva worked as a machinist in a factory and Patrick worked in a shop repairing refrigerators. He then moved into printing. In 1976, after Patrick's father died, they returned to Botswana and set up home in Molepolole. Here Eva worked for the Roman Catholic Mission, as a housekeeper, while Patrick worked as a printer in Francistown from 1978 to 1982.

That was when the problems started. Eva recalled, "We were happily married from 1960 to 1982," but when Patrick came back to Molepolole in 1982 he "started behaving differently." She attributed this to his beginning an affair with his uncle's wife, who was living next door to them in the village. The family put pressure on the woman to end the affair, but it continued, and Eva explained, "We started fighting. I went to the kgotla [Kgosing] to report the matter to the kgosi." It was here, on 17 May 1982, that Mr. Masimega and I first met Eva in a dispute. Eva was forty-nine then and Patrick was fifty-two. For an abridged account of the case refer to appendix E.

Hearings

As is common in such disputes, Eva did not directly address the issue of her husband's infidelity. Her statement began by alleging ill treatment by her husband, through his failure to support her, his disrespect for property, and his habit of locking her out of the family home. The arguments marshaled by husband and wife follow the same form established in the Kgosidintsi dispute.

Once again, the kgotla's response, channeled through Mr. Kgosiensho, the deputy chief, was to emphasize their need to restore peace and harmony and to admonish them to behave in the appropriate manner. Yet again the issue of reporting played a central role.

In his ruling Mr. Kgosiensho proclaimed:

> The defendant [the husband] is strictly ordered to go and stay with his wife and treat her kindly and do all things a good a man is expected to do for his wife. There must be no practice of locking her outside or leaving her to stay alone. In conclusion the order still stands. If ever the defendant finds something unusual in his wife's practice, he must report to his wife's parents in the first place. His wife also, in noticing his bad behavior, should report immediately to her husband's parents. That is the traditional and customary way of working together as married

people so that when misunderstanding arises between you in future there can be proof to confirm who is in the wrong.

However, as with Manaka, things did not improve, and another case was raised in 1983 (MO 511/83 heard 10 June 1983). This time the ill treatment referred to physical violence. She accused Patrick of assaulting her with a sharp stick and chasing her away from the family compound. On his part, Patrick raised the issue of divorce, stating his wish to divorce Eva "because she does not have children."

The kgotla was unsympathetic to the claim for divorce. Mr. Kgosiensho held, "This is against Tswana law and custom. No one can make a woman bear a child [i.e., she should not be penalized on this ground]. Another thing the court finds is that the two people are not living peacefully. If the two of them cannot make an effort to come to a peaceful settlement no one else can. The mistakes they have made with one another need to be straightened out by themselves. You, Patrick, are given an order that you should go and live with your wife in peace."

When Eva was interviewed in 1984, she expressed surprise that Patrick had sought to divorce her for childlessness, as he had never raised this issue in the kgotla before. She could not "understand why he brought it up in the kgotla case." Their relationship remained fraught.

Access to Law: The Woman's Voice Discounted

According to Eva,

After the case [in 1982 and 1983) we did not stay in peace together. There were problems and I went to stay with friends because of violence. Then I went to see the D.C. Mr. Roland in October 1983. I did this because I went back to the kgotla many times but the people would not listen. Mr. Kgosiensho just told me to go home and live with my husband. Mr. Roland tried to get us together. He told my husband that if he didn't want me he must divorce me instead of hitting me every day.

My husband decided we must go back to the kgotla. I decided then to invite [Kgatla] Kgosi Linchwe [she is a Mokgatla] for the case. I asked him because I felt that the people at Kgosing were favoring my husband. They always put me "off side." They did not want to listen to me and when I went to show them my bruises and beaten face they simply told me to go home. Kgosi Linchwe said they must hear the case or send it to him. When they read his letter they sent the police to go and fetch my husband. They read the letter to him. This was on 22nd October 1983. They said I must give him one more chance to see if we could live nicely. We went home together with two men from the kgotla who asked him to open the door of the house and we went in.

When asked about her current situation in 1984 she said, "From the day we went home together we stayed together nicely and he has never said anything to date [i.e., he does not beat her]. When we were at home I found he had sold most of my clothes but I said nothing as I felt that as long as we could stay together nicely I would not complain."

Unlike Manaka, Eva did not regard her treatment at Kgosing as motivated by her husband's political connections. In her opinion, the officials at Kgosing "are just not interested in such cases." She commented on other women she knew who had complained: "they are just told to go and stay at home." In her view the kgotla failed to affect Patrick. "It was he who changed his behavior."

When asked why his behavior had altered, she claimed to have no idea. However, she did comment that since becoming involved in a Y.W.C.A. horticulture scheme in Molepolole at the start of 1989 he had become a different person and was "not just sitting around." Before that, from their first dispute in 1982 until 1989, he was unemployed and "used to drink." Eva, like Manaka, set up a small dressmaking business in 1984, using family contacts in Johannesburg to provide her with secondhand clothes. By 1989 she was concerned that "business is poor. I do not have enough money to buy stock and people do not pay very well. They take clothes on credit and do not pay." Like Manaka, she has outstanding debts which need to be cleared.[5]

A CHANGE IN VENUE: BORAKALALO WARD

The strategies and arguments deployed in marital disputes at Kgosing also occur at the local kgotla and ward levels. This is affirmed by a marital dispute from Borakalalo ward which also underlines the important role that a wife's male relative can play in such a dispute.

Borakalalo Valley, which has hosted various factions among Bakwena from the reign of Sebele I (1892–1911) onward, is now the location of one of the major wards in Molepolole today. It is not regarded as one of the traditional wards, as it is said to have evolved historically out of a concentration of disparate groups of individuals who did not belong elsewhere in the village or who had abandoned their natal wards for various reasons. Otswataung from Mosotho kgotla, who deserted his wife Shadiko, is just such an individual, since he gave up membership of Basimane ward in favor of Borakalalo. Certain villagers have commented that it houses the "riffraff" element in Molepolole. Many Bakgalagadi, often regarded by Batswana as having inferior status, live there.

It is a place where all sorts of people congregate and where most of the trading stores, many owned by Asians, are centered, though new sites are developing with the village's continuing expansion.

The Role of Kin in Local Networks

In a hearing that Mr. Masimega and I attended in 1982 the brother of a woman Mmathari brought a matter before the wardhead Abraham and other kgotla members. For an abridged account of the hearing refer to appendix F. As head of the family (now that their father was dead), the brother refers to Mmathari as "my daughter" until the very end of his address, when (reverting to his status as Mmathari's brother) he refers to her as his sister. This was one of the rare occasions when I saw a male member of kin initiate a dispute and speak on a woman's behalf in the kgotla. Mmathari's brother was not only fulfilling his role as kin, but also appearing as headman of their kgotla, which had tried unsuccessfully to deal with the couple's problems. Patlo was carried out in 1965 when Mmathari was seventeen. The couple had five children, three of whom died. Mmathari was thirty-three at the date of the hearing.

At the end the familiar ruling common to all disputes of this kind was given: "You must go and bring back all the household property and take your wife and children and go and live with them at home in peace. If you fail to do this, this kgotla will transfer the case to the chief's kgotla."

Features Common to Marital Disputes

The same concerns that are articulated in the chief's kgotla were raised here at ward level. What action was taken to report marital unrest to their families and how did they respond; why were the parties living apart and who was responsible for this; what role did the other woman play—was she a wife or a nyatsi; and what was the position regarding household property? The issues raised were typical of those that surface in such a dispute, but the audience's response was unusual. A young woman (twenty-three) voiced the opinion that the dispute had not been properly handled, because the man's nyatsi had not been called to the kgotla to account for the property and to be admonished for her role in disturbing marital relations. Women are often present at kgotla meetings, but they rarely participate directly like this unless specifically addressed. Even then those who speak are generally grandmothers, who by virtue of their status are more empowered to speak than younger women. This was the first and only time in my experience that a young woman made her views known publicly in this kind of forum.

It is clear from these disputes, with their emphasis on reporting and relatives' participation, that it is not only the spousal relationship that is under scrutiny, but more general family relations. The tensions within such relations, contrasted with the harmony accentuated in ideal affinal or marital bonds, may well be acted out in the spousal domain. Just such an example is provided by the Bakwenas, whose case is considered next. Here the disputes entered into between husband and wife were fueled by the wife's mother-in-law. In this case, Ninika, the wife, found herself making the same allegations as Manaka and Eva and engaging in the same type of marital skirmishing.

All these women had unsatisfactory experiences with the kgotla system, but Ninika suffered the greatest disadvantage because she is less educated than the others and has fewer skills and resources to rely on. While life is hard for them, it is even tougher for Ninika. She has much in common with Diane (whose life history was discussed in chapter 3), and like her, with limited resources, she has been forced to look to a series of male partners for support. Both women fall within the most vulnerable category of female-headed households that gives rise to concern in Botswana today.

THE BAKWENAS

The first time I met Ninika Bakwena was in Mokgalo ward in 1982. At that time kgotla members were dealing with an ongoing dispute between Ninika and her mother-in-law. On this occasion (16 April 1982), Ninika had come to the kgotla to complain that her mother-in-law, by locking her out, refused to give her access to the dwelling her husband, Moagisi, had built for her. The source of tension between them arose from the fact that Moagisi's mother did not regard Ninika as a suitable wife for her son and did all that she could to disrupt the marriage. Mr. Bakwena Kgosidintsi, the headman of Mokgalo ward, observed, "Moagisi fell in love with Ninika but his parents wanted him to marry another woman who was half deaf. He refused and went to live with Ninika at her parents' home. He eventually married her by special license at the D.C.'s office in 1975. Patlo was not done. His parents reluctantly accepted the marriage. They disapproved because when he became involved with her she already had a child by someone else." There was a formal marriage, but it was vulnerable because patlo, a crucial aspect of familial approval, was lacking. In fact, Moagisi's family's disapproval was well known. Without the family's support Ninika was at risk because her own family connections were less powerful than those of Moagisi (fig. 5), who is related to the headman of Mokgalo ward and to the royal Kgosidintsi family descended from Motswasele I. Moagisi not only has the benefit of those connections, but his status is enhanced by local kgotla members' perceptions that his family is an able one because its members have acquired stable government employment. Moagisi's two sisters are teachers, and he himself, unlike many in his generation, has been employed in Molepolole as a messenger for the Veterinary Department since 1972.

In contrast, Ninika comes from a more humble family in Thato ward. They are not in the same class as those royal ward members with whom Radipati from Mosotho kgotla allied himself through marriage. Ninika's position is weakened by the fact that her father divorced her mother and distanced himself from his daughters when they left school and began having children. In contrast with Moagisi's sisters, Ninika and her sister, Mmamonyanaka, only have a Standard 2 primary school education. Neither is in regular employment, but both work only intermittently, picking up odd domestic or agricultural laboring jobs from local people or institutions. Ninika and her sister have grown up on the fringes of the peasantariat. It is a world that is far removed from that of the educated civil servant or member of the salariat.

Both women had children young. Ninika's sister has three children with three different fathers, only one of whom provides any support. Within their family, both women had close links with their mother until her death in 1988, but their male relatives take no interest in them or their children and do not provide any form of support. According to a headman of Thato ward they have no cattle and "Ninika and her mother lived under very poor conditions." When Ninika and Moagisi got together she already had a child by a man she met in Gaborone while working as a domestic. She came back to Molepolole and had children with Moagisi. They had Moltenyane (a girl, fourteen), Samuel (twelve), Malebogo (a girl, eleven), and Barongwa (a girl, nine). Moagisi disputes paternity of the youngest, who he claims is the child of Ninika's lover from Borakalalo, conceived during the period of their incessant quarreling, when Ninika was moving back and forth from Mokgalo to her mother's home in Thato ward (or as Moagisi alleged, to her lover's place in Borakalalo).

When Ninika and Moagisi first experienced problems, the families attempted to mediate. However, as these attempts proved unsuccessful, the matter was raised several times over a two-year period in the kgotla. It was during this time that Mr. Masimega and I came upon them in Mokgalo ward, when Ninika was complaining about her mother-in-law locking her out and lack of support for herself and the children. Though the kgotla members appeared to support Ninika in the face of implacable opposition from Moagisi's mother, no progress was made over access or support.

Access to Law: Strategies for Survival

The matter was eventually raised at Kgosing in 1984. Here Ninika raised not only the issue of neglect, but also that of another woman. She did this by referring to Moagisi's appropriation of household property for use by his lover. This was one of the few times when a hearing was adjourned to bring the other woman, Kgomotso Masomo, into the process. During the hearing, which followed the typical pattern for marital cases of this kind, Kgomotso admitted that she had had a child with Moagisi but maintained that this had happened before he married Ninika and before her own marriage. Now widowed, she explained that his visits to her home were to see his child and not because of an affair between them.

Mr. Kgosiensho found in Ninika's favor that "Ninika is telling the truth. Moagisi her husband does not really take care of her. This kgotla has shown Moagisi that he is neglecting his wife and children." After publicly upbraiding him he concluded as usual that "you [Moagisi] are ordered to go and stay with your wife peaceably at your dwelling home."

This hearing occurred during a period when Ninika was shunted between the magistrate's court and Kgosing in her attempts to take the matter beyond the jurisdiction of Mokgalo ward. In her own words

> I went to Kgosing and was referred back from there to the D.C., where the case [under the Deserted Wives and Children's Protection Act 1963][6] has not yet been called. I went to Kgosing twice this year. Kgosi Sebele [senior chief's representative] told me to go back to the D.C. He phoned the D.C. and told me to go there. Nothing happened. I told the kgotla people [Mokgalo] and they fixed a date for the hearing. My husband was called and instructed [at Kgosing] that he should stay with me and the children and that he must support us. That was the order my husband was given but he did nothing. The matter was then dealt with once more in Mokgalo because Mr. Kgosiensho referred it back to the ward. However none of my relatives were informed.

She had reached an impasse with the kgotla system, and "Mr. Sebele said it was better to claim support through the magistrate's court. He explained that it would be easier than to keep on discussing the matter in the kgotla when the kgotla men order Moagisi to support and he does not."

After the 1984 Kgosing hearing Ninika received some support. "He bought sorghum flour worth 6 pula and flour for bread worth 3 pula 75 thebe. He also gave me a small tin of coffee worth 75 thebe and some sugar worth 1 pula 33 thebe and small tin of powdered milk worth 2 pula 20 thebe."

This was all that Ninika received during the two years from 1982 to 1984. Throughout this period she was still waiting for the magistrate to call her case. Support was hard to come by. The self-help project she was involved in was a failure. "We reaped very little because the vegetables burned [due to the severe drought]. The soil was poor and they got scorched by the sun. We stopped cultivating after that." Ninika was reduced to begging in order to survive. "I live by begging food from other relatives, mostly my husband's sister, who gave me 4 pula a few days ago to buy food. Sometimes I go to the clinic and they give me some mealy meal for me and the children." She looked for work, and "last year [1983] I was working for one Neo at Borakalalo making fat cakes for sale. I was able to buy food then." But this was temporary. "The other women and I left because our wages were low and our employer would not increase them." She has become dependent on others for her existence. In 1984 she commented, "It is a problem living from day to day. I am not working now. I depend on going to my mother for food or to other relatives or friends."

A Husband's Perspective

Moagisi, who was interviewed during his lunch hour in 1984, presented a very different account of their marital history. He maintained the problems began when Ninika took the children and left him to stay at her mother's home. "We had not quarreled and I had not beaten her. I think it was her own idea [to move] because she was not interested in living with me." He stated that when asked about his lack of support by Mr. Kgosiensho he stressed that he would only provide food if his wife and children were living at home in Mokgalo. He was told that "I must see to it that my wife and children come back home and that I support them." In his view Ninika caused all the problems because she would not remain in Mokgalo but returned to her parents home every few days. He could do little about this, as "my wife never tells me anything. She never responds to my questions." No mention was made of his mother's role in all of this. The constant vacillation was, he implied, to enable her to visit her lover. She would leave the children with her mother and then disappear. To his mind she was ignoring the kgotla pronouncement that they should live together: "She is not actually doing that. At sundown she goes away to sleep at her home." He vehemently denied allegations of nonsupport, explaining that as Ninika was absent so often, he bought the food which his mother cooked for the children.

He firmly denied allegations about his lover on the basis that "this is invented my wife. When a woman's panicking or in sorrow she will say anything that will make people believe that her husband is a bad man." He knew about the case Ninika had lodged with the magistrate's court and commented that he had also gone to the court. "After I caught her sleeping with another man I went up to District Administration and asked the clerk of [the magistrate's] court what he would do." He was informed that Ninika had registered a complaint against him and "that I had to go home and support her and the children." In interviews with Ninika and Moagisi in 1989 it transpired that after the hearing in 1984 the case in the magistrate's court was finally heard. Moagisi was ordered to pay support. This was seventy pula a month, according to Ninika, and forty pula per child, amounting to 160 pula, according to Moagisi. He supported them for two months and then filed for divorce in the High Court. Ninika did not know this at the time. He asked her to sign a form, which she did, unaware that this was connected with divorce proceedings. She did not know that the paper required a response from her.

Formal Divorce: Knowledge and Access to the Process

Shortly after, Moagisi presented her with a piece of paper from the High Court saying that they were now divorced. He stated that he had been granted a divorce and that he had been given custody of the children. Ninika was amazed and went to the D.C., who explained that her case was over. The children's custody had been awarded to Moagisi. She opposed this, but on a visit to Moagisi's mother they were detained by his family and she has not seen them since.

Moagisi divorced his wife for desertion and adultery with a another man in Borakalalo with whom he alleged she had two children. He claimed that she was already living with this man in 1984 when she claimed support. Once again in 1989, Moagisi stressed, "I made arrange-ments for her to stay in Mokgalo. She did not stay, but went back on her own to the man in Borakalalo with the children." That Ninika did have a lover seems to have been common knowledge in the community, but whether this was due to Moagisi's neglect was unclear. The allegations of Moagisi's affair with Kgomotso in the 1984 hearing also proved to be valid. In 1989, he openly admitted to living with her in the house she had built below Borakalalo Primary School. Kgomotso is regarded as a much more suitable partner for Moagisi because she is a teacher and is related to him. She is from Moabello kgotla, which is headed by Baruti's son (fig. 5), who is a junior relative of Bakwena Kgosidintsi's and of Moagisi's father.

For the divorce Moagisi hired a lawyer from Gaborone. Ninika had no legal representation. Moagisi observed that Ninika did not defend the divorce. "She did not even appear. The judgment was in my favor." The fact that she knew nothing of what was happening did not concern him. He interpreted her lack of response as admission of facts pleaded. Such a response is common and is depicted in the Busang dispute, which will be presented in chapter 7. Although the High Court awarded Moa-gisi custody of all the children, he has allowed Ninika to look after their youngest daughter "because she is still small." Nothing was said about property, and the matter has not come up at Kgosing.

Access to Resources: A Woman Without

Moagisi confirmed that Ninika did not get property from him and that he did not have any cattle or livestock. He even observed, "We have never had a field to plow." Ninika never considered division of property, as "nobody told me that there was any property to be divided." How-ever, she recalled "a bedstead, a table, [and] four chairs" at home, which had remained with Moagisi. She was less concerned about these items than the loss of her clothes. In 1984, she claimed that Moagisi changed the locks on their door so that she had to go and stay with her mother in Thato ward. When she went to collect her clothes, which were in a tin trunk, she was told that Moagisi had taken them to the house of the headman, Bakwena. She went to collect them, but the trunk was no-where to be found.

From 1984 onward, Ninika tried to gain support through a series of temporary jobs. She worked as a laborer in the drought relief scheme until that ended, and then took on a temporary job as a cleaner for

District Administration. After that she went from place to place wherever short-term labor was needed. She even worked for Mrs. Masimega at harvest time in 1986 and was paid three bags of corn. Her liaison with the man from Borakalalo ended, and since 1987 she and his offspring have been living with her current partner, Ketshabakgang, with whom she also has two children, at the Phatlheng lands. They find it hard to survive, living off subsistence agriculture and the occasional odd job.

Ninika interpreted the kgotla's disinterest in her case and that of her own relatives (who stopped attending hearings early in the process), as due to the fact that "my marriage with Moagisi was not founded properly." By this she meant that patlo had not taken place. She believed that "Moagisi had no intention of living with me permanently as his wife. The Kgosing people wouldn't do anything because he had no intention of living with me." In her view, "Moagisi planned to divorce me for a long time. He wanted to get rid of me long ago."

When Ninika obtained a hearing, she was supported, in theory, by kgotla members at all levels, who ordered Moagisi and his mother to give her access to their home and provide support. All this was couched in terms of the couple living together "in peace and harmony." From at least 1982 onward, however, the parties were in reality living separate lives. It was hard for Ninika to gain access to hearings, and when she did so little was achieved. She was clearly disadvantaged, not only by her family background and inability to mobilize kin in her support, but also on account of her lack of knowledge. Unlike women such as Mmashaoudi and Mathilda, who are considered in the next chapter, she lacked knowledge about the system she faced, and this acted to her detriment, particularly where divorce proceedings were concerned. This is not uncommon. Others, such as Gofetamang Busang, whose case is discussed in chapter 7, have also had this experience.

In marital negotiations, Manaka Kgosidintsi and Ninika Bakwena depict what happens in the early stages of dissociation from a man. Eventually, a stage is reached at which there is some form of public recognition that the relationship is over. This may be through divorce, or a division of property, as in Manaka's case. A division of assets provides grounds for public assent to the parties going their own ways, a recognition of something that has, in fact, been a reality for years.

It is clear that women as wives operate within a gendered environment where they find themselves in unequal power relations with their husbands. In most cases, men's enhanced ability to draw on all forms of resources essential for a family base places them in a stronger position than women to accumulate what is necessary to form a household, and thus to elevate their power and status in the social world in which they live. Women who are married not only face the constraints of motherhood and limited economic opportunity (in some cases due to their husband's dissipation of assets) but also have to contend with their role as wives. Such a role situates women in a different position from that of their husbands in the family hierarchy, due to the different social conceptions that inform the roles of husband and wife. In this context, it is not just control over resources that is important, but also the ideological component that attaches to spousal roles, which generally operates to the detriment of women in their dealings with men.

When tensions arise between spouses which devolve into disputes, such disputes represent women's attempts to overcome their unequal position with respect to power in relation to men. In cases involving family property used by their husbands for other purposes women seek to set aside the constraints placed on them in order to preserve that family property and thus retain access to support for themselves and their children. Yet again, the difficulties that women encounter in handling this situation are reinforced by their experiences of courts and the legal system, both of which continue to uphold the social basis upon which women's partnerships with men are constructed and interpreted, in this case (unlike those of the previous chapter) in the context of marriage.

SIX

Untying the Knot: Public Dissolution and Division of Property

It is not only during the course of a marriage that women as wives may encounter problems with their husbands over provision for support or management of property. Such problems may also arise on divorce or termination of a marriage, especially where the parties have a history of quarreling over these issues. Among Bakwena, estrangement from a marriage takes many years. As the narratives and cases in the previous chapter show, it takes time for personal dissatisfaction to enter into the public domain and to produce public recognition of breakdown through divorce and division of property. In some cases parties never pursue a formal closure but just part informally and go their own ways. This was the case with Makokwe's granddaughters, the eldest daughters of his eldest son, Motlotlegi, whose life histories were traced in chapter 3. When their families failed to reconcile their marital difficulties, they left their marriages and moved on to other long-standing liaisons.

But in this and the subsequent chapter the focus is on formal closure and on those unions in which there is public recognition of a marriage's dissolution. Such recognition not only marks the social significance of such acts, but also invokes legal regulation concerning status and division of property. The narratives and cases of those unions selected for discussion involve a range of parties, both rich and poor, whose assets vary from a few possessions, mostly household goods acquired over a lifetime, to more substantial property including cattle, bank savings, and businesses. Not only do these accounts cut across the social spectrum (so that it is not only the experiences of a propertied elite that are represented), but they also arise from a number of locations which extend beyond formal legal forums such as the chief's kgotla and High Court to include local wards.

Local wards play an integral part in the process of uncoupling, which, as the last chapter demonstrated, takes place over many years. Because of this and perceptions of acting on behalf of the kgosi, wards may elect to dissolve a marriage and to divide whatever property is avail-

able between the parties, although they in fact lack the formal legal powers to do so. This disjunction displays a tension between the formal legal
system and what other scholars refer to as living (Ehrlich 1936) or folk
(Woodman 1988) law. It derives from the period of colonial overrule,
when a distinction was drawn between legal and administrative duties,
with the former restricted to only those wards and dikgotla, such as
Kgosing, that were authorized to handle law through the process of publication in a government document referred to as a gazette. But when it
comes to the handling of marital disputes there is a marked degree of
continuity in what takes place in local wards and at Kgosing. In other
words, what occurs in the chief's kgotla as a customary court in this
context, as well as other local forums, follows the same pattern which is
common to the customary system as a whole.

So although these selected narratives and cases cover the social spectrum, they also underline a continuity derived from common forms of
argumentation that revolve around the gendered roles of husband and
wife. The way in which parties construct and manipulate these roles in
relation to one another determines the terms under which dissolution
will take place, including rights to property. In this case, what is at stake
in the public dissolution of a relationship and distribution of property
is displacing the burden of fault onto the other spouse. In this process,
women's and men's strategies differ with respect to the ways in which
they seek to achieve this end in the context of their spousal roles. The
accounts that follow and the discussions surrounding them show the
way in which law is perceived by the divorcing parties and the communities to which they belong. These perceptions shape parties' strategies,
actions, and responses to institutional encounters and thus integrate
law, in all its dimensions (both national and local), into people's lives.
Such integration is at odds with any centralist notion of law, especially
as it pertains to the juristic, weak, or traditional model of legal pluralism.

CONDUCT: THE GENDERED ROLES OF HUSBAND AND WIFE

In this process, the spouses' dissociation from each other's conduct is as
important as it is in the marital disputes discussed in chapter 5. Each
party must appear as the one aggrieved, the one who has fulfilled his or
her marital role, while simultaneously undermining the other spouse's
conduct. Such characterization involves a manipulation of the traits associated with a good husband or wife. In this way, both parties seek to
escape blame for marital breakdown and to secure their share of prop-

erty. But the claims that are open to them differ; for as the previous chapters have shown, husbands and wives are differentially situated in terms of the structure of familial relations and access to resources.

It is particularly hard for a wife to displace the burden of fault. She is often forced to take action—leaving home, for example—that immediately exposes her to allegations of misconduct. This is because a wife may not leave home without her husband's permission or without cause. So where she adopts certain actions, such as leaving home, she must first overcome the appearance of negative conduct before she can begin to assert any kind of claim to marital property. This is difficult to accomplish given the ideological constraints under which women operate and the authority of men, which predominates not only in practical terms, but also in respect of prevailing attitudes (Alverson 1978).

Both spouses contribute to household development and both have their own spheres of authority, but women, nonetheless, find their authority subordinated to that of men for the reasons put forward by Kinsman (1983). This is due not only to material factors but also to the way in which women are socialized into existing power structures. Many women today find themselves temporarily or permanently in charge of households, yet they operate in a world where access to resources is still largely mediated through men.

A wife must defer to her husband's authority as head of the household. That she may find ways to circumvent his authority is not the issue; the fact is that in structural terms her power to act is not the same as that of her husband. This is underlined by the kinds of links existing between households and local politicians embedded in the kgotla system. Only a man who can establish his seniority within a community can become headman or wardhead. Women are essentially excluded from these positions, and only in rare cases involving elites do they serve as regents. The kgotla system is built on a system of male authority; while women today—unlike their forebears—may present their own disputes in the kgotla, they are still operating within a predominantly male ethos and domain. For this reason, the support of male relatives is often crucial to their standing.

The disputes in this chapter depict how gender shapes expectations of marital conduct, which vary for men and women, and how it frames men's and women's respective claims to property. Even where a woman overcomes the problem of apparent negative conduct and is accepted as a good wife, her claim to property is still limited because of the structure of family ownership. This favors her husband because he is the one who is publicly accredited as head of the household and family and as their children's custodian. Among Batswana, the position of children and the issue of their inheritance is a major consideration when it comes to division of property, especially where there are substantial assets. Where there is property, this consideration often effectively restricts or subordinates women's claims to property as wives, unless their spouses have lost the support of those who would normally uphold their positions, as in Pepere's case, which will be discussed shortly. Thus, women, as wives, find themselves doubly disadvantaged as regards property claims compared with their husbands, not only in the social domain of the family but also in those cases where they appear before the kgotla in their ward.

Such appearances, in the form of disputes, mark key moments in individuals' lives and in their narratives. As well, they take on the character of cases and acquire all the legal implications that follow from their handling within particular institutional domains. Thus, cases—which underline episodes in individuals' lives—represent critical junctures for integrating social and legal worlds; particularly, cases involving distribution of property on marital breakdown test women's abilities to overcome the burden of fault.

THE BAIPOKAS' DISPUTE

The first dispute arose as a case in Borakalalo ward. It involved parties living at subsistence level with few assets. Nonetheless, the parties opted to publicly dissolve their relationship and to divide the existing property between them. As in other cases, the relationship between Mmanku-dinyane and her husband, Barontsheng, was the subject of numerous kgotla hearings in Borakalalo ward. Abraham, the wardhead, recalled Barontsheng's complaints that his wife had abandoned their home and was running around with other men, while Mmankudinyane complained that he beat her. Barontsheng finally spoke out in the kgotla on the grounds that "now that she has deserted me she must repay the expense for the upkeep of the home during the lifetime of our marriage." After negative responses to questions about reconciliation, based on a history of failed attempts to reunite the couple, Abraham stated, "The way he puts his case makes it a divorce case and the problem must be solved by the kgotla."

Divorce Hearing in the Kgotla

The divorce hearing took place on 24 March 1982 and was attended by Mr. Masimega and myself. The hearing began where the previous discussions ended. Abraham recalled that Mmankudinyane had been ordered to go home and asked her, "Why do you not return to your dwelling house after you have been ordered to do so by this kgotla?" To justify her conduct she responded, "It is because I am afraid of my husband. He is always beating me and has threatened to chop me with an ax. I have been twice in hospital seriously hurt after he assaulted me. I am afraid that he will eventually kill me. I do not want to be married to him any more. I want to separate from him." Such allegations of domestic violence are often made in these hearings, as in Manaka's and Eva's disputes in the previous chapter.

Having established Mmankudinyane's position, Abraham asked Barontsheng, "What do you have to say to what your wife has stated? What do you say to the fact that your wife says that she is not prepared to live with you because of your violence.?" The ball was back in his court, and he tried to circumvent the issue of violence by focusing on the right to divorce after being in dispute for seven years. He replied, "We have been separated since 1975, and this matter was dealt with some time back at Kgosing. It was arranged that this matter would be referred to this ward. If my wife is not prepared to return home, I have nothing to say; I give up."

Having made his position clear, he was then asked what he wanted, and this was where the property issue was raised. He stated, "I cannot say that my wife must return to me against her will, but she must return the property that I acquired for her during the period that we were living in peace together." This initiated a discussion of marriage and the conventions that surround it as Abraham asked Mmankudinyane's father, "Do you know what action is taken against the woman's parents according to Tswana law and custom if a wife divorces?" This was in fact a rhetorical question aimed at establishing the conventions that come into play. When the father, by replying in the negative, did not acknowledge this, Abraham raised the issue directly: "Do you know that in a situation like this, the wife's parents are required to return the property that was acquired from the man who is being divorced?" Despite the fact that it is the man who raised the issue of divorce, it was attributed to the woman, who was seen to be at fault because of her refusal to obey the ward's request to return to her husband. This was so even though her allegations of violence provided her in theory with good reason for not doing so.

Mmankudinyane's father eventually accepted divorce, and the question of property was discussed in greater detail. Barontsheng laid claim to two cooking pots and one empty water drum. He tried to claim small livestock, but when pressed about this admitted that they had died many years ago during the drought. For her part, Mmankudinyane maintained that there was more property involved: "My husband had bought a plow, two cooking pots, a sewing machine, and two drum water containers." These, she alleged, were removed by Barontsheng to his parents' home. When asked when this occurred, she replied, "In 1975. There is also a tin trunk and two buckets. I still have one of the pots and one drum water container and one sewing machine. That is all I have at present."

Barontsheng was questioned about this property but denied that he appropriated it as she claimed: "I did not take it from her by force as my wife maintains because I took these things with the permission of the subward because she was refusing to go and stay with me at our dwelling house." His explanation put another interpretation on his actions. It established Mmankudinyane as the one in the wrong. His version of events was endorsed by a kgotla man who confirmed that he was present when this was done.

Discussions then centered on their children and on what to do about the division of property "when the other property held by the man was not here." It was agreed to postpone the division of property until it was all brought to the kgotla. How it was to be divided was hotly debated. According to one kgotla man, "The household utensils are not to be shared between husband and wife only, but the children are to have a share. That is why those things must be brought here and divided in the presence of the kgotla people." Two other kgotla men supported him on the basis that "it is necessary that the property which the husband holds should be brought here and that in accordance with the law the husband will pick one item after another and distribute it evenly to his wife, the children, and to him." Here there is a concept of sharing, but the husband retains control over the allocations. Others, however, did not support this view and considered "that the person who is divorcing needs to be fined. This is because she is breaking the law of marriage."

Their views highlight the problems women encounter over conduct outlined earlier, that is, of being found at fault where a relationship fails.

But Abraham did accept that Mmankudinyane had grounds for parting and as third party used his position to stress this: "According to the law is it right that if this woman establishes that she is afraid of her husband it is right that we fine her for that reason?"[1] His intervention finds support from another man: "There cannot be a fine because there is a reason. The woman is afraid of her husband."

The kgotla decided on divorce, and proceedings were adjourned until all the property was assembled. This was done by 20 May 1982, when the division took place. Most of this property was of a modest nature, comprising domestic and other small items, but to the parties concerned, who had very little, it was significant. It represented the fruits of all their efforts in a long-standing union. Their position is representative of that large group of people who live at subsistence level on the fringes of the peasantariat. The items distributed were "one tin trunk, a two-hundred-liter water drum, one size 1 cooking pot, one size 2 cooking pot, one size 20 cooking pot [large], one basket, four basins, one kettle, one big basket, one small enamel bucket, one wooden brick mold, one stamping block for sorghum, one tub, one sewing machine, one lantern, two plates, one saucer, two teaspoons, and one big earthenware pot." The kgotla awarded Barontsheng the hut in Borakalalo. He also received the tin trunk, the sewing machine, the kettle, the lantern, one basin, the big cooking pot (which had come from his mother), the enamel bucket, the tub, the basket, and the wooden brick mold. In contrast, Mmankudinyane, who was returning to her parents at the lands at Mosinki (six kilometers from Molepolole), was given the stamping block, one small cooking pot, one small enamel bucket, three basins, one plate, the saucer, and the two teaspoons. She was also offered the big earthenware pot, but refused it because it had been given to Barontsheng by his mother.

Underlying Considerations: Gendered Familial Relations

In this case the children were not included in the distribution, except for the eldest adult daughter, who was given the water drum, a plate, and a bowl (not listed) because her parents had bought these for her. But their position is often considered when a division of property is made, as will be demonstrated in the Seitshiro and Busang disputes to be discussed in the next chapter. Bakwena, like other Tswana merafe, view parents as custodians of family property to be handed on to the next generation. This concern for the next generation colors the way in which a division of property is handled when a man and a woman divorce. This is so even though there may not be many assets.

The male line is privileged here. If their parents are married, children are affiliated with their father's kin group. In this context, as the man is head of the household, it is considered fitting to award him most of the property, because he is the one responsible for handing it on to the next generation. Thus, control should remain vested in him. Such a perspective undermines a woman's position, since she not only has to establish that she is not at fault as a wife, but has also to contend with a system which limits the scope of her claims to property. So it is clear why Barontsheng received the major share of assets, including the most significant, the hut and the sewing machine.[2]

THE MONOKGOTLHAS' HEARING: MAUNATLALA WARD

This approach to marital property is endorsed elsewhere in Molepolole. In the Monokgotlhas dispute in Maunatlala ward, the parties made claims similar to those of Mmankudinyane and Barontsheng, invoking the same terms of reference. Like them, Efitlhile (the man) and Keleisetse (the woman) had had problems for years. The headman claimed the husband's grievances included being "chased away from his wife's parents home," that she forbade him to visit when she was sick, and that she removed all their property from Masimo (plowfields) to Molepolole without his consent. For her part, Keleisetse maintained that her husband "was too troublesome in that he was forever quarreling with me and complaining about nothing; that he was not supporting the children; that he denied paternity of some of my children and that he would torment me by telling me that the twins are not his children but have two fathers." Finally, when she was ill he did not take care of her or seek medical attention.

As with Mmankudinyane, the kgotla tried to get Keleisetse to return to her husband. The headman recalled she was asked, "If we would punish your husband for not having supported you, for tormenting and always quarreling with you, would you agree to return to him and begin to live peacefully?" She refused to contemplate this, stating that it was of "no use" because she "knew of her husband's behavior for quite a long time. Even if he was punished he would never improve." She stressed that she "is not prepared to live with him any more" and that she "does not love him."

The kgotla did not consider this acceptable: "We told her that according to Tswana custom you are a person who is divorcing and so you require to refund the property the man has provided for you during your marriage." Unlike Mmankudinyane, the headman was of the view, "In this particular case the woman did not have reasonable grounds on the facts for according to Tswana custom, if her husband has been ill treating her in any way she should have reported the matter to her husband's parents." Once again the importance of reporting is crucial. The headman noted that Keleisetse "was not telling her parents-in-law, and even her parents knew little of her ill treatment. They had never met before to solve the problems she was experiencing."

The Wife's Account

Keleisetse contested this account, and in fact the headman commented at the start of our interview that the parties had come to the kgotla "after they had dealt with the matter in the family compound, where they did not reach any conclusion." Whatever the position regarding familial involvement, the union was dissolved and their property was divided. The headman noted that, like the previous couple, "the parties hadn't much property. They had a plow and one beast, a large empty water drum, one bath, and other household articles such as basins, pots, and other articles." What they had was essentially awarded to the man, including "the beast, the plow, the drum, and the bath." In contrast, the woman received only a few household articles which the headman conceded were "small things, not many, such as basins, dishes, and pots." That she was given anything was only due to the fact that "she had to do the cooking for the little children, who got some blankets and mats." Keleisetse expressed a real sense of grievance, stating that the distribution "was not fair."[3] She felt the kgotla had ignored her version of events in favor of her husband's. They had not properly taken his behavior into account. She was bitter about what had occurred, as in her view, he was the one who had abandoned the family. This started in 1980 when she was forced to remove her first son from school because of lack of money and had to send him "to go and look after cattle." Her husband entirely gave up supporting her "from 1981 onwards." Since the divorce she has been living with her family in Maunatlala ward.

The Husband's Account

Efitlhile told a different story.[4] In his view, "Our misunderstanding arose in 1982." On return to Molepolole from the cattlepost, "I found her changed altogether. She would not speak to me when I spoke to her. At night she went away to sleep." He implies here that she had a lover, as a good wife does not sleep away from her home without her husband's permission. He maintained that it was he who "reported the incident to her parents." He also claimed that when she was ill he had taken her to the doctor and that it was she who had told him that "I must never come back to her again." He presented himself as the model husband, reporting to her family when things went wrong and taking her for medical treatment when she required it. When she got sick, "we had to find a traditional doctor to find out what was wrong with her. She refused to submit to the traditional doctor's examination, saying that he would bewitch her and that I too was a wizard and she did not want my services. Then I gave up." Once again traditional medicine was alluded to in a marital dispute.

Efitlhile's account contravened that of his wife. He asserted that "when the parents called us together to try to make us settle in peace, she would not allow me to come." He alleged she was a bad wife because she rejected him and would not let him take the children to Masimo at plowing time. She also removed all the property from Masimo. When confronted, she admitted this but argued "that the property was hers and not mine." As to the division of property, he, like Keleisetse, "was not satisfied. I told the kgotla men that I wanted all my property." But they drew attention "to the fact that I was ill-treating her." He did not interpret his behavior this way. In his view his wife needed to be disciplined: "I often reported to her parents, but they wouldn't check her behavior towards me [i.e., they did not control her]."

Both parties interpreted events differently, but ultimately, it was Efitlhile who succeeded in the property stakes. In the process Keleisetse considered that the kgotla favored her husband over her by ignoring her account altogether. Mr. Masimega's interpretation of these events was that the ward had no interest in supporting Keleisetse. Because she had already had three children with different partners when she met Efitlhile, they did not take the marriage seriously, and, as in Ninika's case, they did not unduly concern themselves about her claims to support or property.

WARD VIEWS

These cases depict the reality of life. They contrast with dikgotla's observations on what parties, in the abstract, are entitled to when they break up. Such discussions were regularly pursued in dikgotla throughout the village in 1982. They not only displayed a diversity of opinion, but clearly accentuated the problems of attempting to define this process in terms of rule-based propositions.

People vehemently disagreed about a woman's rights to residence and property. In this discussion marriage (usually patlo) was often, but not necessarily, a determining factor. Many villagers were adamant that, where there was no patlo, the woman was perceived of as a nyatsi who would be sent back to her family. She had no claim to any property but might receive something for her services. As one headman at Kgosing put it, "Where a woman is married to a man without patlo but a marriage which the two of them agreed upon, the only remedy is that the woman is sent home." Another supported this view, claiming that "people who marry on their own without the knowledge of their parents on both sides and the kgotla people, are not married. She is seen only as a nyatsi." But another disagreed. When considering Mmashaoudi and Pepere's relationship (to be discussed shortly) he argued, "Even if patlo had not taken place, she has the right to remain and retain the dwelling house for the sake of the children recognized as children of the family kgotla." They all agreed the current situation was problematic, as "it is not always possible when a young man comes from somewhere with a woman whom he has picked up as his wife, to turn her away." However, many members took the view that in such a case the kgotla will "give the young man an order, either live with her and support her as your wife, or take her back to where you got her from."

The Relevance of Fault

Even in the case of patlo, views varied about the woman leaving the family home where it was located in the man's family kgotla. In this case a member of Ntloedibe ward opined, "All the house property and cattle which they jointly acquired would go to the woman and she would go back to her parents." But this was only if the man was at fault and divorcing the woman for no reason. One cynical kgotla member commented that this never happened because "the woman is always found to be at fault." Mr. Kgosiensho, the deputy chief in 1982, disagreed with this view. In his opinion, where the wife is not at fault and it is the man who is divorcing without cause, she may remain "because she has kept her marriage promise." Others at Kgosing disagreed, arguing that she must be returned to her family as, whatever the reality, "it is considered sensible, even if the man is at fault. If the man does not love her or wish to live with her she must be returned safely to live free rather than suffer the strain of isolation." However, she must, regardless of fault, be "provided with carriage by her husband. The household property is loaded and some people drive cattle to the wife's home." This is so because "on patlo ceremony when agreement is complete, there is a set of words coming from the wife's family which say, 'If this woman could in future be too troublesome, there would be no objection if she could be returned to the custody of the parents unhurt.'"

Property issues arise here. Many who took the view that the husband must provide her with transport, which is normally an ox termed lekaba (beast of burden) saw this animal as property given to the woman and her family, regardless of fault. Mr. Masimega confirmed that this position had been adopted by Kgosi Kgari Sechele II (1931–62) while he was working for him. More recently Kgosi Linchwe II has endorsed this approach, which will be presented in the Seitshiro dispute in the next chapter.

A woman's claim to more than one animal was also contentious. Many recognized that she was entitled to those cattle that she had acquired from her own labor from the proceeds of selling homemade beer or agricultural produce grown on her own land. But this did not feature in actual awards. Though accepted as her property (in theory) during the marriage, this was often ignored when it came to division on divorce. Even where blameless, a Maunatlala kgotla member explained, "if a woman divorces on reasonable grounds she gets a share of the division of property but a smaller share than the man." In assessing what this potential share might be, reference was made to Kgari Sechele's practice of awarding up to eight head of cattle. When introduced, it was regarded as an innovation necessitated by the sudden increase in men abandoning their wives for no reason. It represented the kgosi's attempt to control family life during a period of intensive labor migration when his authority was in danger of declining.[5] The figure of eight head of cattle, currently also awarded for pregnancy claims, is one that many kgotlas regard as setting a maximum. It only occurs where "a man has sufficient cattle." Many were of the view that this applied only where a man had a herd of at least fifty to one hundred head. Under fifty would only give her a potential claim to one. Conversely, where there were two hundred cattle or over she would still only be entitled to eight because "the eight head of cattle are subject to law. The law says eight and she will receive eight, as under the old law she received one beast and no more." Even this view is open to question. The Mogkalo headman forcefully argued that "it is only one beast that is paid out, and the household property, the things that the wife uses for domestic purposes, that goes with her." A Maunatlala ward member stressed that the cattle remain with the man and that "if a woman divorces on reasonable grounds the cattle will remain in the original place, the man's kgotla, and the children remain there. The woman will return to her parents." Though "the property will be divided fairly," this will be "in a different way than division where a woman divorces of her own accord [without reasonable grounds]."

The Position of Children

Many kgotla members agreed that on division of property "a woman gets a lesser share than a man." The general view is that a woman always gets less than a man—and where there are children, she gets an even smaller share. This is largely due to consideration for the children, who normally remain with the man. Where they are in existence, as is normally the case, the perspective alters to focus on the children rather than on either of the separating parents. A member of Tshosa ward, when asked about a woman's entitlement to property if she had grounds for divorce, said, "That is not a simple question. If you mean a woman who has children in the kgotla, when a division of property is undertaken, much consideration is given to the children who are bona fide residents of the kgotla." In other words it is children's interests which make for an unequal division. "The woman will go with limited property. It depends on how much property will remain in the kgotla for the children's heritage."

MMASHAOUDI AND PEPERE GABARANE

Such debates accentuate how hard it is to formulate a rule-based set of prescriptions to cover dissolution of a relationship and division of property among Bakwena.[6] This is underlined by the fact that many of these discussions centered on Mmashaoudi and Pepere's relationship, which was talked about throughout the village. Everybody knew of them and had their own views of this relationship, which they were eager to express. This was particularly informative, as general views were often reformulated when they were applied to Mmashaoudi and Pepere's actual relationship. Many who argued that a woman must return to her family suddenly altered their position when it came to Mmashaoudi. Here they were prepared to let her remain in Pepere's kgotla, even though they believed that patlo had not been done in that relationship. Indeed, the question of patlo was itself an issue of debate.

Official Versions

There is a complex history surrounding the hearings on their relationship. The official version begins with the headman of the Senyedima kgotla (subward of Kgosing), where they lived, observing that the first hearing occurred in 1973 and

> it began in this way: Pepere's wife Mmashaoudi complained that her husband was selling cattle and spending the proceeds on a second woman, Goajewa, his nyatsi. In her complaint Mmashaoudi demanded to be allowed to use some cattle in the herd which originated as her own cattle from her parents when they married. Pepere [in response] asked Mmashaoudi if she would leave the kgotla and go back to live with her parents if he would let her have the cattle she demanded. The major complaint according to Mmashaoudi was that Pepere did not stay with her at their home but was spending most of his time with the other woman he loved, Goajewa. . . .
>
> In out first hearing we did not concentrate much on the question of cattle but ordered Pepere to come back and stay with his wife [and ordered them to] remain in harmony and work together and share the proceeds of whatever property they have.

Once again the kgotla attempted, as in chapter 4 disputes, to maintain the relationship. But this presented a problem from the very start, because even at the first hearing "Pepere stubbornly said he would never abandon Goajewa and Pepere's wife also stubbornly objected that if Pepere continued to stay with Goajewa there would be no peace at all in the family and that she was not prepared to accept the situation as it was." This was an unusual occurrence, as parties rarely contest the kgotla's pronouncement directly. Recognizing the intransigence of the parties, the headman explained, "We, as a junior kgotla, transferred the case to Kgosing kgotla. Then it was accepted here [Kgosing], and I think Mr. Kgosiensho has much to say about it because he heard it in the kgotla several times."

Mr. Kgosiensho then took up the narrative: "When we examined the case, we found that there was no fault with Pepere's wife Mmashaoudi. We found fault with Pepere because in terms of Tswana custom it is wrong when a man has a nyatsi to move out from his family and stay at the nyatsi's place and forget his wife and children altogether." He was not saying such a relationship is unacceptable, merely that Pepere's behavior had gone beyond what was acceptable in such cases, and so "this kgotla ordered Pepere to return to his wife and stay with her and the children and [that he] should not continue selling cattle to provide for Goajewa."

Such orders are typical in marital disputes, but they do little to alter the status quo in a relationship or to redress the balance of power with regard to alienation of assets that is of concern to so many wives. Indeed, in this case the kgotla's censure had little effect and there was not even the semblance of compliance as "Pepere refused to carry out the order of Kgosing kgotla." The case returned to Kgosing later that year and was referred back to the subward. It reappeared at Kgosing on numerous occasions: "They would come two or three times a year to complain. Mmashaoudi would complain that he stays away from the family and does not support them (and) Pepere was so stubborn that he told me in the kgotla that I could take a gun and shoot him. Eventually, because this case took a long time to be heard, the Commissioner of Customary Courts advised that a kgosi from another tribal area should come and decide the case. Then Kgosi Linchwe [II] from Mochudi was approached to deal with the case and he did." This was in 1976, when Kgosi Linchwe II "ordered all the cattle to be brought to the kgotla. His aim was to divide the property between them. He divided these cattle so that Pepere's wife might have responsibility for a certain number of cattle for her maintenance and that of the family and Pepere likewise. That meant that each one of them would be free to use the cattle for whatever he or she needed." As a result Mmashaoudi got eighteen and Pepere somewhere between twenty-two and twenty-five head. Those present at the division could not remember the exact numbers. However, they were at pains to point out that "this was not a division of property for permanent ownership; they [the cattle] still remained joint property. The idea was that both of them should have free use of the cattle"—in other words, that Mmashaoudi should have some control over the cattle so that Pepere could not dispose of them at will. When the herd was divided, Pepere was asked once more to return to his wife but he refused. He then claimed "he was suing for divorce." This was in order to defeat his wife's rights to management of the cattle, which would have to be renegotiated on divorce. But Mr. Kgosiensho rejected such a claim: "It is impossible for this kgotla [Kgosing] to accept or recommend divorce because, on the strength of the evidence given by Pepere's kgotla men, there are no grounds for divorce. He often came here [after the division] to request divorce. Chief Mac [the chief regent] has not yet agreed to take it up [in 1982]."

By 1984 Mr. Kgosiensho had long since given up handling the matter. In fact, no further official action had been taken by the time of Pepere's death in May 1984.

Pepere's Rejection of Male Networks

The reluctance to entertain divorce fits with a general disinclination to recognize that a marital union has come to an end. In this case, it must also be viewed in terms of Pepere's own particular situation, as a man who had forfeited the support that would normally have been forthcoming from his male contemporaries. As a boy he was extremely close to Kgosi Kgari Sechele II and it was well known that he was like someone "adopted" by the kgosi, living in the royal compound. He acted as a court councillor in kgotla hearings during Kgari's reign and became known through this. He acquired a reputation as an arrogant man who despised the younger officials at that time, namely Mr. Kgosiensho and Mr. Mac Sechele. When Kgari died he fell from grace, and those who were promoted following Kgari's death discontinued his patronage.

His open defiance of the kgotla exacerbated the situation. People may have considered that Mmashaoudi had been badly treated, but their real concern was with Pepere's rejection of established structures of male authority. His kgotla members would not support him because they felt he had rejected them by failing to participate in his kgotla's affairs. His permanent removal to Goajewa's kgotla without consultation demonstrated his lack of respect and did not help matters. Such actions cut him off from the male networks that he would normally have associated with. This undoubtedly affected his position in the hearings. In Mr. Kgosiensho's opinion there would have been no problem if he had brought Goajewa to his kgotla and built accommodation for her there. But his actions created a situation where "they will never allow him to do that now." This was the major source of friction in these disputes, as "a wife has no real power to object to her husband marrying a second wife [under customary law]." In other words, in this situation it was not that Mmashaoudi had greater power to control the outcome of kgotla proceedings than her husband, but rather that Pepere had been stripped of any power that he might have had by his male cohort.

Mmashaoudi's version of events, given in 1982, 1984, and 1989, presents another perspective contained in the narrative below. Unfortunately, Pepere was rarely in the village, and when he was he evaded attempts to discuss his position. By 1984 he was dead. Mmashaoudi's narrative begins with her first marriage before she met Pepere.

Mmashaoudi's Narrative

Mmashaoudi was seventy when she was first interviewed in 1982.

> When I was a child I went to primary school and left when I was in Standard 2. After that I helped my mother at home until my family arranged a marriage with a relative who was the son of my mother's mother's sister. He came from Mollale kgotla attached to Goo-Pula ward. I was not in love with him but I had to obey my parents' orders. After our marriage we lived with my mother. After our two sons were born we moved to the house that my husband had built for us in Mollale kgotla. We had three more children but they all died. My husband was a traditional doctor who was well known.
>
> Then I met Pepere. I decided to separate from my first husband because he was forever beating me. Our parents kept trying to reconcile us until the final hearing [around 1950] when divorce was granted. Kgosi Kgari [Sechele] divided the property. I owned one kgomo [cow] which I had bought with sorghum given to me in exchange for clothes that I made on my sewing machine. I did not claim my share of the beasts that I had acquired with my husband. I said that they should go to my sons along with this beast.

In her case, "the fault was found with the man. The kgotla tried to persuade me to return to him. I would not agree, and then I was granted the right to leave him." But nonetheless, although she was not at fault, "if a wife insists on divorcing she is not given anything. The fields that I plowed with my husband stayed with him. The same with the huts." Thus, lack of access to and control over scarce resources creates problems for a women even where there is a finding of fault on the part of her husband. This is usually justified on the grounds of preserving the children's inheritance under the control of their father as head of the household and representative of the male line with which they are affiliated. After her divorce, Mmashaoudi went to live with Pepere and they had five children, four girls and a boy. The youngest child was born in 1955. Patlo was carried out while she and Pepere were living at her mother's house.

Pepere became involved with Goajewa, and this was when he started to neglect Mmashaoudi and the children. She reported the matter to

Pepere's family and to his eldest brother, Gabitse, and when they failed to sort out the problem it went to Sekamelo kgotla and from there to Kgosing. At that time, "I'd never queried his wish to marry a second wife. My concern was with his neglect of me and the children."

Official Encounters

This was a wise move. The other women was only brought into discussions via the allegations of neglect, in keeping with social practice that wives do not publicly complain about their husbands' lovers unless this results in their deprivation or abuse. When Mmashaoudi first raised the matter at Kgosing, Bonewamang was kgosi (1970–78). Two senior kgotla men, Tlhagiso and Koonyatse, accompanied her to make her report, so she had strong male support. Not only that, but it was known in the community that her relations were well connected in the world of traditional medicine. Nonetheless, she recalled in 1982, "What is curious about this case was that Kgosi Bonewamang avoided or dodged listening to the case." It fell to Mr. Kgosiensho, who "could not arrive at any decision because at that stage he asked my kgotla men [from Pepere's kgotla] if they found fault with me. They said they didn't, and when asked if in their opinion they found fault with my husband they stammered [prevaricated] and he referred the case back to this kgotla [subward]."

Her experience was similar to that of Eva Makoka and Manaka Kgosidintsi, who found it hard to activate the kgotla system, not only to acquire a hearing, but to follow through on decisions reached there. Unlike these women, however, Mmashaoudi felt in a position to challenge this state of affairs, and she contested the referral because "traditionally, if a case could not be decided by the junior kgotla, it cannot be returned [there] when it was impossible for the junior kgotla to make an order." Mmashaoudi continued pressing for a hearing at Kgosing, but when "I realized that the senior Kgosi was clearly avoiding hearing my case, I was then forced to go and report to the D.C. at that time, Mr. Sikwane, [who] returned the case to Kgosing and told me that he was going to speak to Kgosi Bonewamang."

There was a great deal of to-ing and fro-ing: "When I reported again to Kgosing after the District Commissioner's instructions, Kgosi Bonewamang went to the D.C. I went back to the D.C., [who] also refused to consult with me. When I realized that the kgosi and the D.C. were both avoiding my case, I went to Gaborone to consult with the Ministry of

Local Government and Lands [where the Commissioner of Customary Courts is situated]." Mmashaoudi was the prime mover in initiating a hearing before another kgosi. Unlike many other women, she knew that she could go to Commissioner of Customary Courts and where to find his office in Gaborone. This knowledge combined with her determination not to be put off by those at Kgosing led to Kgosi Linchwe II being engaged to deal with the dispute. When Kgosi Linchwe II heard the case in 1976 (there is no written record of his decision),

> I stated the facts. I said that my complaint was in connection with my husband's desertion and lack of support for me and the children. I stated that I had never been found at fault in any way [and] that my people have also proved that I am a law-abiding kgotla woman. My grief is that I and the children are starving. Amongst the head of cattle which my husband had there were cattle which I brought with me from my parents when we married and that my husband was making use of all cattle property, including mine, selling them and taking all the proceeds to spend at Goajewa's place.

Her presentation in this case adhered to the terms of conventional discourse. For it was based on Mmashaoudi establishing that her behavior was that of the exemplary wife, while at the same time highlighting all Pepere's faults and his failure as a husband. But this in itself might not have been sufficient to tip the balance in her favor. What was more significant was the fact that Pepere himself was in no position to contest Mmashaoudi's claims, having forfeited that support from his male networks that was vital to his position.

As a result, at the end of the case, "Kgosi Linchwe [II] decided that all the cattle were to be brought to Molepolole so that I could be given some cattle from the herd. [I received] fifteen cattle and three calves." Mmashaoudi did not know how many cattle to claim, as "at the time they were called for I did not know how many there were. For a long time my husband had been restricting me from going to the cattlepost, so I had no knowledge of how many there were from the beginning of 1973." Mmashaoudi confirmed that the "eighteen head of cattle were for my free use while Pepere enjoys life with Goajewa." But she also stressed that the award ignored the livestock that she had brought into her marriage and that she had purchased. These included two head of cattle and four goats. Her brothers had given her the two head of cattle from her mother's estate after she died, and the goats she had bought. According to Mmashaoudi, Kgosi Linchwe [II] "did not take account of livestock of that nature, even those which I made it clear I bought out of sorghum [profits]." Mmashaoudi was not complaining, but merely voicing how hard it is for women to establish specific claims to livestock. She was well aware that her award surpassed any that might have been made by Kwena officials. She was also pleased that "in his decision, apart from cattle, he ordered that I remain in my premises with the children and that the plowfields should be kept by me." Though no mention was made of agricultural produce, this was not an issue, as "I was using whatever I could get while Pepere lived with Goajewa."

The Handling of Property

Mmashaoudi was aware that she had fared far better under the judgment of Kgosi Linchwe II than she would have done had the case been dealt with through the normal channels at Kgosing. But she still had to accept a division of property that did not accurately reflect the value of what she was entitled to in her opinion, given the specific contributions that she had made to family assets during her marriage to Pepere. Many women who have been through such a division have had the same experience—that is, one of inadequate recognition or accounting of their contributions during a relationship which derives from their position within the household. This position is perceived of in different terms from that of their husbands, and on a practical level, gives rise to a lack of control over resources such as cattle which their husbands may dispose of without their knowledge or consent.

What is vital for women in this situation if they are to overcome the constraints that face them is how they are positioned with respect to male support from those networks of which they form part. In this respect Mmashaoudi was fortunate in that she had such support, which was enhanced by Pepere's deficiency in this area. Support, however, only represents one aspect of the challenge that faces women. They must also deal with the discourse that confronts them in terms of unequal power relations that derive from the sexual division of labor within the family and the gendered coding that adheres to the roles of husband and wife. In this case, not only was Mmashaoudi able to establish herself as an exemplary wife, but more importantly, Pepere had lost the ability to contest her claims because of his failure to maintain his relations with those male networks that were so central to his existence.

In other cases, women have been successful, but only where they have had the power to shift or alter the terms of the discourse with which they are presented. That power can be seen, for example, in the case of Radipati's daughter, Goitsemang, who challenged her brother's claim to the natal household (examined in chap. 2), and in the case of Mathilda Seitshiro, to be discussed in the next chapter. In both these instances the women concerned had access to resources beyond the ordinary realm of domestic and agricultural labor and could draw on experiences in a world that is not available to many women.

The Issue of Divorce

After this case Pepere raised the issue of divorce. This came as a shock to Mmashaoudi, as "I never had the feeling that Pepere was going to sue for divorce until he announced it in the kgotla. After that I just waited to see what action he intended to take. From then until the present day I've never thought of suing for divorce." In her opinion Pepere thought that by deserting her in 1972 he had indirectly divorced her and expected her to move. However, with the support of the kgotla people, Mmashaoudi stood firm, and that was why Pepere had exerted so much pressure over the years. From one of the few existing texts of the hearings it is clear that Pepere began to raise the issue of divorce as early as 1975 (MO 384/75).[7] The fact that Mmashaoudi did not favor divorce did not mean that she felt their relationship could be maintained. In 1982 she commented, "I've despaired of any hope of marriage with Pepere. I consider our marriage has broken down completely because it is eleven years since separation." By that point they had participated in disputes in 1972, 1973, 1974, 1975, and 1976. Yet another occurred in 1983. In 1982 Mmashaoudi recognized that her position would be jeopardized if she were formally divorced because she would lose the cattle apportioned to her for her use during their separation and she would have to return to her family and forfeit her existing homestead. People at Kgosing were aware of this, and their adamant refusal to grant Pepere a formal divorce operated in her favor. The kind of vulnerability and hardship that women may encounter on divorce is underscored by Mmashaoudi's observation that, whatever her relationship with Pepere entailed, a divorce would have been "worse because when Pepere brought me to this kgotla he had no hut to live in, no cattlepost, and no field which he had prepared for plowing. As a result of my having to toil developing this place [in his kgotla] my parents huts broke down [fell into disrepair]. It would be worse if I returned [if I had to return] to find the dwelling house [my parents' dwelling] extinct."

Since the 1976 apportionment Mmashaoudi has supported herself by hiring "people to plow, depending on whether any of my children have given me money to assist myself." Her children are all adults now. Those who provide the greatest support are her eldest unmarried daughter, who is employed as a primary school teacher in Molepolole, and her married son, who works as a miner. Although Mmashaoudi was left with the plowfields, there were problems because Pepere continued to plow that land for Goajewa. When Mmashaoudi went to Kgosing to complain about this the officials there would do nothing, and in 1982 Pepere was still plowing that land. In looking back on her situation in 1984 she observed, "Pepere was away for fourteen years [until he died in May]. During this time I struggled all by myself to maintain the family. I got used to living the hard way. Things are better now because I have the whole field to myself. The trouble is that the field is not worked because I have been sick for a while. Since 1979 I have been under medical attention and am unable to plow." By 1989 Mmashaoudi's situation had altered, and she was able to do some plowing for the first time in years due to a government agricultural assistance scheme. However, many of the cattle that had been earmarked for her family's use had died during the prolonged drought.

Although the relationship between Mmashaoudi and Goajewa was presented in conflictual terms in the disputes, when Pepere died they came together to organize his funeral. Goajewa provided Pepere's coffin as well as an ox for the meal that forms part of the funeral ceremonies. This shows that it was property that was at stake in the disputes and that there was no personal animosity between the two women as the disputes implied. When it came to Pepere's death, Goajewa behaved and was treated like a second wife. This demonstrates the extent to which relationships between women may be dependent upon their relationships with men.

Ward Discussions

When it came to Mmashaoudi and Pepere's situation, people had very different perspectives on their relationship, and this affected how they viewed the parties' property rights. Some in Ntloedibe claimed that patlo was not done, so that on breakdown "it is not the responsibility of the kgotla people but of Pepere [to deal with the situation]. According to law he would have to give her personal effects and some of the household property. In a case of this nature [concubinage] it is Pepere's responsibility to see to it that she gets some of the property that they acquired when they were together, such as livestock." By this they meant that it would very much be up to his goodwill to give Mmashaoudi any property and to recognize that "this woman [Mmashaoudi] had sons working at the mines and they would bring money. Out of this food and cattle were bought, so she would be entitled to some cattle because they had been bought by her children." But others argued that patlo had been done. One intervened to say, "According to my knowledge, after he [Pepere] brought this woman to the kgotla, he told his parents and went and effected patlo. Patlo was done to enable her to stay as a member of the kgotla." In this speaker's view, "the fault lies with Pepere because he has broken the law of patlo. He has no ground, according to Tswana custom, to divorce his wife because he is in love with another woman." On this view "he would get nothing from the joint property."

Some in Tshosa ward challenged this view. They were adamant that patlo had not been done and that she was not entitled to remain in Pepere's kgotla. All she was entitled to was a hut to be built for her by Pepere at the parents' home.

Tshosa ward members did not approve of Kgosi Linchwe II's handling of the matter, as "according to pure Tswana custom it was wrong. It was in the interests of whoever decided the case." They were prepared to go further than many others and stated that in their kgotla "if Pepere wanted to get rid of the woman we would have removed her from the premises." They were not the only ones to comment on Kgosi Linchwe's handling of the case. Members of Maunatlala ward commented that they were shocked by what he had done and that "the decision over the matter was not based on old traditional Tswana ways of doing things; it was done by modern ideas." They did, however, understand the tensions, observing that the problem as they saw it in Pepere's case was that "from the time he fell in love with the second woman he had the practice of coming to the kraals, selling cattle, spending some of the money to maintain his first wife and some for the second woman. That is why according to the feeling of people today they had to divide the cattle between them so that his wife could support the children and herself." However, they argued that "according to traditional ways of doing it, a Motswana man is free to marry more than one wife. Normally if a man marries a second wife and neglects his first wife, the cattle which are in his particular kgotla are his property and he may use them for his personal and other needs because they are his property."

These debates depict the complexities of dealing with property issues which are so closely bound up with personal and familial ties within a community. Such ties form an integral part of a party's persona and affect their claims to property. The "I" of the individual has a broader referent as man/husband/father or woman/wife/mother and all that means in the context of social relations. Thus, Mmashaoudi was able to marshal support for herself. Her family's standing, with connections to traditional medicine, gave her some status and authority, which was enhanced by a level of formal education which was unusual among women of her generation. This empowered her to challenge Pepere, especially as he had alienated those male networks that were crucial to his support. As a result, Pepere could not divorce Mmashaoudi, although the separation of assets amounted to a divorce in all but name. In this instance, Mmashaoudi clearly had more support than Pepere, even though Kgosi Linchwe II's property division was generally viewed as a departure from mekgwa le melao ya Setswana.

Women as Wives and Their Rights to Property on Divorce

Mmashaoudi was relatively successful in her property claims, largely due to Pepere's disenfranchisement from male networks. However, as the disputes in this and the previous chapters demonstrate, women as wives generally find themselves at a disadvantage compared with their husbands when claims to property arise. This is especially true for women who are part of the peasantariat. Operating within a domestic and agricultural matrix as part of a network engaging in lands and cattle activities and intermittent migrant labor, the women's position is a vulnerable one fostering dependence on men. In this context, it is hard for women to dislodge prevailing models of discourse on familial relations and property, to shift the terms of debate and put them on another footing.

But when women, such as those associated with the salariat, can expand their horizons to draw on another set of reference points, they may alter the discourse and gain greater control over the process. Some examples of this have already been presented in earlier chapters involving discussions over ordinary processes of negotiation. How this can be achieved in the context of divorce is illustrated in the next chapter. What is crucial is how women are located within networks. For the activities they pursue not only shape the course of their everyday lives but also influence their experiences of legal process.

In Mmashaoudi and Pepere's case, cattle, land, and the family compound formed the property at issue. When other assets such as money, businesses, and vehicles are involved, they add to the complications, particularly where divorce encompasses common law through the High Court. The diverse ways in which a division is approached in these circumstances is highlighted by the Busang and Seitshiro disputes, which will be discussed along with the interface with common law in the next chapter. This raises important questions about law that go beyond a narrow focus on pluralism of the juristic kind associated with legal centralism, which upholds a division between common and customary law according to the institutional forums in which law is applied. What is crucial is not the formal classification of law in terms of common or customary law, but rather the power of individuals to construct a discourse that will effectively represent their claims. Such power is not confined to, or solely derived from, the formal legal settings in which it operates, but derives more generally from the broader domain of social life. In this context, women, as individuals, find themselves at a disadvantage in pursuing their claims against men because of the gendered social world that gives rise to differential relations of power between them. By taking account of these considerations, which are absent from a legal centralist account of law, a more accurate understanding of people's access to and use of law is acquired, one which highlights the obstacles that women face in a legal arena.

SEVEN

Final Partings: Institutional Encounters and the Shifting Boundaries of Law

The difficulties that wives encounter in pursuing their property rights at the end of a marriage are reinforced by their experiences in courts and the legal system in general. For those institutions continue to uphold the social basis upon which women's partnerships with men are constructed and interpreted. In other words, such institutions continue to underwrite the unequal power relations that exist between the sexes in terms of their gendered roles as husbands and wives, which derive from the sexual division of labor within the family and the household.

Thus, social and legal worlds intersect in ways which are crucial for women's access to, and use of, law. For those factors which inform social processes of negotiation, such as access to resources, status, power, and gender, continue to have an impact upon legal process. This is so not only in terms of constraining or facilitating access to legal process, but also with respect to the legal process itself (regardless of whether the legal arena in which it is located is a customary or a common law forum). The old, legal centralist model of pluralism cannot be sustained, because an ethnographic approach to the study of law defeats any analysis of law which conceives of these forums as representing separate and autonomous legal systems embedded in the dual systems theory of law endorsed by Hooker (1975) and others.

Within this framework women challenge the terms of reference with which they are presented, but their ability to do so varies. Membership in a network not only allows women to mobilize support, but even more significantly empowers them to shift the terms of the discourse. The women who are in the best position to do so are those who can draw on resources that lie beyond the ordinary realm of domestic, agricultural, and unskilled labor associated with the peasantariat. Such women stand a greater chance of being heard and of establishing their claims to property.

Gofetamang Busang and Mathilda Seitshiro found themselves differentially situated when it came to establishing their rights to marital property. Mrs. Busang's connections were firmly located within the world of the peasantariat, while Mrs. Seitshiro's education, professional training, and government employment put her on a par with the salariat. The effect of such connections and what they mean for women with respect to their ability not only to command a hearing but to do so in terms favorable to them are highlighted in the disputes to be discussed in this chapter.

THE FORMAL LEGAL SYSTEM

Divorce at Common Law: The High Court

Before turning to these disputes, however, it is necessary to say something about the formal legal system, as both disputes involve aspects of common law. In the previous chapter none of the parties had married in church or had had their marriage registered under the Marriage Act 1970 [Cap.29:01]; for them, the divorce process did not proceed under the statutory provisions provided by common law. On the other hand, as the Molepolole marriage data discussed in chapter 2 show, numbers of couples who marry opt for a church wedding or for a civil ceremony and registration. In such cases, when these couples wish to dissolve their union, the marriage must be set aside in the High Court under the Matrimonial Causes Act 1973 [Cap.29:07], which is modeled on English divorce law. The act is framed in terms of the concept of irretrievable breakdown (1973:s.14), which may be established on one of several grounds laid down under the act, such as adultery, unreasonable behavior, desertion for two years, and two years' separation with consent (1973:s.15). The grounds cited in both cases relates to behavior such that "the plaintiff cannot reasonably be expected to cohabit with the defender" (s.15 (1)(b)).

These provisions draw yet another institutional forum, the High Court, into the divorce process. For many of those who must go through the High Court this represents an additional aspect of the process rather than a complete alternative to the customary system. As previous case histories and the two disputes to be discussed show, customary agencies are still very much engaged in the process of uncoupling in dikgotla and at Kgosing. They continue to play a key role in ascertaining whether spouses can reconcile their differences, and where divorce in the High Court occurs, it is usually after many years of wrangling in such forums.

On granting divorce the High Court has power to make an order determining the mutual property rights of husband and wife (1973:s.13) and to award a capital or annual sum of money and maintenance to the wife (1973:s.25). When the court does so, under its common law jurisdiction in terms of the Married Persons' Property Act 1970 [Cap.29:03],[1] the position varies according to whether the rules relating to community of property or a separate property regime are applied. This depends on whether the parties married before or after 1971. For parties married before 1971 the rules relating to community of property are applied, but for those married after that year the rules relating to a separate property regime apply (Married Persons Property Act s.3). Parties had and continue to have a choice under the act of opting out of the prescribed forms, so that they can opt out of community of property and into separate property and vice versa (ss.3 and 4).

Formal Legal Pluralism: Property

Under community of property, derived from Roman-Dutch law, the parties are jointly responsible for debts and share joint ownership of assets, with minor exceptions. Under the original system, the husband took charge of the assets by virtue of his marital power, which was one reason why many women opted out and in favor of the separate property system. The marital power in favor of the husband has been abandoned in South Africa, but it continues to operate in Botswana. Under the separate property regime, marriage is held to have no effect on the ownership of property (in theory), which is held by the spouses as individuals and devolves according to their individual ownership rights, subject to the High Court's powers to determine mutual property rights between husband and wife on divorce (Matrimonial Causes Act 1973:s.13).

When, however, the parties are African and domiciled in Botswana, the property will devolve according to customary law on the basis of section 7 of the Married Persons Property Act. This is so unless the application of customary law is expressly or impliedly excluded. The former occurs when the parties themselves sign a document prior to marriage expressly excluding the application of customary law. This happened routinely when parties came to be married at District Administration in Molepolole in 1982 when as a matter of administrative practice they were presented with such a document—written in English. In most cases, the parties signed the document without having any real idea of what it meant.

In the absence of such a document, it has been argued that customary law may be impliedly excluded on the basis of the mode of life exemption contained in section 2 of the Dissolution of African Marriages (Disposal of Property) Act [Cap.29:06]. This provides that "where on the dissolution of marriage . . . a question arises as to the disposal or devolution of any property . . . such question shall be heard and determined by a Magistrate . . . if it shall appear to the court . . . that regard being had to the mode of life of the spouses . . . it would not be just and equitable that such property should be dealt with according to Customary law." The application of this exemption (Molomo case [Court Transcript Matrimonial Cause 90 of 1979]) has been questioned by the Chief Justice (Moisakamo case [Court Transcript Matrimonial Cause 106 of 1978])[2] on the basis that such an exemption can only be applied to marriages in existence before the Married Persons Property Act was passed and before the provisions for exclusion in that Act could take effect.

When customary law is applied, it is normally done through customary agencies, which in the case of divorce involves the chief's kgotla or the customary court of appeal. The Moisakamo case has, however, established that the High Court has jurisdiction to apply customary law to a division of property on two grounds. The first ground is that where the parties have been married under common law, such a division is ancillary to the divorce proceedings, which are expressly excluded from the ambit of the customary courts by section 12 of the Customary Courts Act. The second ground is that the High Court has inherent jurisdiction to deal with customary law under section 95(1) of the Constitution of Botswana and this "original jurisdiction cannot be limited or ousted by Parliament or any law" (Moisakamo, High Court Transcript 1978, p. 16).

THE BUSANGS AND THE SEITSHIROS

This chapter focuses on two divorces that took place in both the High Court and the chief's kgotla, the first involving the Busangs and the second the Seitshiros. They have been chosen for discussion because they highlight an intersection between parts of the formal legal system involving common and customary law. The forms that this takes when it comes to division of property in the chief's kgotla vary according to the power to set the terms of the discourse that is applied. As these divorces show, the types of discourse which fall under the rubric of customary law are variable. Their variability derives from the parties' power to construct terms of reference that draw on different frameworks for their validity. Such power stems from the different types of network to which parties belong (such as the peasantariat and salariat), which provide them with differential access to resources. This has important implications for women, as these divorce disputes will show, given the gendered nature of the world they live in and the ways in which this affects their power to command a hearing and to pursue successful property claims.

Both the Busangs and Seitshiros were granted divorces in the High Court. The matter was then referred back to the chief's kgotla for a division of property under customary law. Mr. Masimega and I attended both cases, which involved substantial assets covering a broad range of property set out below.

Busangs:
    Modern dwelling house
    Vehicle
    Bank savings: 1,500 pula
    Furniture
    Domestic items
    Plowfield at Maologane
    Ten head of cattle
    Ten goats
Seitshiros:
    Modern dwelling house
    Bar/cocktail bar
    Bottle store/butchery
    Furniture
    Domestic items
    Plowfield at Tlokweng
    Cattle
    Goats
    Rondevaal at Tlokweng

Here the similarity between the cases ended. The parties were differentially situated in terms of the type of claims that they could make and the responses they received. This was due to their affiliation with the kinds of networks which channeled their access to resources and thus to assets in different ways. So Mrs. Busang, whose education and occupational activities fit a profile for the peasantariat, found her power to maneuver severely circumscribed compared with that of Mrs. Seitshiro, whose profile is closer to that of the salariat, with the result that the former was unsuccessful in her property claims while the latter was awarded a substantial share of the assets.

THE BUSANGS

When Gofetamang and James Murray Busang attended the division of property in the chief's kgotla in Molepolole on 16 July 1982, they were both forty-five years old. Like many women of her generation Gofetamang had been educated only as far as Standard 5 of primary school and left to pursue domestic activities at home as well undertaking some casual work. At the time that she met Murray she was working as a domestic for one of the traders in Molepolole. He was working as a government clerk. Both had connections in the village, though his were more powerful in terms of links to ruling Kwena families. Gofetamang's father was the headman of Koodisa ward, one of the major subwards to Kgosing.

She became pregnant, and when the matter was raised with Murray's family, his father agreed to marriage.[3] They were married in church in 1960 and subsequently had eight children. Over the years Murray's career progressed. He was appointed D.C. in Tsabong and at the time of divorce and the hearing was an undersecretary in the Ministry of Works and Communications. In contrast, Gofetamang remained ensconced in domestic activities. The basis of her world was referred to in the context of the divorce. Irretrievable breakdown was cited on grounds of incompatibility due to the fact that since marriage "she has not worked and thus her educational knowledge has deteriorated over time" (plaintiff's declaration to High Court, dated 13 June 1980, p. 3).

When their relationship deteriorated, attempts were made to resolve their difficulties at family level and finally at the chief's kgotla in 1979. These were unsuccessful, and as the parties were married at common law they had to go to the High Court for a divorce. This was granted in Mr. Busang's favor in 1982 on the grounds of Mrs. Busang's behavior. Mr. Busang was awarded custody of the six children under eighteen, ranging in ages from seven to fifteen. They had two adult children over the age of eighteen. The eldest son, Mokwadi, aged twenty, was working for the Botswana police force, and his unmarried sister Polokego, nineteen, and her baby daughter lived with Gofetamang.

Hearing in the Chief's Kgotla Molepolole, 16 July 1982

Claims and counterclaims. As the parties argued over the distribution of property and had not excluded the application of customary law, the matter was referred by the High Court, at Mrs. Busang's request, to Kgosing. Like other disputants she began by stating her claim: "I am complaining about the property which I acquired jointly with Mr. Busang. I say this because it is he who divorced me. I have asked him to let me have some of the things which we acquired jointly: a home, a vehicle, bank savings amounting to 1,500 pula (about £1,000), ten head of cattle, ten goats, and a plowfield." She listed other property including chairs, saucepans, and hoes, as well as 135 pula, "which is the proceeds of jerseys I was knitting." Mrs. Busang was then questioned by the third party hearing the dispute, Mr. Sebele, the senior chief's representative. He inquired about the specifics of this property. "Is this money in the bank at the moment?" "You said there were ten goats. We would like a full explanation as to how you arrived at the number ten."

After Mr. Sebele, she was questioned by Mr. Busang, who also queried his wife's account of the property. He inquired, "Since all the money deposited in the bank [is recorded], have you a book for this money?" In further interrogation he discredited her by forcing her to admit that she was making a claim for animals based on an ox (in this context a gelded bull), which could not reproduce. The interchange was as follows.

Mr. Busang asked, "You claim that we were compensated for crop damage in 1961 by a beast—what was the gender and the color of the beast?" Mrs. Busang replied, "It was a brown ox." Mr. Busang continued, "So this ox reproduced eight calves?" Mrs. Busang hesitated and Mr. Sebele intervened to say, "You must be specific in answering questions. Did this ox actually reproduce eight calves?" Mrs. Busang was forced to accede: "No, because it was an ox." Mr. Busang reinforced his point: "When you said this ox reproduced nine cows you know an ox never reproduces. Do you think you are telling this court the truth that you are claiming ten cattle from me?"

This interchange severely damaged Mrs. Busang's credibility. The Busang case followed the usual kgotla procedure of opening up discussion to all members. A lengthy debate ensued in which kgotla members focused on the issue of fault. The first question to Mrs. Busang was posed by the chief regent, participating as an ordinary kgotla member: "Your husband divorced you. My question is did he just divorce you without any cause?" Mrs. Busang replied, "He just divorced me." The chief regent pursued the issue: "Since you say he divorced you without any cause, have you ever heard of a case of that nature where a husband divorced his wife without any reason?" She was forced to concede, "No, I've never heard of such a case."

This exchange was crucial as it established fault on Mrs. Busang's part in the eyes of the kgotla. It set the tone and the strategy for Mr. Busang and his supporters for the rest of the dispute. Mr. Sebele then questioned Mrs. Busang intensely, which resulted in her dropping a substantial part of her claim to the property. It was only after this that Mr. Busang gave his statement.

When he responded to Gofetamang's claims, he ignored the specific property details and concentrated instead on the issue of fault, which he claimed excluded her from any entitlement to property: "In connection with the case I do not see anything that entitles this woman to the property she is claiming. She is not entitled to anything according to traditional custom. I'm saying this because she is the person who created all the troubles in our married life since we married on the 12th of November 1960." He then read verbatim from the statement that he had submitted to the High Court for divorce. This detailed ways in which her conduct had been at fault including allegations that (1) she practiced "witchcraft," (2) she was a "harlot" and after one of her affairs had to have an abortion, (3) she contributed nothing to the home, (4) she assaulted him, (5) she deserted him and the children, (6) she refused to cooperate in efforts made at reconciliation and when divorce was inevitable, with the arrangements for divorce.

The erring wife and the accommodating husband. Like the husbands in marital disputes in chapter 6, Mr. Busang used these allegations to present a picture of behavior that was fundamentally inconsistent with that of a good wife. In contrast, he stressed how reasonably he had behaved, that he forgave her the affairs and abortion, that he tried to cure her of witchcraft, and that he offered to make arrangements over property. Not only that, but he was willing to settle matters amicably:

> I told her she did not have enough grounds to claim a share of the property because the matter will be referred to the kgotla to be settled in accordance with our tradition and you are going to lose the case. Then I suggested that she should let me know what items of property she wanted and I would give them to her. I wanted her to list what she wanted so that I could tell the kgotla the division that we had agreed to. I even gave her the option that if she wanted to take all the property

I would let her have everything willingly. Then we listed out the items and I came to Molepolole with the list on the 25th of July 1980 so that we could both sign an agreement which included the custody of the children. Then she refused to sign the list and then and there I knew that someone had advised her not to sign. Then on wrong advice she made a different list with her lawyers which included things which did not exist.

He not only stressed how reasonably he behaved, he used the High Court to endorse his conduct and her fault:

I presented all the evidence to the High Court to Justice Hannah. She did not contradict all this. She was represented by certain lawyers who I paid for. I had only paid the legal costs—she consulted lawyers all on her own; all I did was pay for the lawyer. This indicates that she was aware of everything that I presented to the court and she accepted it in toto. It now astounds me that she, being aware of the fact that she had been instrumental to the breakdown of the marriage in collusion with her parents as previously stated, claims any property.

Mr. Busang was then questioned by his wife, who attempted to clear her character. He was not questioned at all by Mr. Sebele.

Kgotla deliberations and judgment. After this the kgotla members attempted to see if he would concede anything to her. One member asked, "Is it right that a woman should forfeit everything because of a mistake she made in her past? Haven't you got any sympathy for your wife?" to which he responded, "No." He was adamant in all his replies that he was not prepared to alter his position.

Finally, the kgotla members were asked for their counsel. In this they were guided by Mr. Sebele, who stated, "What we want to do is deal with the merits of this case." What was the response? Some felt Mrs. Busang should receive something, others disagreed on the basis that she had been at fault. To present some of the more forceful views, one member argued,

In this present case the reasons advanced were not contested by the wife. As he said, she was not an asset except so far as bearing children. When considering cases of this nature, usually we base our consideration on the position of the children—whether they are minor or grown up. But in a case where a woman left the husband and left the children with the husband, as is the case now, she is just like somebody who is dead. I do not think her claim to property is justifiable. With whom is she going to share this property when all the minor children are under the custody of the husband? I can only go as far as that.

Another kgotla member disagreed: "We've been listening to this case all day, and it is difficult for us to base our decision on customary procedure—all we can do is to ask Mr. Busang to be sympathetic and give her something." But another opined,

> I don't see any reason why the woman should be given a share of the property. Our Tswana expression is that she has committed suicide and someone who does so you don't cry for. When her husband wanted to sympathetically consider her position and give her property, she turned that offer down. She did not see the implications in the offer made by the husband that he was willing to give some property voluntarily but did not want to argue about it. It is on those grounds that I see no reason why this woman should be entitled to any of the assets. I contend that they belong to all the children she has deserted together with the husband. If she had been submissive to her husband and cooperated with him when he made her an offer there would not have been all this trouble. She is instrumental to the divorce, so I contend that she should get nothing.

Mr. Sebele adopted the sentiment expressed by the majority of kgotla members and concluded that

> when the court considered Tswana law and custom, the kgotla found that Gofetamang was not entitled to any property due to the fact that she was instrumental to the divorce, and further that when the marriage was dissolved at the High Court the children were given to the father. This property should be used for their maintenance. It is true and at the same time in accordance with customary law. I agree with the kgotla members that Gofetamang is not entitled to anything. It is reported that she has all her clothing. Nevertheless, this court pleads with Mr. Busang to be sympathetic. It is not a court order, it is a request. He must take into account the duration of their marriage and how many children they had together. He must try and consider her position sympathetically; it is not an order but a humble request.

Mrs. Busang's Experience of Gendered Power Relations.

The hearing was packed with people from all over the village. Many women attended but none of them participated in the kgotla's deliberations. The fact that Mrs. Busang had very little family support was evident. Only a sister, a cousin, and her brother were present. In contrast, there were at least eleven relatives of Mr. Busang present, including two aunts, an uncle, his mother, a sister-in-law, and one of his mother's cousins.

When asked about this in 1989, Gofetamang surmised that her relatives had been taken by surprise. Not only were they unaware of the date of the hearing, but "they were confused, sad, and disappointed that they had never been consulted. Normally a dispute of this kind is heard by parents before it goes to Kgosing." In her view Mr. Busang had never gone through the proper channels, and her family was not prepared for a hearing of this kind to take place. Another relative present at the interview indicated that Gofetamang's mother had not been present "because it was a great shock and caused her grief." She implied that Gofetamang's mother did not want to have anything to do with the divorce, no doubt because Busang's family is so influential in the village.

In talking about her experiences Gofetamang considered that she "was prejudiced from the very beginning." She denied deserting Busang and explained that after they quarreled in 1979 she had moved to her mother's home in order to demonstrate the gravity of her grievances, in line with accepted Kwena practices. As was appropriate in this situation, members of Koodisa ward informed the Busangs and asked them to come to discuss the matter, but they did not. Instead, Gofetamang claimed she was issued a summons to appear at the High Court. Her family was never presented with the allegations made by Busang of "bewitching or adultery." When she went to the High Court she felt excluded from the process: "No one paid any attention to me and I was never asked any questions." This did not improve when the location moved to the chief's kgotla, as in her view "Sebele was prejudiced. He would not allow me to ask questions or to make comments. It was clear that he was in favor of Murray because he would not let me say anything against the statements Murray made against me."

Gofetamang never did receive any property from Murray after the hearing, but she managed to retain the knitting machine. She felt aggrieved: "The saddest thing is that I was making money with Busang and gave him the money which he was saving for me. After the divorce he did not give me the money back. The money was in his name in the bank book." After the divorce she was supported by her mother and used her knitting machine to sell things locally. Her brothers, who were working at the mines at that time, provided some support for her and her mother in the form of agricultural produce. In 1987 Gofetamang got a job through her sister-in-law (the wife of Busang's elder brother) as a cleaner at Tlhobologo Primary School in Gaborone. This provided her with accommodation. She was also helped by her two daughters, who, unlike their mother, have managed to acquire a higher degree of education and pursue careers as a nurse and a court clerk. Unfortunately, Gofetamang no longer sees the younger children because "he has prejudiced them against me. They are supposed to come in the school holidays but it became too difficult."

Gofetamang graphically illustrates how a woman may be judged as a wife and denied rights to property. Contrary to general kgotla discussions, she was not even given one ox, lekaba, to accompany her to her family home. Her situation was worse than that of a nyatsi, who would at least have been entitled to some household utensils. Gofetamang was permitted to state her claim, but she never succeeded in commanding the attention of the kgotla. In this respect she was trapped by gender, unable to overcome the hurdles surrounding the social construction of fault and the restrictions placed on women's property rights by Kwena succession. She was constrained by her own position as well as by the power relations with which she was confronted. Her own operational sphere, centering on domestic activities, restricted her ability to establish specific contributions to assets. It also confronted her with the more general problem of having her claim assessed on the basis of her conduct as a wife, judged according to certain standards.

Politics of Knowledge and Power

Gofetamang was not as articulate or adept at controlling the proceedings as her husband, but given the difference in their educational and social standing this was hardly surprising. Lack of knowledge was important here. Where this was crucial was in the discussions relating to the High Court. The court's decision to grant Mr. Busang divorce and to award him custody influenced the kgotla's attitude toward her. It was viewed as upholding Mr. Busang's allegations of fault and endorsing them in its judgment. Through her lack of knowledge about the legal concept of "irretrievable breakdown" Mrs. Busang failed to undermine Mr. Busang's and Mr. Sebele's references to the High Court decision. Otherwise she could have argued that divorce on this basis is meant to be free from the concept of fault and that the one which took place was merely administrative in nature. Indeed, prior to the High Court divorce proceedings Murray had persuaded Gofetamang not to contest the divorce on the understanding that she would be entitled to a share of the property. Her lawyers therefore did not contest the divorce, and the allegations concerning witchcraft were never subject to proof but accepted at face value.

Judges in the High Court, who often come from the United Kingdom, are reluctant to become involved in assessing evidence of witchcraft, though there are procedures for appointing assessors in these situations. In this kind of case judges are happy to grant an undefended divorce without subjecting the grounds of divorce to a proof. Unfortunately for Gofetamang, she and her husband failed to reach agreement over the property, and that was why their dispute ended up being dealt with in the chief's kgotla.

However, it was not simply personal characteristics, such as lack of knowledge, which placed her at a disadvantage. She also had to deal with power relations over which she had no control. These were located in the structure of the hearing itself, through the authoritative role attributed to the third party handling the dispute. The third party controls the proceedings in the sense that he has the power to decide how long a party may speak, what form interventions may take, and what lines of argument may be pursued. In this case, Mr. Sebele played an active part, and it was one which operated to Gofetamang's detriment.[4] For example, he pursued an aggressive policy toward her statements concerning property and managed to put pressure on her to withdraw her claims to certain items, such as the plowfield and the bank savings. At the end of this process, when she stood firm and refused to withdraw her claim to the 135 pula acquired from the sale of jerseys, he confronted her by saying, "At the High Court, who won the case?" immediately closing off any further discussion of property and shifting the emphasis onto conduct and the underlying assumption of fault on her part.

On another occasion when Gofetamang was attempting to clear her name by questioning Murray's allegations, he intervened several times and this confused her. For example, she addressed several questions to Murray aimed at dealing with conduct. "You stated that at a certain time I deliberately had an abortion; when you noticed this what action did you take; in connection with the statement about bewitching what action did you take; if it's true that I contributed nothing towards the maintenance of the home how is it that I was knitting jerseys for which you have the money?" It was at this point that Mr. Sebele intervened to tell her that she must deal with the reasons put forward for the dissolution of marriage in the High Court. She was informed that her questions were irrelevant.

When she carried on questioning in the same way—"Was I wrong to go to our people and tell them about our trouble?"—Mr. Sebele again intervened to say that such questions were irrelevant and that she must base her questions on distribution of property. "Your husband has divorced you and has given his grounds as to why you should forfeit everything in connection with the marriage, so you must concentrate on this if you think that you should get a share of the assets." This, however, is what she was doing. By asking the questions she asked she was addressing herself to the general question of conduct on which her husband refused her claim to property. Her questions were not the ramblings of an incoherent woman. When she asked Murray, "Since you say I'm a harlot, what action did you take?" this was highly relevant, because if he really considered her to be unfaithful he should have arranged meetings with her family or the kgotla to discuss the matter at the time, rather than raising it as an issue a long time after the event. Her questions concerning action, with their implied reference to family notification, are precisely the same as those we have seen chief's kgotla personnel, wardheads, and kgotla members asking disputants time and time again in previous disputes. In this case, however, Mr. Sebele's interventions shifted the focus of debate, and Gofetamang finally ceased to say anything because she became confused.

THE SEITSHIROS

A very different form of proceedings in tone and style took place in the Seitshiros' dispute. At the time of the hearing they had been married for fifteen years and had two sons aged twenty-one and fourteen. Mathilda was in her fifties and Seitshiro was sixty. Like the Busangs, they had married under statute and therefore were required to be divorced in the High Court. By agreement, custody of the son under eighteen was given to Mr. Seitshiro. Like the Busangs, they were subject to a division of property in the chief's kgotla under customary law.

Mathilda became friendly with Seitshiro in 1960 while she was a trainee nurse. He had been previously married, had divorced in 1952, and was living with another woman in Molepolole at the time, with whom he had four children. He and Mathilda had their first son in 1961, and in 1967 they married in Mahalapye. No bogadi was transferred.

Serious problems arose in their relationship from 1975 onward. Mathilda explained that "according to Tswana custom, whenever I had any complaint I would go to Mr. Seitshiro's uncle and he came to the house and discussed it with Mr. Seitshiro and myself." This occurred on numerous occasions. In January 1980 she finally left the family home in Tlokweng (adjacent to Gaborone) to live in Molepolole, where she was working as the matron of the hospital.

In March that year, Mr. Seitshiro wrote and informed Mathilda that if she did not come home within fourteen days "he would divorce me and charge me with desertion." She notified her parents and her lawyer to say that she would not return home. Seitshiro then phoned her in November to tell her to collect the furniture that she had bought. Mathilda then "went over to my parents in Mahalapye and told them; they advised me to see my lawyer, as Seitshiro's family had never said anything to them."

Mathilda's lawyer advised her to collect the furniture, as Seitshiro had only given her thirty days to collect it. He advised her to do this through Kgosi Gaborone, who was the Tlokwa kgosi of the morafe to which Mr. Seitshiro belonged. Kgosi Gaborone tried to persuade Mathilda to give Seitshiro one more chance, but she was adamant. When the furniture was collected, it was done in the presence of witnesses representing the interested parties. These were two representatives from Mahalapye, representing Mathilda's family, two representatives from Tlokweng kgotla, representing the interests of Seitshiro's community, and two representatives from a subward in Tlokweng, specifically representing his interests.

The High Court

After the property was collected, Mathilda instructed her lawyer to sue for divorce in the High Court. "I charged him with adultery, having fathered two children with different women in 1968 and 1970, ill treatment, and that he did not maintain me." They were summoned on 21 September 1981 to the High Court in Lobatse, where the judge advised them "to talk about the property before the marriage was dissolved." The case was postponed until 22 October. When they were recalled to Lobatse, they failed to reach agreement on the property, and "as we did not agree on anything we were asked to sign a paper stating that the property would be dealt with by Kgosi Gaborone according to customary law at Tlokweng."

The divorce in the High Court was granted in Mrs. Seitshiro's favor on the grounds of Mr. Seitshiro's behavior. It was undefended. Kgosi Gaborone then began to deal with the property. Mr. Seitshiro kept postponing meetings. He did this three times and then finally wrote to the Commissioner of Customary Courts claiming that Kgosi Gaborone was prejudiced against him, that, as Mathilda reported it, "he hates him and told one of the women in Tlokweng that he would fix him." As a result Kgosi Linchwe II was called in to deal with the property. One two occasions Mr. Seitshiro failed to turn up, but finally the division took place on 14 and 15 June 1982 with Mr. Masimega and myself in attendance, together with various headmen from Molepolole. Mathilda came with "my two brothers, a male cousin, and my three sisters" while Seitshiro came "with his uncle, two sisters, and his brother-in-law from his first marriage."

At the date of the division Mathilda, a well-educated woman who had qualified as a nurse and spent part of her training abroad, was matron of the hospital in Molepolole. Seitshiro, who was less well educated, was manager of the bar and bottle store that they had established. Before that he had concentrated on lands and cattle activities and been intermittently employed as a borehole mechanic. It was known that he intended to marry again.

Claims and counterclaims. In the Seitshiro division the focus was not on fault but centered on establishing particular claims to property. Mathilda, like Gofetamang, began by staking her claim. "I am married according to community of property. I demand a share of property involving cattle, goats, and a house at Tlokweng. At the cattlepost I claim the pumping plant engine which was meant to water cattle and make income by fees paid to people to water cattle. I claim all this property because my husband turned me away, he did not want to live with me as his wife." Unlike Gofetamang, however, she presented more of a presence and she was not subjected to detailed questioning by the kgotla. Kgosi Linchwe II never opened the matter up for kgotla participation but kept control of the discussion to himself, Mathilda, and Seitshiro. He only questioned her about the number of children that she had had with Seitshiro.

When his turn came, Seitshiro constructed his statement in the same vein as his wife, concentrating on specific items of property and how they were acquired. He began, "This lady bought the bricks as soon as she arrived from England. There were more than two thousand brick blocks. I had bought the corrugated iron in 1965. There were nine sheets and I stored them at my mother's place. I was allocated a yard site in 1965 by the kgosi with my headman named Mokete. I came there and began to build there after my marriage with Mathilda."

He then tried to argue that Mathilda was not entitled to property, but on the basis that she never contributed financially to its acquisition. He claimed, for example, "We had already paid the first builder the sum of 140 pula. I don't know how much more money he was paid, because

my wife had the money. She was the person to do the payments. I struggled about the money to pay for the building and my wife never contributed anything." Indeed, he accused her of stealing their joint property:
"When I got home from Ghanzi I found that she had taken some blankets, plates, cups, and some other things from the house. Also, the children told me that their mother had taken a number of things from the
house. Sometime later I phoned her to tell her that I was surprised to
find the house almost empty. Then she replied that it was herself who
took the house property."

Seitshiro tried to establish that his wife was at fault and responsible
for the breakdown of the marriage, but all his attempts to do so were
firmly quashed by Kgosi Linchwe II, who steered the dispute back to
issues of property. Like Mr. Sebele in the Busang case, he firmly controlled the dispute. In contrast to the Busang case, however, he allowed
Mathilda to fully develop her case. She was not cut off in midstream,
nor was she subject to abrupt shifts in reasoning. When it was time for
him to deliver his decision, Kgosi Linchwe II based his argument on a
notion of fairness. He did not introduce the notion of fault at all.

Kgosi Linchwe II's judgment

> When a woman is to return to her parents' home, a man is ordered to
> give her some property, any property including cattle, in other words,
> a reasonable subsistence. A woman should not go back to her parents
> with nothing at all. Reasonable subsistence is a matter to be decided by
> the kgosi and the men who are listening and discussing the case in the
> kgotla. In the case of Makoke versus Makoke which was presided over
> by Kgosi Linchwe II, we gave the woman 140. We found that it was a
> reasonable share because she also was entitled to live a better [decent]
> life.

He was of the view that a woman should be able to maintain her
standard of living: "In this case between Mrs. Seitshiro and Mr. Seitshiro,
I find that Mrs. Seitshiro's position has been simplified because she
wants only sixty head of cattle and ten goats." He went on to explain,
"She doesn't demand estate cattle. She demands the cattle which she
worked for, because, according to law, if people separate they have to
share the cattle which they jointly acquired when they married." He
commented that estate cattle are "cattle which have been handed down
from father to son," from "generation to generation," and which "must
remain with the man." They are "not to be divided between the man
and his wife." In fact, at the cattlepost at Lephephe, Mathilda was given

twenty-three head of cattle while Seitshiro was left with 161 head of cattle in his kraal (excluding calves).

In terms of the immovable property acquired during marriage, Kgosi Linchwe II emphasized an equitable division:

> I listened to your case regarding your immovable property. You have two fenced yards here; one yard is for dwelling premises. I therefore decide that Mrs. Seitshiro shall take the bottle store and butchery. The toilet will be used jointly by them, each one will keep a separate key. The office goes to Mr. Seitshiro. The dwelling house belongs to both Mr. Seitshiro and Mrs. Seitshiro. When they die the premises shall go to their last born son, whose name is Kesebonye. If Kesebonye should die while you two parents are living the premises will go to your first born son, Ramarettwa. If he should die before he is married the premises shall go to the first born son of the first wife; that is the rule according to Tswana custom.

Kgosi Linchwe II made it clear that if Seitshiro married again he must build a separate house for his new wife and "not bring her into the mentioned premises." He also compensated Mathilda for her loss of enjoyment of the premises with three oxen.

Different Perspectives on Division

The headmen from Molepolole who attended the division were astounded by the division made in Mathilda's favor. While they considered that Seitshiro was not to be trusted and was the one who was at fault in the breakdown of the relationship, they would never have awarded Mathilda the number of cattle that Kgosi Linchwe II did. Nor would they have awarded her a half share of the property other than cattle. It was the talk of Molepolole for weeks afterward. In their view, referring back to Kgosi Linchwe II's handling of Pepere, it was not based on "old traditional Tswana ways of doing things; it was done according to modern ideas." Within Botswana Kgosi Linchwe II is viewed as a very distinctive personality with particular views, who has made his own mark on chiefship.

Mathilda, like Mmashaoudi, was well aware that she had fared better under Kgosi Linchwe II than she would have under Kwena judges, but like Mmashaoudi she had brought cattle into the relationship and felt she had suffered under Seitshiro's control. In a later interview (22 July 1982) she confided that Seitshiro had sold and hidden many of the cattle so that those found at the cattlepost did not reflect the true size of their holdings, which in 1977 had numbered over three hundred full-grown animals.

COMPARISON: ACCOUNTING FOR DIFFERENCE

The Seitshiro dispute was handled in a very different way from that of the Busangs. These disputes raise questions about what activates the types of arguments that are utilized and the forms of procedure that are employed, which can, despite sharing the same location, reflect radically different processes and lead to the denial of any share of the property to one woman and the award of a substantial share to another. Mathilda was able to command attention in a way that Gofetamang could never do. How can we account for this? Was it simply that she was more articulate, more knowledgeable, that she had more status, or that she was appearing before a more sympathetic third party?

Frameworks for Interpretation: Common and Customary Law

To provide an explanation solely on the basis of individual or personal difference is to ignore the framework within which social relations are articulated. A more informed analysis takes account of this framework, which in this case engages with law. In this context these disputes could be interpreted in terms of different legal models. In doing so it is tempting to fall back onto those models provided by the formal legal system which distinguish between customary and common law—to associate the Busang case with the former and the Seitshiro case with the latter.

The discussion and decision in the Busang dispute concentrated on the issue of fault, which is viewed by Bakwena as central to a division of property under customary law. In the Seitshiro dispute, however, attention was concentrated on the ascertainment of assets and their division between the parties, which seem to reflect a "European" approach based on community of property. Although Kgosi Linchwe II's responses controlled the scope of discussion, they may also be interpreted as a subconscious incorporation of European ideas through his references to community of property. Indeed, this was the perception of wardheads from Molepolole who viewed what Kgosi Linchwe II was doing as something associated with "modern" ideas and "common" law. One might argue that the Seitshiro division took the form it did because Mr. Seitshiro was considered to be at fault. Although the issue of fault was never expressly articulated, it was implicit in the process, and it was clear that

Kgosi Linchwe II regarded Mr. Seitshiro as an untrustworthy man who sold cattle without consulting his wife. However, even if fault played a role, it cannot be used as the sole rationale for the decision, which astounded the wardheads from Molepolole. These wardheads, even allowing for the fact that Mr. Seitshiro was at fault, would have nonetheless awarded him a far greater share of the property.

In giving his decision Kgosi Linchwe II expressly referred to cases heard in the High Court as authority which he would follow, even though they concerned "people who married according to community of property." He also made references to "the hard rule of common law and equity." His division of property followed that of cases drawing on different legal roots, namely, the Molomo case (which involved common law and the application of community of property) and the Moisakamo case (which involved the application of customary law by the High Court).[5]

The influence of common law, however, is not limited to the Seitshiro dispute. It is also present in the Busang dispute. Mr. Sebele, like Kgosi Linchwe II, was aware of its existence and used it at various points to control proceedings. We may recall Mrs. Busang's insistence on maintaining her claim to 135 pula, representing the proceeds from knitting jerseys. When she refused to drop it Mr. Sebele shifted his argument to one that may be seen as European, demanding proof of the money's existence with reference to a bank statement. Immediately following this interchange, when a kgotla member raised the issue of "the cause of their divorce" he was silenced by Sebele, who informed him, "The time for that question has gone; this case was tried at the High Court and that was where all such questions were asked. All the questions must be based on the distribution of property. Since they are married in community of property what belongs to one belongs to the other; that is why she is asking for distribution of property." While Mr. Sebele's response controls the scope of discussion, it may also be interpreted as a subconscious incorporation of European ideas. He talks of "community of property" and limits questions to those concerning "distribution of property." Matters that have been dealt with in the High Court must not be raised again because they are res judicata. When another kgotla member asks about the alleged abortion, this is dismissed as irrelevant on the same grounds, that "we must bear in mind that this question was raised in the High Court. We are here to listen to Mrs. Busang and why she thinks she is entitled to the property."

References to common law are not limited to Mr. Sebele. Mr. Busang also referred to it in terms of the High Court to support his arguments in the kgotla. It was as influential in the Busang case as it was in the case of the Seitshiros. However, common law is utilized for different purposes. In the Busang dispute it was used to endorse the kgotla's finding of fault; in the Seitshiro dispute it was used to used to support a "no fault" approach based on the parties' actual contributions to marital property. The fact that common law may be used for different purposes demonstrates its flexibility and undermines any attempt to confine it to a particular institutional setting, such as the magistrate's court or High Court.

Confounding Formal Legal Models: Reconfiguring Law

This does not mean that what is happening is merely an extension of common law within a customary setting—in other words that customary law has been overtaken by common law and that the influence is all one way. Close attention to detail reveals that the Seitshiro dispute, which purports to represent a model of common law, exhibits aspects which are inconsistent with such a model. While Kgosi Linchwe II talked about cases in which the system of community of property endorsed by statute applied, he did so in his own terms. He did not divide the cattle equally, according to the principle of community of property based on European and Roman-Dutch law. The estate and serotwane (endowment) cattle which Mrs. Seitshiro's family had provided for the marriage were excluded. In excluding such cattle he was following traditional Tswana practice. He may have borrowed the language of community of property and talked of joint division, but he did so within his own context. The same is true of his approach to immovable property. The parties were not given outright ownership of assets as they would under a community of property system. Instead they only received a right to use with ownership reserved for their children after their deaths. To provide for the children's inheritance, during the parties' lifetime, is also common Tswana practice often done through the earmarking of cattle, but it is not an aspect of divorce within a European or South African system of community of property.

Such actions illustrate the complexities of defining legal models according to certain fixed criteria and prescribed rules, a problem that is underscored by the fact that the Molomo case, dealt with in the High Court on the basis of a common law jurisdiction involving community of property rules, also excluded estate cattle from the division of property. In doing so the Molomo case can be seen to be upholding Tswana custom within a common law setting. Similarly, the Busang dispute, said to represent a customary model of law, contains elements which reflect a European or common law influence.

In his handling of the dispute, Mr. Sebele spoke in the language of joint property and community of property, although like Kgosi Linchwe II he placed his own interpretation on these terms. His handling of the dispute can be said to reflect a continual shift from a European to a Tswana mode of inquiry. When he silenced the kgotla member who asked about the cause of the divorce and declared that all questions must relate to the distribution of property, he was acting like a European judge, treating the matter as one that had already been adjudicated upon. When he allowed Mr. Busang to restate the case he raised at the High Court, he was acting in a Tswana mode which considered that such conduct was relevant to Kwena perceptions of fault and distribution of property.

Both the Busang and Seitshiro disputes illustrate the way in which law is integrated into people's lives and, given this integration, how the processes at work cannot adequately be described in terms of customary or common law models. Based on outdated conceptions of difference, arising from a distinction made between Europeans and Africans during a period of colonial overrule, such models do not provide an adequate explanation for what is currently taking place or for the diversity of outcomes that exist.

An alternative and more meaningful explanation is provided by considering the parties and third parties in such disputes not only as individuals, but also as social beings linked to networks with access to certain kinds of resources. These cover a variety of spheres. How individuals are situated within such networks and in terms of their sphere of operation has a bearing on the kinds of claims they may make, how these are articulated, and the kinds of responses they receive.

Resources and Terms of Discourse: Salariat versus Peasantariat

From this perspective Mathilda and Gofetamang were differentially situated. Through her education, Mathilda was able to pursue a career as a nurse. This has given her social status particularly in her position as matron of a hospital. It has also taken her into full-time and secure employment guaranteeing her direct access to money. She is one of those people who fall within that privileged group, the salariat. In this position she was able to acquire assets and to point to the specific contributions that she had made with these assets to family property. Her life experience provided her with an opportunity to develop another line of argument with respect to her property claims and bypass the notion of fault, which so bedeviled the Busang dispute.

Through her sphere of operations she has had access to a world that lies beyond the reach of Gofetamang Busang. She has been able to construct a status for herself that does not depend on where she fits in a kin network, although such connections may enhance a person's position, as they did in the case of Mr. Busang, who not only has access to the world of Mathilda by virtue of being a highly placed civil servant, but is also linked through kin to the ruling Kwena elite. Murray Busang is able to operate in both worlds, embracing kin networks linked to a domain of lands, cattle, and domestic activities as well as to the domain of regular employment, government structures, and finance. In contrast, Mathilda's husband, Seitshiro Seitshiro, is more closely connected to the former domain, although he had some links with the latter through his employment as a borehole mechanic, and more significantly through exposure to the financial world in connection with the family businesses. However, Mathilda has much stronger links with the latter than he does, and she was able to use this to strengthen her position.

In comparison, Gofetamang Busang, with her minimal education and containment within the domestic sphere (although she was just beginning to branch out into the commercial sphere by knitting jerseys), found herself operating within the peasantariat's domain of lands, cattle, and domestic activities, which operates as the predominant paradigm within which wardheads and many other Kwena officials in Molepolole operate. Within this setting she did not have the power to challenge Murray, as her kin networks were less prestigious and she found herself bound by the gendered coding of a good wife.

Through their spheres of operation, these women found themselves in very different positions when it came to articulating their claims in the kgotla. When asked to outline her claim to property, Mrs. Seitshiro was able to talk in terms of the financial contribution that she had made to the assets in question. Indeed, the whole focus of the discussion between her and Mr. Seitshiro centered around who had provided money and what assets had been purchased with it. By concentrating on such issues Mathilda was able to engage her husband in a debate which cen-

tered on material factors and which bypassed the more elusive considerations of a fault-based perspective. This was a different means of engaging in the discussion, one which found sympathy with Kgosi Linchwe II.

Gofetamang was not unfortunately in the same position as Mathilda. She was unable to establish any direct financial contribution to the
property except with regard to the money she acquired through knitting
jerseys. This was something which Mr. Sebele was initially prepared to
consider, although he rejected the claim on the basis that the source of
her profit had derived from her husband, who had purchased the knitting machine and the wool. Unlike Mathilda, Gofetamang did not have
the same resources at her disposal to bolster her position or manipulate
lines of argument within the dispute. As she was only educated to an
elementary level, she was unable to pursue a career beyond the domestic
sphere, except as a cleaner. As her sphere of operation situated her
within the domain of lands, cattle, and domestic activities, this made
her much more susceptible to assessment of her claims on the basis of a
different set of criteria from those which were applied to Mathilda.

These criteria shifted the focus from material contribution to the
assets in question, to an evaluation of contributions of a different
nature, namely those stemming from her conduct as a wife in her per-
formance of the marital role. We are made aware of this at the very
beginning of the Busang dispute. Gofetamang was provided with an opportunity to establish her claim to the assets, but her inability to develop
this along the lines of financial contribution not only reduced the scope
of her claim to the assets—because she had to establish a specific contribution—but also made her vulnerable to discussions of her marital conduct, which opened up the question of fault. She was unable to control
the form that the dispute took, and the rapidity with which discussion
centered on her conduct as a wife laid her open to allegations of fault.

The Busang and Seitshiro disputes present different processes and
forms of manipulation which are centered around different spheres of
operation. The abilities of the women in these disputes to participate in
the disputing process presented a stark contrast. In one case, Mathilda
had status, knowledge, and confidence, whereas in the other, Gofetamang had none of these attributes. Such attributes are socially constructed and draw heavily on an individual and his or her family's
political connections and his or her experience of education and employment. Through her education, employment, and experience beyond
the domestic sphere, Mathilda was able to hold her own in the kgotla,
whereas Gofetamang, with her limited experience, was subjected to ma-

nipulation by others and was unable to create the space within which she might have been heard.

Constraints of Gender

However, even where woman are able, like Mathilda, to make themselves heard, they still have to accept that they are operating within a gendered environment, that is, one where women in their roles as wives find themselves differentially situated compared with their husbands in terms of claims to property. The Busang dispute provides a clear illustration of this, demonstrating the structural hurdles that women are required to overcome. However, it is also at work, less visibly, in the Seitshiro dispute. Through her sphere of operations, Mathilda had more scope to develop her property claims than Gofetamang, but she was still operating under some constraints.

She was unable to lay claim to any of the estate cattle, resulting in Seitshiro retaining 161 fully grown animals compared with her award of twenty-three. Male control over cattle can lead to reclassification of some animals to bring them within the estate category; this is often accompanied by underhanded fixing of brands.[6] It also makes it very difficult to establish how many cattle there are, because men hide and sell them. Mathilda was well aware that Seitshiro had been doing this, as was Kgosi Linchwe II, who made allowances for this in his award. However, it is difficult to establish the scale on which this takes place, and Mathilda wisely did not emphasize her real losses for fear that this would undermine her credibility. To be seen to be claiming too much would place her in the role of the unreasonable woman. While Mathilda's half share of the modern dwelling house in Tlokweng was recognized, it was Seitshiro as head of the family who was to hold it in trust for their children. She was denied control, and the three oxen awarded to compensate her for her lack of access to and use of this asset did not really reflect the value of what she had lost.

What counts as law in these two disputes reflects a repertoire of differing forms of normative ordering on which individuals may draw. Given the conditions under which most Batswana live, more women are likely, in reality, to find themselves subject to the normative framework governing Mrs. Busang's dispute than are likely to find themselves operating within the terms of reference informing Mrs. Seitshiro's world. But even where they are successful in shifting the terms of reference, as Mathilda Seitshiro managed to do, they are still constrained by the gendered construction of Tswana family relationships and property. How this gendered construction is formed and how it affects women have been absent from earlier ethnographic studies of law in Botswana.

Implications for Legal Analysis

In Botswana, it is clear that any analysis of law must incorporate the legal system as a whole and that any attempts to focus on customary and common law as discrete entities that stand apart from one another cannot be sustained. Earlier ethnographies on law (including those written in the postcolonial period [Comaroff and Roberts 1981; Kuper 1970]), failed to address the national legal context, thereby limiting their study of village life to certain forms of local ordering divorced from the broader national dimension and their relationship with the state. In some cases (Comaroff and Roberts 1981), this was predicated on the premise that engagement with the formal legal system would inevitably privilege a particular legal perspective associated with legal centralism, which in turn would dominate and distort the interpretation of Tswana law.[7] But equally, to leave it out of the account is to ignore an important aspect of law in Botswana. For Kwena narratives show that ordinary people pursue claims against one another in particular forums—the chief's kgotla, magistrate's court, and High Court—which form part of the formal legal system. This raises questions about how Western law is to be perceived and to what extent its analysis must rest upon the form of analysis associated with legal centralism.

It is true that recourse to institutions associated with the formal legal system brings them within the orbit of centralist legal discourse outlined earlier in this book. In this discourse, power and authority are constructed from specific sources and institutions which set law apart from other social domains and which uphold an image of autonomy, neutrality, and equality. But this separation between legal and social domains, which is crucial to a centralist model of law, is one that cannot be sustained in the Kwena context. For the narratives underline the extent to which social understandings, expectations, and values permeate law—regardless of whether law is located within a customary or Western setting. This is illustrated through the ways in which women's partnerships with men are viewed and handled in the ordinary world of everyday life as well as in legal forums associated with courts.

Such observations are not new, forming part of an anthropological or sociological perspective as they do. But they are important. This form of analysis, which takes account of individuals as social beings linked to networks with gendered attributes, provides a perspective which looks beyond the confines of common and customary law. It provides for an evaluation of disputes with contradictory outcomes (represented by the cases of the Busangs and Seitshiros) which does not simply treat them as the products of different chiefs applying their own perceptions of customary law. Rather, it analyzes these disputes in terms of differentially situated networks which vary according to the parties' spheres of operation and which may be located at different points on a social scale drawn from everyday life. Such networks, exemplified by the peasantariat and salariat, give rise to varying forms of discourse. How individuals are situated with respect to those networks will affect their power to construct a form of discourse in support of their claims.

This type of analysis, which takes account of individuals as social beings linked to networks with gendered attributes, provides a perspective on law which looks beyond its classification as common or customary to the world of economic and social differentiation. Such an approach adopts a socially oriented perspective which moves away from a law-centered approach to disparity. Rather than locating law as the central reference point for the construction of difference, it places the focus on the ways in which social processes themselves give rise to such difference and configure or reshape law. In this account of law, it is essential to recognize how power and the discourses to which it gives rise are constructed. Only with this knowledge can an understanding of the conditions under which such discourses may be altered or transformed be acquired.

Such a dimension is absent from a centralist account of law, but it is an especially important consideration when dealing with a legal system that endorses overt pluralism. This is because where such pluralism exists, there is a tendency to align different forms of discourse with the different classificatory forms existing within the formal legal system. This is misleading, for by focusing on the formal classification of law it renders invisible the power of individuals, arising out of their position in social life, to engage in varying forms of discourse. This is significant because the terms of reference and forms of dialogue they create transcend boundaries of the type set up by the formal legal system, which focuses on regimes of rules and institutional settings. Engaging in this form of analysis rather than a legal centralist one makes possible a more sophisticated account of legal process—an account that provides for an understanding of concurrence and difference both within and between social domains, as well as their relationship with law and the circumstances which may give rise to change. As the narratives and life histories in this book demonstrate, such an understanding is an essential component of any analysis concerning women's access to, and use of, law. For women's power to construct any form of discourse, regardless of the forum or court in which it is located, is framed by the gendered world in which they live.

EIGHT

Reconfiguring Law: A Differentiating Perspective

My study of gender and justice in an African community centers on two interrelated themes. These are women's experiences of the world in which they negotiate their status, on which claims to property and resources in family life are based, and their encounters with law, as represented by both official and customary institutions and practices. These themes are integrated through a study of the relationship that exists between procreation and marriage, a study common to both social sciences and law. This study is based on a discussion of everyday life derived from women's and men's life histories and narratives of dispute highlighting the whole range of relationships and the diversity that exists in heterosexual partnerships in actual practice. The study raises questions about the extent to which marriage merits or continues to merit the central role in family life accorded to it. Thus, it highlights the need to address this question through an analysis of power and an understanding of how power operates to facilitate or constrain individuals in their negotiation of heterosexual partnerships with one another and how this affects the kinds of choices available to them.

An analysis of power is critical to understanding the options open to Kwena women, given the gendered nature of their world and its social and legal domains. This world is one in which inequality between the sexes, derived from the sexual division of labor within the family, operates to place women in a less powerful position from which to negotiate their status with men generally, not only within the family domain but also in the social world at large, which includes formal legal institutions. The composition of families and the organization of households in which women live have a direct impact on women's abilities to mobilize the resources on which power in social life is based.

In this context, marriage plays a role in setting the parameters within which procreative relationships between women and men are negotiated, even if only to establish their nonmarital status. Thus, marriage operates as a catalyst for social understandings of and legal ap-

211

proaches to women's partnerships with men. Where the law is concerned, women find that their access to and experience of legal process bring them into a confrontation with a dominant discourse that reinforces social inequalities based on gender existing between men and women in their roles as unmarried partners or spouses in daily life. While it is true that gender intersects with a whole range of other factors which come together to situate individuals in their negotiations with one another, it is one that consistently operates to place women at a disadvantage in their dealings with men, except in certain circumstances. Women actively seek to overcome the restraints placed on them by adopting their own legal strategies differing from those of men and, where possible, by challenging the terms of the discourse with which they are presented. But they are usually successful only where they can set aside the normal constraints facing them, an undertaking which is only viable in situations where their male counterparts are correspondingly unable to rely on those resources that would normally be available to provide support for them. Such constraints may be due to a man's race or class, which may vary significantly from that of the woman and impinge on his authority in ways that would not affect him were both parties of the same racial classification or class.

For these reasons my analysis of power in relation to law is not limited to the study of formal legal institutions, or officeholders, or disputes, but is grounded in everyday life. It considers how individuals are situated in networks of kinship, family, and community, and the features which affect their position within material and symbolic hierarchies, including whether or not they are members of the peasantariat or salariat as well as their gender. For such elements form part of the multiple ways in which individuals are restricted in their forms of expression, including their ability to negotiate status and to articulate claims against one another. An analysis of the way in which these elements frame individuals' powers of expression is not simply limited or confined to observing what goes on in formal legal settings, whether central or local, that are upheld by the state. My analysis not only highlights the circumstances under which people do or do not have access to these legal forums, but also accounts more generally for the conditions under which individuals find themselves silenced or unable to negotiate with others in day-to-day social life.

This perspective is crucial when it comes to assessing the relationship that exists between a formal legal system and people's access to law.

It makes visible what is otherwise ignored in analyses of law that stem from a centralist paradigm, in which issues of power and authority are addressed from a particular standpoint. This standpoint is derived from a specific set of sources, including statutes, cases, courts, and legal personnel, that are associated with a Western model of law. But one challenge posed at the beginning of this book is the extent to which any analysis of law in a postcolonial context that engages with such a model is bound to reproduce and reinforce a centralist paradigm of law. Or rather, whether it is possible to provide for another account of law. The difficulty in adopting this approach is that a certain legal framework must be acknowledged. It must be incorporated into any analysis of law that is presented. So the texts, institutions, and personnel that are associated with a centralist model of law continue as part of the legal landscape and as such retain legal status. But that does not mean that the centralist vision of law must be upheld or that a more integrated perspective on law cannot exist. As this study shows, it does not necessarily follow that working with these terms of reference inevitably reproduces a centralist vision of law. Another perspective is viable.

The challenge lies in working with a framework that focuses on the bounded nature of law and that makes a distinction between law and nonlaw. This framework creates a dilemma for all legal pluralists of the nonjuristic variety who adhere to the "strong" (J. Griffiths 1986) or "new" (Merry 1988) form of pluralism because they are confronted by a powerful paradigm which has already established the ground rules for a study of law. By upholding a distinction between law and nonlaw, this paradigm meets any attempt to undermine it with the claim that what is presented is not law for it does not meet the criteria set by such a model. So what does not fit is cast aside. Not only that, but pluralists have to overcome the accusation of being imprecise theorists who, in their attempts to reconceptualize law in broader terms drawn from an array of normative orders operating more generally in social life, fail to make a distinction between law and nonlaw and thus to provide for an analytical concept of law.

My study of law cannot be dismissed on these grounds, as it engages with those aspects that qualify as law in centralist terms while at the same time undermining any image of law that is accredited to this model. In my discussion of law, the features associated with legal centralism are incorporated into a broader set of social relations where the focus is placed on points of connection between these elements and the varying forms these take. Thus, this is an inclusionary approach rather than an exclusionary one of the kind a centralist model favors. One consequence of this approach is that the issues of gender and social status cannot be ignored. This is particularly important when dealing with centralist claims to legal equality and neutrality which fail to address either the gendered or socially divided world within which law operates. These aspects are made visible by accentuating, as I do, the movement across boundaries rather than adopting a more limited, centralist perspective focused only on the confines of such boundaries and what takes place within them. It is through a focus on the latter, more narrowly defined terrain that the centralist model has been able to sustain so successfully the kind of exclusionary claims that it makes in relation to law.

My approach undermines the centralist perspective, but not at the expense of leaving law in some uncharted territory. The elements that come together to form points of connection are not all defined as law existing in their individual state. In this way, not all norms or components that make up the elements under consideration qualify as law. Those elements that I regard as law do derive from those aspects of law (e.g., sources and institutions) associated with a centralist model. However, what is crucial to my model is the processes through which all elements (both legal and nonlegal in centralist terms) come into contact with one another and the points of connection that emerge.

It is at this stage, where the focus is on processes and points of connection, that the way in which those elements previously defined as law in centralist terms is transformed. Those elements associated with a centralist model of law, such as cases, institutions, and personnel, acquire another meaning. They adopt another character through the processes of exposure to and integration with other sets of elements. They become redefined through the processes of interconnection. While these elements continue to have a legal character, it is not the one ascribed by a centralist model. This is because the processes referred to above form an integral part of a reevaluation of legal institutions and present law in another dimension.

The accompanying analysis leads to a reconfiguration of law, one that draws on certain centralist and pluralist aspects of law but in a way which diverges from both these paradigms in important respects. This approach is alien to a centralist model because it undercuts a perception of power solely derived from these sources. In other words, it does not accept these features as being the only reference points from which relations of power are established and interpreted. It is this latter perception of power vested in law (in the centralist sense) that has given rise to the instrumental approaches to social engineering which have failed so miserably in Africa.

In my analysis of power, those elements associated with a centralist model of law are situated in terms of their relationship with other factors that form part of ongoing processes of social relations. This provides different contexts for the exercise of power and its interpretation. From this perspective the claims to autonomy put forward by the centralist model, with the image of law as suspended, dissociated, and immune from social life, cannot be upheld. In this respect my study has much in common with the work of legal pluralists in the strong sense, who seek to reorient our perceptions of law toward a more pluralistic model derived from normative forms of ordering that are a feature of everyday life.

However, through my approach, law does not lose its specificity. Nor does it retain its specificity at the cost of endorsing a centralist perspective on law. Legal centralists lay great claim to specificity as one of the features they employ to exclude challenge from any other accounts. On this basis centralists dismiss much of legal pluralism, on the grounds that what the latter puts forward is too nonspecific or diffuse to count as law. In my approach, law retains its specificity without adopting a centralist image, even though my account of law incorporates certain elements that are present in a centralist model.

Although such aspects are present, my approach does not reproduce an essentialist or reductionist vision of the kind associated with legal centralism. This is because I examine the interrelationship between legal and nonlegal domains in ways which completely undermine such a vision. This examination incorporates a whole range of features which, although nonlegal in origin (in centralist terms), have a bearing on and transform the ways in which law is perceived through the processes of exchange and integration that take place. It is precisely by taking account of all features and the specificity of their forms of interaction that differential forms of access to, and use of, law are made explicit. This is done by explicating the multiple ways in which numerous sources of power in everyday life are configured and reconfigured to converge with law.

ACCESS TO THE RESOURCES OF LAW

The Sources of Power

Power is derived from the networks with which individuals are affiliated. In the Kwena case this is presented in terms of the families and house-holds of which men and women engaged in procreative relationships form part. Locating individuals within these broader terms of reference follows the classic approach adopted by historians and social scientists, especially social anthropologists. However, the connections made and the range of resources taken into account in my analyses of individual, household, and family relationships transcend the public/private divide erected by many earlier studies, particularly those grounded in capital-ism. I will come back to this point, which feminist scholars highlight because of the way in which this artificial divide operates to disempower women through its failure to make explicit the gendered nature of the world in which both women and men live. As H. Moore (1988:2) among others (Boateng 1994; Harris 1981; Robertson 1991) has pointed out, it is not that women fail to feature in empirical studies but rather the way with which they are dealt on theoretical and analytical levels that is problematic.

History and the Past

One key to understanding the present is to look to the past. Indeed, the past of historical accounts and ethnographies reinforces the current perception that what exists in present-day Tswana procreative relation-ships is a growing alienation of procreation from marriage, with links between the two no longer assured or unproblematic. This perception arises because accounts of and from the past stress the importance of marriage in upholding the role of kinship as being central to the social, political, and economic life of Tswana merafe (the same, of course, is said of many societies). Such accounts highlight the ways in which kin-ship once provided the idiom within which social relations were negoti-ated and in terms of which status and hierarchy were established and embodied through the domain of the household. In situating these accounts it is important to recognize the extent to which they reflect a dominant discourse or represent ideological considerations set against social reality—with all the problems that this entails with regard to the use of historical sources (Vaughan 1983). But it is also true that changes occur over time, and understanding the present with reference to the past also involves a recognition of the transformations that have come about and their integration into the discourse.

With kinship operating in the past as the sole—or at least principal—matrix for social, political, and economic relations, marriage assumed an importance not only for elites within a social group but also for more economically successful if less politically prominent commoners. Marriage provided the basis upon which kinship relations were fashioned and manipulated, and scholars have stressed the different kinds of marriage strategies adopted by elites and commoners associated with different means of access to power. The multiple ways in which individuals may be related continue to provide scope for negotiation with regard to the kinds of social relations that parties wish to establish or uphold at any one time. Not only that, but the social processes that provide for the inherently negotiable status surrounding kinship also endorse the kind of ambiguity that surrounds the status of a customary marriage.

The basis for these accounts of marriage strategies is an ideological conception of the household founded on the concepts of agnation and matrilaterality that define the social universe. These concepts construct relations in society through male and female lines and are invested with gendered attributes which relate to the qualities associated with maleness and femaleness.

These sets of relations complement one another and have symbolic significance in the ideological realm attached to marriage. They underlie the reasoning behind marital strategies. The models of marriage strategy put forward reflect a male-centered universe where women exist only to create links in a set of relations primarily formulated around men and male access to power. Such models associate men with the public or politico-jural domain and with the competitive, aggressive relations of the market, while relegating women to the nurturing, supportive, private domain of the family. Feminist scholars challenge this view of the social universe where it upholds a rigid separation between public and private, and male and female domains. Instead, they stress the ways in which public and private spheres are inextricably interrelated. They do, however, recognize the importance of the public/private division as an ideological construct underlining the way in which men and women are associated with specific but different spheres of sociality invested with different sets of attributes.

Feminists highlight the ways in which gender stereotypes are developed and used in strategies which individuals of both sexes employ to advance their interests in various social contexts. H. Moore (1988:37), for example, notes how the power of such statements such as "Women are like children: they speak before they think," although they do not reflect an accurate social representation of women, is nonetheless pervasive and operates not only to provide a strategic reason for women's exclusion from activities such as politics but also to ensure that they will be so excluded. The clearest example of this kind of ideological manipulation in this book is presented in the gender stereotypes of husband and wife and the ways in which these are negotiated by the parties and communities concerned in both social and legal terms.

The historical and ethnographic accounts of Tswana family life presented in previous chapters indicate that the gendered role attributed to women in the Tswana ideological realm also found expression in the material world through women's differential access to and control over resources compared with that of men. This difference derived from differential patterns of ownership attached to the products of men and women's labor, which affected a woman's ability to accumulate the kinds of resources that produced status and power within a community. For a number of feminist scholars (Sacks 1979; Leacock 1978; Delphy and Leonard 1992), access to and control over resources is a key element in accounting for the gendered position in which women find themselves. However, these scholars acknowledge that productive and reproductive processes cannot be understood in isolation from the cultural perceptions which people have of those processes. In other words, it is a question not just of who has access to what resources, but of both what people do and the cultural understandings that underlie their actions (Collier and Rosaldo 1981:276).

Among Batswana, as in certain other societies, the ownership in question was based on a system of land tenure, cattle keeping, and rights to property through inheritance which centered around men and the passing of such property from father to son through each generation. Although women could acquire rights to such property, their scope for doing so was more limited than that of men, and even where such scope existed control over property was often mediated through men, as for example in the case of cattle, where taboos excluded women from the domain of herding at the cattlepost.[1] In addition, women faced discrimination through their exclusion from local political life and the holding of political office (except on rare occasion), to which their fathers, brothers, and husbands had access as a matter of course through household affiliation and the kgotla system.

Within this setting, marriage was a key element in the acquisition of status and authority. It marked the transition to adult status, often accompanied by greater control over resources. However, although important for both sexes, the terms on which it operated for men and women were not the same. Labor within households provides one crucial example of the difference. While men could use the unremunerated labor of their wives and other women in the household, the only way in which women could use the labor of male household members was by paying for it with food and drink. In other words, women were obliged to work for the senior members of the household, but men worked for women only if they could exchange labor with them. As noted elsewhere (Guyer 1984), women's dependence on the conjugal relationship for access to resources is linked in complex but historically changing ways to their labor obligations to their husbands, because it is as wives that women gain most of their access to land, labor (male and female), and capital. The different positions men and women occupy with regard to their ability to mobilize various forms of labor is an expression of their social power (Whitehead 1994; Moore and Vaughan 1994); this, as Harris (1981:59) and Vaughan (1985) observe, derives from their position both within the household and within a wider set of social relations outside it.

Transformations in Terms of the Past

This wider set of relations included prolonged contact with Europeans in the nineteenth and twentieth centuries. Such contact precipitated changes in the structure of Tswana merafe through the imposition of colonial overrule. It also brought about transformation through exposure to Christianity as well as the introduction of a cash economy and sustained participation in migrant labor over many years. Such contact created changes in existing structures of authority and had an affect on the ways in which social networks operated.

Within this broader picture, marriage was inevitably affected. Changes in marriage practices included the decline of polygyny (Schapera 1950:45; Schapera and Roberts 1975:266; Comaroff and Roberts 1977) and an increase in the average age at marriage for both sexes (Schapera 1947:173; Timaeus and Graham 1989:392). The prevailing rationale for marriage was undermined (Kuper 1987; Gulbrandsen 1986). Such a rationale had formerly revolved around the structure of the political system based on male hierarchies constructed out of households established through marriage. Marriage, politics, and access to resources were inextricably linked.

Under the pressures of colonial overrule, with the introduction of alternative administrative structures and new means for acquiring resources, this link became more tenuous. In this context, polygynous marriage no longer provided the returns that it once did. Not only that, but access to means of support through migrant labor also placed constraints on marriage. This was because significant numbers of adults (particularly men) were absent from their natal households for extended periods of time. Their prolonged absence helped make marriage partners harder to come by, a situation exacerbated by a decline in polygyny, also under attack by missionaries seeking to impose Christian monogamous marriage, because women were increasingly barred from plural unions with a smaller pool of men. Under these circumstances, both men and women tended to engage in a series of relationships, investigating the potential of various marriage partners and testing the benefits of such associations before committing themselves to one partner. Instead of investing in a number of marriages through polygyny, the pattern became one where only one out of several relationships, contemporaneous or serial, acquired the status of a marriage (Comaroff and Roberts 1977). This led to a situation in which many women had children in a relationship the status of which was unclear.

Over time, a relationship might develop into marriage, but at a much later stage in the parties' lives than had previously been the case; on the other hand, it might never acquire marital status. The effect of such postponement, or alternatively no marriage at all, was an increase in the numbers of adults associated with the natal household. There was also an increase in the generational component of households as many young unmarried women remained at home with their children. According to Gulbrandsen (1986), the economic reorganization of the household that took place in response to these changes created an environment where marriage no longer assumed the central role that it had once possessed for either men or women.

Current Affairs

These kinds of analyses are used to explain the extended life cycle of the household already apparent in the late 1930s and in evidence today. Such analyses generate different perspectives on the significance of marriage. Scholars such as Comaroff and Roberts (1981) continue to stress the importance of marriage and affinal links as a resource, while others such as Gulbrandsen (1986) stress the extent to which marriage no longer provides the access to resources it once did and consequently has fallen out of favor.

These debates underline the dangers of assuming that there can be only one perspective. My research demonstrates that such perspectives need not be incompatible, but must be addressed in the context of the specific circumstances in which individuals and their family and household networks operate. Moving away from the study of ideal types to look at detailed life histories highlights the conditions under which marriage remains an important resource for some while not for others. Although all individuals may be social actors, they are not all endowed with the same status or position within the social hierarchy. This has implications for the ways in which marriage is viewed and operates. As Mann (1985), working on another part of the African continent, demonstrates, responses may prove to be contradictory in respect of one another, depending on the different marital strategies pursued by different social groups. Not only that, but a social group may alter its responses over time to reendorse a position previously marginalized. This underscores the point that marital change cannot be viewed in linear, unidirectional terms as a progressive move from one state to another but must always be kept under review in the light of changing economic, political, and social conditions.

For the members of the peasantariat, who represent a substantial portion of the population in Botswana, marriage may still play an important role in providing access to the broader networks of suprahousehold management and cooperation on which they rely for their subsistence. But it is not uniformly true for others, such as the rural and urban squatter poor. Bakwena life histories mark the varying conditions in which individuals live and the role that these conditions play in shaping their marital perspectives. They also underline the ways in which different responses to gender, procreation, and marriage come back to the issue of power in all its dimensions (Hirschon 1984:1). They bring us back to earlier discussions on gender and how this affects the position of women and men when it comes to negotiating the content of the procreative relationships in which they engage.

H. Moore (1988:46) and Guyer (1981) observe that households maintain their importance for feminist analysis because they organize a large part of women's domestic and reproductive labor. As a result, both the composition and organization of households have direct impact on women's lives and in particular on their ability to gain access to resources, to labor, and to income. Robertson (1991:9) views past failure to make the links between production and reproduction as arising from an inadequate analysis of the social significance of reproduction. This is due to the way in which discussions surrounding reproduction have been confined to the family, lumped together with domestic activities, and then effectively ignored. In Robertson's view (1991:94), inattention to the organization of reproduction has driven a wedge between our understanding of what goes on in households and our understanding of what goes on in society at large. Yet as Harris (1981:59) and Vaughan (1985) observe, the relationships between household members are not defined by the household itself but by the social, economic, and ideological relations outside the unit.

Building on these approaches to analyses, I am able to demonstrate how the family domain, represented through individuals and households, reflects both private and public dimensions. These public and private aspects are an integral part of family life and cannot be separated from one another or treated as conceptually separate, as some scholars (Rosaldo 1974; Lamphere 1974) have attempted to do. They shape the context in which individuals and their families operate in terms of their everyday existence as well as in relation to disputes.

Households form part of the network with which individuals are associated within the broader social domain in Botswana today. Despite transformations that have taken place, there is still a gendered universe operating at an economic and ideological level impinging on the negotiation of procreative relationships. At one level, this is underlined by family relations constructed through the system of inheritance. As Delphy and Leonard (1992:157) observe, transmission of property not only produces effects across time, but also at a particular moment by situating individuals and the powers they possess in relation to one another within a family hierarchy. In this hierarchy, women find themselves accorded subordinate status because—despite modifications of the inheritance system in Botswana which allow women to inherit an increased share of their family's or husband's estates—they are still faced with limits not applicable to men.

These limits on the control of resources place women at a disadvantage when they negotiate their status within and beyond the family. Even when inheritance is not a factor in material terms, men still have better access to and control over land, cattle, labor, employment, and cash. These are the resources on which families and households depend for their existence. In many cases these resources are acquired through suprahousehold pooling and cooperation. Within this kind of network, women are often at a disadvantage because men's work, within and beyond the agricultural sphere, is accorded a higher value than that of women. Because of this, women find that their position in relation to one another, and more generally to society at large, depends on the kind of male networks with which they are associated. They rely on the degree of support for and mutual cooperation with them existing within such networks. There are exceptions, especially among those women associated with the salariat to be discussed shortly, but for most women it is still crucial to maintain links with men.

This is not to say that links between women are not important. When it comes to procreation and child rearing, which women incorporate into their working lives, they also rely on one another for support (Ingstad 1994). This situation encourages intensified links between women, especially mother and daughter. Such links turn on mutual support, with a woman returning to her natal household, giving birth, and leaving her child with her mother or another female relative when she returns to work. While a woman's relatives provide child care she is free to work and to send back money, which is so vital to the rural base. Her child provides labor for the household as he or she develops until mature enough to seek employment. This set of links between women, especially mother, daughter, and grandchild, sustains the different bases that are necessary for survival. However, such links are most effective when incorporated within a network that also operates in association with men.

This is made clear by the impoverished position in which many female-headed households find themselves. These are the households that lack adult male affiliation or support because husbands, other male relatives, or partners are dead or have dissociated themselves from a household, for whatever reason. In this situation, female-headed households (particularly among the peasantariat) are at a severe disadvantage because of the enhanced difficulties they face in acquiring resources. For some households this is only a temporary state, but the more it is prolonged, the worse the situation becomes. While the life cycle of a household devolves and children mature into adults, children who have experienced extended deprivation continue to find themselves disadvantaged as adults. This affects their ability to establish and maintain households (Motzafi-Haller 1986). In this way, the cycle of poverty perpetuates itself, so that this particular kind of household continues to exist on the margins of society.

Women as Wives

Among these marginal households, motherhood and marriage have become separated, a phenomenon widely observed (Izzard 1985) in current Botswana life. However, women as wives still operate within a gendered environment. Men's enhanced ability to draw on all forms of resources essential for a family base places them in a stronger position than women to accumulate what is necessary to form a household; this also provides them with power and status in the social world in which they live. Women who are married not only face the constraints of motherhood and limited economic opportunity, but also have to contend with their role as wives. It is not just control over resources that is important, but also, as Murray (1981b) and Channock (1982, 1985) observe elsewhere, the way in which men construct and uphold tradition, which provides a powerful ideological tool for inscribing women.

Through marriage women may improve their access to resources and enhance their status but still find they are located within unequal power relations with their husbands. These inequalities arise from the different positions men and women occupy in the family hierarchy, which not only involve access to and authority over resources, but also are due to the different social conceptions that attach to the roles of husband and wife. Although these conceptions in Botswana are the product of specific historical and social factors, they accord with feminist findings in other parts of the world that comment on the gendered nature of marriage and these roles (Okin 1989:4; Pateman 1989:131; Smart 1984; Fineman 1991:265).

The Kwena disputes demonstrate this point most clearly and highlight the extent to which marriage continues to inform the way in which procreative relationships are negotiated. Even where relationships are nonmarital, women still find themselves in the shadow of marriage and being judged accordingly. This observation is not limited to Botswana. All kinds of relationships and families find themselves understood, compared, or treated in terms of one form of family life which has its roots in marriage and is endorsed by law, as others have observed (Smart 1984:xii; Delphy and Leonard 1992:4–5). Pateman (1989:131) observes how the status of wife structures the personal circumstances of individuals—circumstances which, according to Smart (1984:xiii), are most clearly exposed on divorce, when women's economic vulnerability caused by marriage and the sexual division of labor is laid bare. Fineman (1991:265) comments on the extent to which this economic vulnerability is a product of the way in which society perceives marriage and on how the relationship of husband and wife profoundly affects the way in which rules governing property distribution at divorce are selected and applied.

Knowing this, Kwena women exercise care in the kinds of issues they choose to make public in confrontations with their spouses and in the ways they present them. Given their vulnerable position, this usually involves establishing credibility over the long term by building on a series of family consultations and hearings over a number of years. Under accusations of neglect and lack of support—which are only too real— wives often seek to pursue a larger agenda concerning the preservation of present and future rights to their family property if this has come under threat from their husbands' relationships with and behavior toward other women and their families. Part of the strategy involves an attempt to preempt what might happen in the future. In this situation, the focus is on potential future developments rather than the past. In the knowledge that the marital relationship might be publicly dissolved through divorce at some future date—with all the consequences this entails—a wife attempts to strengthen her vulnerable position in advance, by establishing prospective credibility and compliance with her role.

These observations on the vulnerability of women have also been the subject of more general comment. Okin (1989:167), for example, marks the way in which asymmetric power relations between husband and wife, based on dependence, affect wives' potential for a satisfactory exit from marriage. This is significant, for knowledge of what is likely to occur on dissolution affects the balance of power within the family and therefore changes the effectiveness of wives' voices within marriage. Women take this into account when deciding what issues to contest with their spouses.

While underlining the constraints women face as wives, Kwena disputes also reveal the differences that exist between women arising through the varying networks of which they form part. These differences make clear the need to carry out detailed case studies so that an analysis of gender is based on specific, concrete experiences derived from people's lives. In feminist scholarship, this marks a move away from treating the category "woman" as a universal and homogeneous entity or from any suggestion that there is a prototypical woman whose interests can shape a feminist agenda (Pateman and Shanley 1991:9).[2] Constructions, like that of Ortner (1974), which universalize the social world in terms of a dichotomy between nature and culture (constructed out of the differing domains attributed to women and men) must be rejected because they set up gendered domains designed to bridge all cultures and historical periods (Collier and Yanagisako 1987; Pateman 1989:125). For as Strathern (1980), among others, observes, the category "woman" is not universal but is always culturally and historically specific.

This raises the problem of the need to recognize the differences of race, class, religion, ethnicity, and nationality experienced by women (H. Moore 1993), while at the same time recognizing that they may also have experiences in common. In other words, it raises the problem of the need to avoid an essentialist perspective based on universals. Bakwena life histories illuminate the diversity that exists among women as well as the points of reference they have in common. The balance lies in taking proper account of difference before establishing common reference points. Women do share similar difficulties and experiences the world over, but, as H. Moore (1988:198) observes, these similarities must be demonstrated and specified in each case and not assumed. While we must accept that women's experiences do overlap, all women are not necessarily at one with each other. That this is so does not invalidate attempts to seek common ground, for again, as H. Moore points out, in order to assert communalities it is not necessary that all women be the same.

The Kwena data reveal the conditions which give rise to differences between families and which foster gender relations. These hinge on the varying types of networks in Botswana today. The differences have implications for women, and for their power to negotiate procreative relationships, not only at the level of choosing whether to marry, but also with regard to the terms in which the choice takes place. Others elsewhere have commented on a growing tendency on the part of women to choose not to marry (Obbo 1980; Allison 1985). What are the conditions under which such options can be exercised?

Women within the peasantariat find their choices mediated through a particular position in relation to male networks and structures of authority which provide the mainstay for their existence. So, for example, through male sibling support, some women find themselves with the power of choice which is not available to other women who lack access to this type of network. Those with choices may opt not to marry, while those without access to the conditions under which such choice becomes available still seek to marry but often in vain. In contrast, women associated with the salariat, who are not so reliant on these male networks, find themselves with a greater degree of power and control over the choices that are open to them. It is among this minority of educated and employed women that negative views on marriage are most often expressed.

Within this framework, women challenge the terms of reference with which they are presented. Their ability to do so varies. Those most able to shift the terms of discourse and to establish their position effectively are those associated with the salariat. The disputes dealing with divorce and distribution of property provide a clear illustration of this. When women can move beyond the terms of reference associated with the peasantariat and their position within a matrix of domestic, agricultural, and unskilled migrant labor, they stand a greater chance of being heard and of establishing their claims to property. For example, little weight is attached to property claims where the woman has contributed her domestic or agricultural labor, as this falls within the sphere of what she is expected to provide as a wife. When, however, she can talk in terms of actions extending beyond this sphere, such as direct financial contributions to family assets, she may be able to alter the way in which her case is perceived and the basis on which a division of property takes place.

Even when it is not possible to shift the terms of debate, women still offer resistance. Once again disputes provide illustrations of the ways in which this is attempted. In many cases, women are aware that the issues of lack of support and rights to property that they raise will not be brought to a satisfactory conclusion. However, going public with a dispute exposes a man's behavior to public scrutiny and renders him vulnerable to public humiliation.

IMAGES OF LAW

Displacing the Centralist Paradigm

So far the focus has been on the forms of power and authority that operate in varying social contexts involving families, households, procreation, and marriage. These shape the kinds of negotiation that occur in everyday life and the types of claims that women pursue with respect to their male partners. In some cases these claims are pursued in particular forums, such as the chief's kgotla, magistrate's court, and High Court, which are part of the formal legal system and, as such, fall within the orbit of centralist legal discourse. In this formal legal discourse, power and authority are constructed from specific sources and institutions which set law apart from other social domains and which uphold an image of autonomy, neutrality, and equality.

But this separation between legal and social domains cannot be sustained in the Kwena context. For the narratives underline the extent to which social understandings, expectations, and values permeate law—regardless of whether law is located within a customary or a Western setting. This is illustrated through the ways in which procreative relationships are viewed and handled in the ordinary world of life as well as in state legal forums. Where pregnancy is concerned, there is a set of social practices which frame negotiations between individuals and their families and which inform legal debate.

What is important here is the points of connection between social and legal domains and on their mutually constitutive nature. For while centralists find no incompatibility between identifying law in formal terms and acknowledging the social sources of its content, their focus remains firmly on the former. The social basis upon which law operates is largely ignored. For the way in which the centralist paradigm defines its boundaries limits what counts as law along with the context in which law is located. As a consequence law is able to maintain its image as a discrete entity. But Kwena ethnography demonstrates that the social contexts within which law is embedded cannot be ignored. These contexts play a crucial role in formulating the kind of perspective on law that is essential for underpinning changes in legal policy and for undertaking legal reform, matters which have practical effects in their implementation. In assessing access to law, for example, it is insufficient to focus on the legal rules that apply (as a centralist would do) and draw deductions from this information alone. This is because such rules of access do not operate in a vacuum. They do not function independently from what is going on around them, but depend upon the social structures on which the legal system rests to give them meaning.

It is clear that among Bakwena, social considerations operate to control access to a hearing. Officials, for example, may deny a person access to a legal hearing if they consider that the appropriate social channels for dealing with the matter, such as family consultations, have been ignored or not yet exhausted. Or the assessment of a person's application may be formed on initial appearances without the benefit of a full hearing and the application denied on that basis. This kind of situation arises when a woman with several children comes to the chief's kgotla to seek support. If the kgotla personnel consider that her relationship with a man is nonmarital, they often send her away saying that she has no case for support, as her claim is of compensation for pregnancy under customary law and she is not eligible because she has had more than one child. However, given the ambiguity surrounding negotiations relating to customary marriage, it may well be that her claim for support is not one of compensation (wherein the case would hinge on the woman's sexual behavior) but is based on the man's marital obligations. In order to clarify the position there ought to be a hearing to establish the status of the relationship. Denied such a hearing, the woman finds herself preempted from raising the issue and thus subject to a form of closure that she cannot contest.

Taking account of such matters makes visible what would otherwise remain hidden from view under a centralist model, which would simply dismiss those denied access to a hearing on the legal basis of having no title to sue. In such a model it is only what occurs in a legal hearing (and not what is excluded) that is the subject of investigation. Yet, as my research demonstrates, women regularly find themselves excluded from the legal domain for a number of reasons which often involve social considerations. Even where they have access to law they may opt not to take legal action, not because they are ignorant of the law but because other factors come into play. Research of the Women and Law in Southern Africa Trust (WLSA) (1991:164–65, 1994:281), formerly the Women and Law in Southern Africa Research Project, highlights the fallacious reasoning behind the assumption that where women are slow to avail themselves of the legal remedies that exist they are ignorant of the law. This type of reasoning, treating law as the motivating factor for action, derives from a centralist approach. To operate on the basis of this assumption is to miss what is really at issue for understanding the underlying basis for action, or lack of action, so critical to an accurate reflection of the role played by law with respect to different interest groups within a community.

Failure to take the social underpinnings of law into account when engaging in law reform leads to unintended consequences, as those states that have attempted to use law as a tool of social engineering in postcolonial Africa have discovered (S. Moore 1978:55; 1989). Law in and of itself cannot change the ways in which people conduct their lives and view their relationships. As the narratives in this book make clear, if women as unmarried partners or wives are to overcome the constraints they face in making the kinds of claims on men that they do, then it is essential that the social underpinnings of power which operate to situate women in relation to other family members, especially men, be fully acknowledged. Such an understanding of power is crucial not only to ordinary negotiations, but also to access to courts and the terms and conditions upon which hearings there take place, with all the implications that this has not just for giving women a voice but for making their voices heard. Failure to engage in this type of analysis leads to a flawed understanding of the legal system and may produce an incorrect assignment of blame when it comes to assessing the role that local law plays within a development context (Benda-Beckmann 1989). There is a danger that customary law will be singled out while common law will escape any significant form of critical examination. Thus, the inadequacies of a centralist model of law not only concern academic debates but also have a social impact. This reminds us that theory is not just of concern in the abstract, but in application affects people's lives.

The Old Legal Pluralism

In the African context, discussions of law have the added dimension of dealing with overt legal pluralism. As initially conceived, such pluralism—which acknowledged the coexistence of common and customary law—did not break the hold of the legal centralist model. This is because the old, weak, or classic form of legal pluralism—a product of the attempt to unify the conception of law from the colonial encounter with that of law in other jurisdictions—identified law in terms that upheld the division between those who were colonizers and those who were colonized. This kind of pluralism endorsed a centralist approach to law, by applying the kind of boundaries that the centralist model constructed between legal and social domains within the legal domain itself. This meant that the kinds of boundaries established between legal and social domains, with the differential authority attributed to the rules associated with such domains and with the hierarchical relations that they engendered, became reestablished within the legal domain. So it was that customary and common law were viewed as separate entities in that the rules of one sphere remained confined within that sphere. Although independent of one another, these spheres existed within a hierarchical relationship in which the rules of common law were invested with a greater degree of authority than those of customary law. Limits of application were imposed on the latter, and often they were accorded a status subordinate to those of the common system when conflict arose.

However, this segregationist account of law also cannot be sustained. As the Kwena narratives demonstrate, rules are not self-contained in the sense that they can be said to be immune from what is going on around them, particularly as they take shape from the contexts in which people seek to apply and manipulate them. They do not exist in a social vacuum. A striking example of this is found in the disputes involving distribution of property on divorce. The rules that apply on divorce are grounded in the different property regimes that give rise to them; this is either a separate or community of property regime under common law, but a customary division according to the rules of customary law. The differences between them are underlined through the institutional setting with which they are primarily associated, with the High Court being the forum responsible for the handling of the first two regimes, and the chief's kgotla for the application of customary law.

From a legal centralist perspective, given this framework, the expectation is that a division of property will be dealt with according to the particular property regime that applies in each case, that is, in terms of certain rules which are distinguished from certain other rules. In other words, it is assumed that the law which operates is bounded by the property regime that is to be applied. The disputes, however, demonstrate that rules do not behave in this way,[3] or rather that those applying them do not confine their application of rules to the system which gave rise to them or to the institutional setting in which they are being applied. What is taking place is a process of cross-fertilization where rules in one system are shaped by and are shaping those in another. This is not a one-way process in which common law imposes its standards or values on customary law. The image of domination in this sense cannot be upheld. The old image of legal pluralism in centralist terms cannot be sustained. Indeed, there is a certain sense of justice in acknowledging this fact and reorienting our approaches to pluralism. For having formulated the concept of pluralism as legal scholars, initially in the context of "others" as colonized peoples, it has now rebounded back on ourselves as objects of study, so that the study of law has come full circle.

Dispelling the legal centralist vision of pluralism, however, is important because, as Channock (1989) and Woodman (1988) observe more generally in the case of family law in Africa, inadequate analyses of customary law and pluralism lead to misinformed approaches to law reform. As legal institutions continue to provide the focus for such re-forms it is essential that their role should be more rigorously evaluated. Such a task is currently being undertaken in South Africa, where in the light of reframing the constitution, issues of law and justice and the role of the peoples' courts are being reformulated. Looking at law in opera-tion among Bakwena not just in terms of varying officials' behavior but also with respect to how ordinary people deal with and use the legal system presents a more dynamic and less bounded image of law—one that is flexible and interactive. Taking account of the social processes at work in the construction of individuals, families, households, and their relationship with legal institutions highlights the ways in which legal and social fields overlap. This approach undermines any treatment of such fields as separate polarized entities. However, the recognition of overlap does not mean that law becomes indistinguishable from the rest of social life. While this book demonstrates why it is necessary to focus on points of intersection and to cross boundaries, it does so in a way that recognizes that boundaries still exist.

Realigning Boundaries: Women's Access to Law in Botswana

Approaches to marriage within social and legal domains provide a strik-ing example of this. The narratives illustrate that what is important in procreative relationships from a social perspective is their potential for development. The open-ended nature of the relationship is valued in many cases rather than its classification as a marriage or nonmarriage. This is why it is the process of becoming—with all the scope for negotia-tion that that entails—that is prized rather than the status of marriage itself. This is why many families do not enter into disputes when a rela-tionship comes to an end but concentrate instead on establishing new relationships. They let the matter drop when "a man turns away from his promises" because there is nothing further to be gained through in-terfamilial support or cooperation by pursuing the relationship. What is at stake are more wide-ranging forms of cooperation which cannot be coerced, rather than specific claims to treatment.

From a legal perspective, however, the issue of classification is an important one. The importance of marriage in ideological terms is underlined in the legal realm, for it is used as the reference point on the basis of which procreative relationships are distinguished from one another and handled accordingly. How parties are dealt with when it comes to the question of procreative relationships—whether in terms of access to third-party forums or with regard to the actual hearings—will depend on whether their relationship is classified as a marriage or a non-marriage. Such endorsement or rejection of a relationship in terms of marriage operates to define and prescribe the content and character of such relationships. Status becomes the key and affects access to a hearing before a third party and to the way in which the matter is handled.

While a relationship subsists, its parties may not be particularly concerned whether it is or is not a marriage, but when it comes to an end this becomes important if there is property and the parties cannot agree on its division. In such a situation, when third-party intervention is invoked, the nature of the relationship becomes crucial. Although women as wives find it difficult to establish their rights to property, without that status they cannot even begin to make certain types of property claims on men whether they are merely unmarried or fall within the status of a concubine.

The issue of classification affects women's access to, and use of, law in a formal legal setting involving courts. The narratives highlight the sophisticated kinds of strategies women and men employ in relation to claims made against one another. However, women find their scope for raising claims in the formal legal arena represented by courts limited by certain factors. They cannot pursue a man for child support beyond the first child in the chief's kgotla in Molepolole unless they can establish that their relationship with that man is a marital one. Given the difficulties in establishing that a customary marriage has taken place this is an onerous task, especially where a relationship has broken down and one of the parties (usually the man) denies that the relationship ever had any of the hallmarks of such a marriage or argues that the potential for marriage never materialized. Thus, social constructions of marriage contrasted with unmarried partnerships have an impact on the legal treatment of such relationships in a court setting. This provides yet another example of the way in which the formal legal system embodied in courts not only draws upon social formulations of family life for its authority but reinforces and upholds the presuppositions on which they are based.

For this reason women as wives do not necessarily find themselves better served by the court system when it comes to claiming maintenance or support. Although married women have the option of raising actions for either, in both the magistrate's court and the chief's kgotla, this may not amount to much in practical terms. While women's status as wives may gain them a hearing in the chief's kgotla, very little comes out of this in practice in most cases, because kgotla officials are reluctant to take any action other than bringing the parties together to discuss their problems and using social censure to apply pressure to alter behavior. Where such censure does not work, as many of the women's narratives in this book demonstrate, there is little that such women can do to enforce their claims to support. This is the case even though the chief's kgotla has the power to attach a man's property to ensure that he carries out his marital obligations in this respect. The same is true for the magistrate's court where specific provisions exist that allow the court to attach a man's earnings on a regular basis after a maintenance order is made. In fact, in my experience in Molepolole no such order was ever made.

At another level, when wives seek to enforce specific claims to marital property they find that in the courts they face the same types of constraints placed on them by virtue of their status in the social sphere, irrespective of whether it is common or customary law forums that are involved. For those women who find themselves denied marital status, there is not even the option of a property claim against partnership assets, unless they can establish their ordinary property rights as individuals and not as marital partners.

Thus, the difficulties women encounter in a court setting are related to the difficulties they face as social actors. That is why it is necessary to take full account of the social dimension of family life when it comes to reforming the legal system if such reform is to be effective (Molokomme 1990/91). This is especially important when considering the issue of legal rights and claims to equality and neutrality made by common law. As the narratives in this book demonstrate, what shapes the power and authority of women within social life also has an impact in the legal domain despite any claims made by the formal legal system. A key element here is gender, which operates to situate women and men in different positions with regard to family life and resources and, more generally, within society. While it is true that individual capacities for power and authority vary among women as well as between women and men, nonetheless, gender cuts across social and economic divisions such as those embodied in the peasantariat and salariat to place women generally at a disadvantage when it comes to negotiating their status with men. The important role that gender plays, not only in the social but also in the legal sphere, has been highlighted by a recent High Court case concerning the citizenship rights of children and thus raises the issue of discrimination based on gender in the constitutional sphere.[4]

REAPPRAISING LAW: ANOTHER PERSPECTIVE

But the challenge to a centralist model of law does not end here. My analysis of law extends beyond the confines of traditional definitions relating to common and customary law and the institutional settings in which such categorization is located. It goes further than simply reformulating and rearranging traditional legal categories. It does this by moving beyond the study of legislation, disputes, and courts to examine the social processes at work in constructing individuals, families, and households and their relationship with the formal legal system. This marks a shift in focus away from the exclusionary emphasis that is placed on the formal sources and institutions associated with such a model to other points of reference that have a bearing on law.

Such an approach provides another perspective on law, one that underlines the points of connection between legal and social domains rather than focusing on the boundaries that exist between them. This is important because, although the centralist model cannot be sustained in reality, the image of such a model continues to exercise power and authority in our thinking about law at an ideological level (Fitzpatrick 1992b). This is so even though scholars such as Harrington and Yngvesson (1990:142) stress that "law as ideology is not a sphere from which meanings emerge and to which meanings are carried back, and practice is not a process separable from law. . . . Rather, law is found, invented, and made in a variety of locations . . . through a variety of practices which *are themselves ideological"* (emphasis in original).

Nonetheless, the image of the centralist model of law as autonomous and immune from social corruption (in the sense of being shaped by the social world) persists through its claim to distance from such a world. How such distance is constructed requires scrutiny, and for Harrington and Yngvesson (1990:144) the task of sociolegal research is to find "how modern forms of power, such as law, get separated from material life—from their role in creating the relations of material life." My analysis of law undermines those earlier claims attributed to a legal centralist account of law. It does so not only with reference to the kgotla or customary system but also with regard to the legal system as a whole in Botswana. It does this by highlighting the real boundaries that people encounter with regard to legal and social relationships. These are concerned not so much with institutional forums or the designation of law as customary or common, as with the social processes which are central to the construction of persons' lives. Individuals form part of networks which shape their world and channel their access to resources. Such resources include the power to negotiate and the terms of reference on which this is based. At this level discussions on power and how it is constituted are crucial. Life histories illustrate the ways in which power operates to produce certain forms of discourse with regard to familial relationships and property. These inform the terms upon which parties speak and how they formulate claims against one another in everyday life. Such discourses amount to law (at the very least in centralist terms) when they are located within particular institutional settings such as the magistrate's court, the High Court, and the chief's kgotla.

But the power to shape such discourses is not confined to, or derived solely from, these legal settings but is generated within a broader arena which carries authority beyond such settings in the operation of everyday life. In other words, law is in fact reflecting and reinforcing social processes and the boundaries to which they give rise. In this context, women as individuals find themselves at a disadvantage in pursuing claims against men because of the gendered social world that gives rise to differential power relations between men and women. As has been noted, such relations derive from the sexual division of labor within the household and the family, as well as differential access to employment and other resources within and beyond the family.

This kind of analysis is in tune with the strong or new form of legal pluralism advocated by J. Griffiths (1986) and noted by Merry (1988) which undermines a centralist account of law within its own jurisdiction. The challenges mounted by pluralism to the dominant centralist paradigm and the ways in which it undermines that account of law have played an important role in leading to more critical forms of legal analysis. However, pluralism itself is subject to critique on the basis that it has failed to take the next step and provide viable analyses of alternative models of law. Some scholars, such as Merry (1988:878–79), doubt that such analyses are possible, on the grounds that when it comes to identifying law in a pluralist model there is a tendency to find it everywhere and thereby to rob law of any value it may possess as an analytic concept; others, such as Benda-Beckmann (1989), argue that an analytical model of pluralism can and should be developed out of the normative systems that inhere in social life.

While drawing on pluralism, my analysis also diverges from it in that my study maintains the specificity of law without endorsing the image or model of the centralist account. At the same time, like a pluralist account, my study examines a whole range of features and focuses on points of connection across social and legal domains. This focus on interrelationship, rather than on divisions, with their exclusionary characteristics is what my approach has in common with many other attempts to reappraise law. It is in tune with studies of law that, as Santos (1987:288) states, place emphasis on "interlaw" and "interlegality." Fitzpatrick (1988:180) carries this farther: "The revival of the scholarship of legal pluralism has much in common with the pervasive post-modern temper even if the links between them have not actually been made." It is a point that has been taken up by others (e.g., Petersen (1992).

RECONFIGURING LAW: THE BROADER DIMENSIONS

My analysis of law is based on research among Bakwena in Africa. But the form that it takes has much in common with the strong strand of pluralism and especially with more general feminist debates on law. For scholars such as Okin (1989:125), the strength of feminist scholarship lies in the ability to cut across disciplines and make explicit what has previously been ignored or marginalized within individual disciplines, that is, the gendered world in which women live. This is accomplished through analyzing the "multiple interconnections" which exist not only between women's domestic roles and their inequality and segregation in the workplace, but also "between their socialization in gendered families and the psychological aspects of their oppression" (1989:125).

This approach integrates aspects which are normally separated. Such separation is based on a model of social relations constructed in terms of a public/private divide. The feminist approach of scholars such as Smart (1989), Petersen (1992), and Pateman (1988) reinforces the exploration of relationships between knowledge and power and between legal status and social context. And as legal academics such as Fineman (1991:xiv) and MacKinnon (1983) have observed of Western-style law, the basic tenets of legal ideology are at odds with the gendered lives of women, a fact which the legal system ignores. This is so not only in Botswana, but elsewhere. As Boyd (1989:136) among others has commented, supposedly gender-neutral ideologies promoted by the principle of equality "render invisible to the legal eye social and economic differences between the sexes." The reasons for this stem from the fact that gender-neutral language obscures the fact that the sexes "have had very different histories, very different assigned social roles and 'natures,' and very different degrees of access to power and opportunity" (Okin

1989:10). For these reasons, according to O'Donovan (1985:105–18), law perpetuates women's economic dependence within marriage and the family.

Nevertheless, while law is undoubtedly powerful, it is not the "barometer of the social world" (Smart 1989:81), as the relationship between law and the disadvantaged position in which women find themselves is an indirect one, mediated through familial and marital relationships. As Smart observes, "Law does not create patriarchal relations but it does in a complex and contradictory fashion reproduce the material and ideological conditions under which these relations may survive." For this reason it is essential to understand what lies behind the exercise of legal power and not simply to focus on the formal aspects of law itself.

My research in Botswana highlights the problems of such a focus. Problems arise because the introduction of formal equality and legal rights within the family sphere do not, on their own, remake patterns of relationships within and outside the family and may instead subtly impose previous patterns of power on those who are most vulnerable. Studies such as that of Weizman (1985) have pointed to the unintended consequences that legal reforms may have, as in the case of the introduction of no-fault legislation and equal rights to marital property introduced by the legislature of California in the 1970s. Instead of benefiting from these provisions enacted to improve the position of wives, women actually experienced the reverse—a setback—due to inadequate consideration of the social and economic conditions under which families operate and how this affects women.

But while it is accepted that law undoubtedly reinforces gendered familial roles which reproduce public and private relations oppressive to women, law may also provide opportunities for women's resistance to such oppressive conditions. These opportunities arise not so much at the level of constructing legal policies which legitimate the legal forum and the form of law that feminists challenge, but at the level which looks beyond these terms of reference to the broader aspects of how power is generated and operates with respect to law and legal discourse (Bottomley and Conaghan 1993).

The issues of power and authority which arise from this kind of analysis not only undermine any legal centralist unitary conception of the state, where the relationship between law and state is presented in uniform and unproblematic terms, but move beyond the confines of legal institutions (however defined) to other bodies and agencies which construct social relations. In my research, the other bodies considered are the structures on which the family rests in everyday life: the conditions under which families come into being, the resources that they have at their disposal, and the effect that this has on the roles women and men adopt in relation to one another. This form of analysis, which takes account of individuals as social beings linked to networks with gendered attributes, provides a perspective which looks beyond the confines of law (whether common or customary) to the world of economic and social differentiation.

Taking account of these factors provides a socially oriented perspective which moves away from a law-centered approach to disparity. Instead of taking law as the central reference point for the construction of difference, it places the focus on the social processes themselves that give rise to such difference and the ways in which they reshape law. In this context, an understanding of how power and the discourses to which it gives rise are constructed provides for analysis of the conditions under which power and such discourses may alter or be transformed. This important dimension is one that is lacking in a centralist account of law, but it is especially pertinent when dealing with a legal system that endorses overt pluralism. Where such pluralism exists, there is a tendency to equate different forms of discourse with the different classificatory forms that exist within the formal legal system.

The danger of this tendency is that it focuses on the formal classification of law (as common or customary) and thus loses sight of the more significant factor: the power of individuals to construct certain forms of discourse. For such discourses transcend boundaries of the kind set up by the formal legal system and affect legal process, regardless of the formal institutional settings in which their individual proponents are located. My approach provides a more sophisticated form of analysis which accounts for concurrence and difference both within and between social domains, as well as the circumstances which may give rise to change. This is of particular significance for women, whose power to construct such discourses is constrained by the gendered nature of the world they live in.

Such an approach transforms the way in which law is perceived, for although the familiar sources, institutions, and personnel associated with a legal centralist model of law continue to be a part of a legal landscape, they do so in ways that completely undermine any claims by the centralist model to represent the only authentic account of law. The challenge lies in reorienting the way in which the well-established sources and tools of formal law are contextualized so that they cannot be used to support or reinforce a centralist account of law. For me, as a lawyer who continues to teach family law, these established sources and tools of law cannot be ignored or abandoned. There is, thus, a pedagogic dimension to the undertaking that is a necessary complement to the praxis dimension that has occupied the bulk of this book. These sources and tools must be incorporated within a broader framework that provides for other perspectives and does not merely pay lip service to the social underpinnings of law. It is not enough to leave the social aspects of law to specialist courses on sociolegal studies, or the sociology or anthropology of law, which—however worthy and worthwhile they may be—through their designation as specialist subjects become pushed to the margins, while leaving the general discipline to represent the corpus from which the majority of students derive their knowledge. This is an issue that must be addressed if we are to achieve a truly integrated social perspective on law, one which gives recognition to all those voices that are currently excluded from legal discourse or, alternatively, integrated on terms that operate to their disadvantage.

APPENDIX A

Procreative Relationships and Marriage in Three Families

MERE'S FAMILY GROUP

There are 34 adults in Mere's family group: 16 women and 18 men. But of the women, 5 are wives brought in. Therefore, in terms of relationships entered into by particular family members we are dealing only with 11 women and therefore 29 adults.

Of these 29 adults associated with the family group, 5 did not have children: 1 woman and 4 men, which leaves 10 women and 14 men in relationships with children, a total of 24 adults.

The 10 women represent the following number of relationships:

	G.3	G.4	G.5
8 Marriages	6	2	
0 Fleeting			
6 Brief	2	3	1
1 Intermediate		1	
1 Lifelong	1		
1 Current		1	

The 10 women represent 17 relationships, of which only 8 are marriages.

The 14 men with children represent the following types of relationships:

	G.2	G.3	G.4	G.5
12 Marriages	3	6	3	
2 Current		1		1

MORERI'S FAMILY GROUP

There are 99 adults associated with this family group. They represent 58 women: 7 in G.2 (7 brought in), 26 in G.3 (7 brought in), and 25 in G. 4. But of these women, 14 represent wives brought in. In terms of the number of adults associated with the family group there are 44 women and 41 men, a total of 85 adults.

Of these 85 adults, 12 have no children: 4 (in G.4) of the 44 women and 8 (5 in G.3) of the 41 men, which leaves 40 women and 33 men with children. Of the 40 women with children, 19 are in G.3 and 21 in G. 4. There were 33 men with children.

The 40 women in childbearing relationships represent the following types:

	G.3	G.4
11 Marriages	8	3
6 Fleeting	3	3
16 Brief	9	7
7 Intermediate	5	2
3 Lifelong	3	
9 Current	4	5

The 40 women represent 52 relationships, of which only 11 are marriages.

The 33 men in childbearing relationships represent the following types of relationships:

	G.2	G.3	G.4
25 Marriages	9	14	2
5 Brief		1	4
7 Current		2	5

The 33 men represent 37 relationships, of which 25 are marriages.

KOOSIMILE'S FAMILY GROUP

There are 75 adults associated with this family group. These represent 45 women and 30 men. But of the women, 13 represent wives brought into the group. In terms of the number of adults associated with the family group we are dealing with 32 women and 30 men in relationships entered into by members of the family group, a total of 62 adults.

Of these 62 adults there are 9 who have not had children: 5 women and 4 men, which leaves 27 women and 26 men with children. Of the 27 women, 6 are in G.3 and 21 in G. 4. Of the 26 men, 3 are in G.2, 14 in G.3, and 9 in G.4.

The 27 women represent the following number of relationships:

	G.3	G.4
12 Marriages	1	11
6 Fleeting	3	3
7 Brief	2	5
5 Intermediate	4	1
0 Lifelong		
12 Current	3	9

The 27 women represent 42 relationships, of which only 12 are marriages.

The 26 men in childbearing relationships represent the following types of relationships:

	G.2	G.3	G.4
24 Marriages	7	12	5
6 Brief		3	3
1 Intermediate		1	
2 Current		1	1

The 26 men represent 33 relationships, of which 24 are marriages.

THE THREE FAMILY GROUPS OVERALL

The total number of adults is 208: 16 women and 18 men in the Mere group, 58 women and 41 men in the Moreri group, and 45 women and 30 men in the Koosimile group. Of these 208 adults, 119 are women and 89 are men. But numbers of these women represent wives brought into the family group. Therefore, in terms of family members having childbearing relationships (in order not to duplicate relationships) we find 5 of 16 Mere wives, 14 of 58 Moreri wives, and 13 of 45 Koosimile wives brought in, which leaves 11 Mere, 44 Moreri, and 32 Koosimile wives, or a total of 87 women left.

Of these 176 adults a certain number have not had children: 1 of 11 Mere women, 4 of 44 Moreri women, and 5 of 32 Koosimile women, which leaves 10 Mere, 40 Morei, and 27 Koosimile women with children, a total of 77. The 16 men without children were 4 of 18 Mere men, 8 of 41 Moreri men, and 4 of 30 Koosimile men, which leaves 14 Mere men, 33 Moreri men, and 26 Koosimile men with children, a total of 73. In total, there are 150 adults associated with Mosotho kgotla who are in childbearing relationships.

The 77 women represent 31 marriages (8 in the Mere group, 11 in the Moreri group, and 12 in the Koosimile group), and 80 other relationships (9 in the Mere group, 41 in the Moreri group, and 30 in the Koosimile group). Of these other relationships, only 22 are current (1 in the Mere group, 9 in the Moreri group, and 12 in the Koosimile group). Therefore 58 of the other relationships are over.

The 77 women break down into the following generations: of the 10 women in the Mere group, 4 are in G.3, 5 are in G.4, and 1 is in G.5; of the 40 women in the Moreri group, 20 are in G.3 and 20 are in G.4; of the 27 women in the Koosimile group, 6 are in G.3 and 21 are in G. 4. There are thus 30 women in G.3, 46 in G.4, and 1 in G.5.

Of these 77 women in childbearing relationships we find the following types of relationships:

	G.3	G.4	G.5	Total
Marriage	15	16		31
Fleeting	6	6		12
Brief	13	15	1	29
Intermediate	10	3		13
Lifelong	4		4	
Current	7	15		22
Total				111

Of the 55 childbearing relationships represented by the 30 women in G.3, we find that 15 are marriages and 40 are other relationships. Of these 40 other relationships only 7 are current and 33 are over. Of the 55 childbearing relationships represented by the 46 women in G.4, we find that 16 are marriages and 39 are other relationships, of which 15 are current and 24 are over. The 1 woman in G.5 represents 1 childbearing relationship, which was a brief relationship and not a marriage.

Of the 84 childbearing relationships represented by the 73 men, we find that 61 represent marriages and 23 are other relationships. Of the 61 marriages, 19 were in G.2, 32 in G.3, and 10 in G. 4. The 23 other relationships were of the following types: 11 brief (4 in G.3 and 7 in G.4), 1 intermediate (G.3), and 11 current (4 in G.3, 6 in G.4, and 1 in G.5).

Overall, there are 92 marriages, representing 61 men and 31 women, and 103 other relationships involving men on 23 occasions and women on 80 occasions. The total number of relationships involving children is 195.

APPENDIX B

Text for Teko Mere's Hearing

As is typical in these cases, the hearing begins with Teko setting out her complaint:[1] "In 1975 Rankolwane talked to me and proposed marriage. I agreed and we had sex. In April 1976, I became pregnant. In December I gave birth to a baby. In March 1978 I had the second child. In September 1980 I was pregnant again. I gave birth in May 1981. He supported these three children well. He supported each one of them from confinement. Now he does not mention anything about marriage and does not support the children. I want him to tell me who the father of these children is and I want to know what does he think they eat because he does not support them. I have spoken to him several times before his parents. He does not take notice of what I say." In her speech she is setting up the validity of the relationship and her appropriate handling of it. She mentions that marriage was promised. She shows that he recognized the relationship and took it seriously by providing support during and after confinement. This is the period immediately following birth, when a women is isolated from men in the community and particularly her husband. It generally lasts for a couple of months. Teko indicates that she has dealt with the matter through the proper channels because she spoke to the man's father. This follows the practice of discussing the matter between the families before raising the matter in the kgotla.

After she makes her statement, Rankolwane, the man, is allowed to question her. He seeks to ask certain questions aimed at denying the relationship. For example, he asks, "What proof do you have?" to which she replies, "My proof is that you have never denied that you are the father." This is a common assertion and is seen as having some cultural validity. Where men do not expressly deny paternity their silence is treated as a tacit admission.

Teko is then questioned by a kgotla member who asks her about the role that her parents played. This is significant because for a relationship to have any social recognition the families of the individuals concerned must be involved in its negotiation. To this she responds, "My parents never went there" (meaning to his parents). This reply would be seen as damaging to her claim of social recognition because it appears that her parents had not visited his parents. She is then asked why she carried on her relationship with him in the way that she did, to which she responds, "I agreed to continue bearing children with him because we had discussed the matter and agreed on marriage." She attempts to provide social recognition by stating, "He was always visiting my mother's place. He did not hide himself."

She is then asked what she wants to do about the situation, to which she replies, "I want him to tell me who the father of these children is."

Mr. Kgosiensho, the deputy chief and third party hearing the case, then asks a series of questions geared to dealing with the recognition of the relationship, to which she responds, "Yes, he is my husband. I was sleeping with him because his parents knew and had met my parents about the matter."

To back up her claim about recognition, her grandfather Tshitoeng then gives evidence. He gives a long statement aimed at establishing that the appropriate procedure has been followed, that is, that he reported the pregnancy on the first occasion to the man's father, that he referred back to the man's parents on several occasions about the marriage, and that he even returned money that they gave him because (the implication was) he was more interested in marriage than compensation. He then states, "After this we brought the case to Kgosing so that they could tell us whether they (the man's family) are marrying or not." For him the issue is one of marriage. The public forum is being used to put pressure on the man and his family by airing the matter publicly. For Teko the issue is now one of compensation and support.

Tshitoeng is then questioned by Rankolwane. His questions are aimed at discrediting Tshitoeng's claims that he followed the appropriate procedure. Asked when he reported seduction, Tshitoeng replies, "I went to tell Keboletse [Rankolwane's father] when Teko had the first child." When a woman is pregnant, the appropriate time to inform the man's family is before birth and just after the child has come out of confinement. He also adds, "I also went and told him when the second child was born." Tshitoeng is then questioned by Mr. Kgosiensho, who pursues the line of questioning concerned with correct procedure. In response Tshitoeng states, "If Keboletse would speak the truth he would assure you that I have always been approaching him about this matter." He is then asked about the position of the two children and whether it is appropriate for his family to raise a case at this stage, to which he replies, "The second child is disputed. Yes eight head of cattle are paid for the second child." This is in response to a question about whether such payment can be made when one has more than one child.

The next part of the proceedings center on the man, Rankolwane, who outlines his position. He concentrates on establishing that he is not obliged to pay compensation because she has already had a child with another partner, in fact two children, before she had his child. When questioned by Teko about his allegations that she was involved with another man, he responds, "I found that man sleeping with you at your mother's place. That man's name is Sephinnyane." He was then questioned by Tshitoeng, who asked about the man, and he replied, "I found that man sleeping inside Teko's home. I questioned Teko as to who he was, and she told me that he was an old boyfriend." He is then asked why, if he found this state of affairs to exist, he did not inform Teko's parents, to which he responds, "I never told you because I knew that Teko was my nyatsi." In this response, by labeling her as his concubine, he is trying to establish that this was not a marriage-type relationship and therefore consultation with her parents was unnecessary. He is then asked what his intention was, to which he replies, "I told you that my intention was to marry." What is meant by that is that when he entered the relationship he intended to marry, but as it progressed he changed his mind, having set up allegations of infidelity to substantiate his position.

He is then questioned by Mr. Kgosiensho along other lines, namely his position with regard to the children. He admits paternity of one child, saying, "I have a child with her." When asked about the care of this child and of Teko, he says, "I took care of her in confinement for the two children." This shows what a responsible person he is. However, to substantiate his previous position he immediately says, "The second child was not mine." When asked why he provided support if the second child was not his he replies, "I took care of her in confinement for the second child because I loved her."

He is then asked how he views his current relationship with her, to which he responds, "She is no longer my woman because of her actions." When asked about the status of the relationship with her parents, in an attempt to see how the relatives viewed their relationship, he tries to portray her family in a bad light, to make it clear that he is not responsible for compensation, by saying, "Teko's parents never told my parents anything when Teko became pregnant with the first child."

Rankolwane, like Teko, produces a witness, his father, who backs up his son's version of events. He maintains, "Tshitoeng never came to report to me when the first child was born. To my knowledge my son, Rankolwane, found Teko with two children already. He had the third child with her. Tshitoeng did not come to me even when the third child was born. I only saw him once when he came to report to me that the child was starving."

When questioned by Teko, he continues to support his son. He shows how his knowledge of the relationship between them was not acquired through the proper channels. He says, "I was led to you by Rankolwane." This establishes that he met her through his sons instead of through her parents. When questioned about the children he responds, "I only know of one child."

He is then questioned by a kgotla elder who asks him how many children had been born when he met Teko's family. He replies, "I don't know which child was born when I went with Rankolwane to Tshitoeng's place." He is then asked about marriage, to which he replies, "I told Tshitoeng that Rankolwane said that he was not ready to marry yet." When asked by kgotla members about his information on pregnancy he says, "Tshitoeng never told me that Rankolwane had made Teko pregnant." This is an attempt to emphasize that Tshitoeng never followed the appropriate procedure for marriage or compensation due to pregnancy. When asked about support for the child he responds, "I have never said that he should neglect her."

When finally both parties are asked to make a final comment about how they view their situation, Teko says, "I want him to compensate me and we part." Unlike her grandfather Tshitoeng, she is not interested in the issue of marriage. She is interested in the social affirmation of the breakdown of the relationship, support for the children, and censorship of the man through a compensation award. He responds, "I do not know what compensation she wants from me, because the first child was not mine." To emphasize this point he adds, "I wonder if she means that I should pay compensation for my own child."

When Mr. Kgosiensho asks a kgotla elder for his opinion, he finds in favor of Teko, saying, "The complainant has told this court that Rankolwane has three children with her. The defendant states in his defense that he only knows of one child. Accordingly, the defendant has to pay eight head of cattle as compensation to her." Mr. Kgosiensho, however, is of a different view. He rejects the recommendation. He puts forward a summary of Teko's position: "Teko has told this court that Rankolwane has three children with her outside the law [without patlo]. She states that she became pregnant in 1976 and had a baby in December 1976." He then goes on to give Rankolwane's version of events: "In his defense Rankolwane states that when he fell in love with Teko she was already pregnant with the second child. Then he went to the mines and says the child is not his. Rankolwane states that the only child he has with Teko is the third child."

Mr. Kgosiensho then goes on to evaluate the claims made by the family members: "The evidence given by the parents [i.e., grandfather and father] on both sides does not show that the first child was reported to the boy's parents [pointing up a failure to adhere to a Tswana norm]. Tshitoeng states that the second child is disputed [i.e., that the dispute is over the second child]. The truth is that it is only the first child that is disputed [i.e., one can only consider raising a case over the first child]. This is according to Tswana custom." He then states what the Tswana custom is: "For the first child compensation of eight head of cattle or 640 pula is necessary." He then goes on to give his decision: "Therefore this court does not find the defendant at fault." He then says, "The defendant is let free [i.e., the case is dismissed]."

APPENDIX C

Text for Nyana Segethsho's Hearing

Mr. Kgosiensho asks Nyana about the nature of the relationship: "What was the agreement your parents reached?" to which she replies, "It was marriage, that he was going to marry me." Mr. Kgosiensho continues by asking, "What proof did they do to show you were to be married to him?" When Nyana hesitates, he explains, "Did they consult? Didn't they bring up anything showing proof that you were engaged to their son?" Nyana knows what is required and responds, "Yes, they brought the necessary things which according to Tswana procedure are always brought to the girl's parents as initial proof that the parties are to marry. The items were three blankets, a dress, a pullover, one bed sheet, a head-dress, a lantern, and a pair of shoes." Mr. Kgosiensho then tries to divine Mokwaledi's attitude to her. He asks Nyana, "Have you ever heard this man propose marriage? Did you ever talk it over together when he said he was in love and wanted to marry you?" She responds, "Yes."

Mr. Kgosiensho seeks to deal with the issue of pregnancy and tries to establish how it fitted into the picture in terms of formal procedure: "How did it come about that he gave you a child before marriage took place?" Nyana is able to establish that the pregnancy (her first) was perfectly acceptable in terms of Tswana procedure because "his parents requested that we should be allowed to live together. They said that we could live together as man and wife until January the following year after plowing." Mr. Kgosiensho asks, "What year was that?" and she responds, "1978." Mr. Kgosiensho then seeks to find out more about the relationship by asking, "What happened after plowing?" She indicates that Mokwaledi's parents were not fulfilling their side of the agreement: "They never said anything. They never took any action towards the marriage agreement." Mr. Kgosiensho seeks more information on this point: "Until when? How long did they allow the arrangement to continue?" Nyana responds, "From that time until today, during which time I had to bear a child." This establishes that she became pregnant only after the parents agreed to their living together and thus accepted pregnancy. Mr. Kgosiensho then asks, "How many children do you have?" to which she replies, "Only one."

Mr. Kgosiensho then shifts the discussion away from Mokwaledi's parents to the role that her own parents played by asking, "During such a long period, what action did you parents take?" Nyana shows that her parents behaved responsibly by replying, "My father went several times to demand to know why the marriage was not yet arranged, and every time they would tell him that they would arrange marriage."

Mr. Kgosiensho asks about the man's conduct: "Then what did this man who intended to marry you actually say?" Nyana shows his behavior in a bad light: "He has never said anything. Since I came out of confinement nursing the baby, he disappeared, and from then until today I haven't seen him."

Mr. Kgosiensho then tries to find out her attitude toward him with a view to reconciliation, "Could you tell me if you still love him?" She, however, rejects any move in this direction by responding, "No, I don't love him anymore." Mr. Kgosiensho tries once more to see if they can mend the relationship. He asks, "Would you take him back again to marry?" She, however, remains firm with her original position: "No, since he disappeared for many years."

The proceedings then center on Mokwaledi, who is asked to state his position. He denies her claim for compensation by stating that he is married to her and that the reason for his lack of contact with her is her bad behavior. She has not been a good wife. He states, "I was married to this young lady. I had a child with her. I took care of her from pregnancy into confinement, and I did all that was needed for keeping her in confinement." This established that he behaved responsibly and in accordance with what is expected in a relationship which is or has the potential for a customary marriage. He underlines the fact that this was a serious relationship by stating, "The clothing which were to indicate that I was to marry her were given to her through our parents." He is also stressing parental involvement and acceptance of the relationship. He then goes on to try to discredit her claim of abandonment by stating, "I was staying with her until the child was nine months after confinement. After that I went to look for work and the kind of work I was looking for was in fact obtained for me by her father." By discussing work he is justifying his absence. He continues, "It was a heavy job and I did not stay long. I had to leave the job. Then I went to look for work at Lobatse. At that time I came to Molepolole in October to see her and the child. That was in 1980. When I came in she never took any care of me; she disliked my presence. She showed the dislike by taking certain personal effects I left in her care. She threw them outside the house. Then I went back to my work and never came back until today." Nyana questions his allegations of misconduct by asking, "Which are the articles belonging to you that I took and threw outside?" (implying that Mokwaledi has simply made this up). He responds, "You took my bag for clothing and you put it outside the hut and then you locked up the hut." She does not ask any more questions.

Mr. Kgosiensho then seeks to find out what the relationship between the parties is by asking, "Who is this?" (turning to Nyana), and Mokwaledi responds, "It is my wife." He is then asked, "Under what law did you marry her?" to which he replies, "I married her according to Tswana law." When asked, "How many years have you been married to her?" Mokwaledi answers, "I have been married to her for two years." Mokwaledi's credibility is then questioned by Mr. Kgosiensho, by his observation, "Do you consider two years to be from 1978 to 1982?" to which Mokwaledi has to reply, "That is not two years." Mr. Kgosiensho builds on this response to ask what he has been leading up to: "Where have you been these four years? Have you been living with her?" Mokwaledi responds, "It is only one year that I have been living with her." Mr. Kgosiensho queries this: "Did you hear her saying that she has never seen you since you disappeared until today?" He replies, "Yes I did hear." Mr. Kgosiensho follows up this line of questioning by asking, "Is there any kind of husband who would stay away from his wife for such a very long time?" Mokwaledi attempts to justify his position by responding, "Yes, there could be such a husband when he was actually expelled."

Mr. Kgosiensho then sets out to test the truth of this allegation. He begins by asking, "If a man or his wife [in the case of a man or his wife], who has authority to expel the other?" Mokwaledi responds, "It is the wife who can reject the man." Mr. Kgosiensho asks a pertinent question relating to the correct way of handling a marital dispute: "Under marriage custom what action do you take if your wife rejects you?" Mokwaledi then states the accepted procedure, which is, "I must tell my parents and then complain to my wife's parents." Mr. Kgosiensho builds on his response: "Have you ever told them of your complaint that your wife has expelled you from your dwelling house?" Mokwaledi replies, "I have never reported to them." He attempts to salvage his position by stating, "I was in a hurry because I had to go back to work," but is rebuked by Mr. Kgosiensho, who asks, "Which is most important, your wife and child or the job you had secured then?" Mokwaledi is bound to respond "My wife comes first."

After extracting this admission Mr. Kgosiensho continues to emphasize his failure to act properly by asking, "Why did you act like that, to just leave them in the lurch without letting them know where you had gone to?" but Mokwaledi attempts to justify himself by saying, "It was because she chased me away." Mr. Kgosiensho is not prepared to accept this. He asks, "What proof can you give [of] the fact that you were driven away, because you have never reported to your parents or the girl's parents?" Mokwaledi stubbornly replies, "It was only because she ordered me out of the dwelling house." Mr. Kgosiensho points out the inconsistency in this position: "Now if you did not report to either parents, who is at fault now?" He is forced to reply, "The fault lies with me because I did not report."

These exchanges emphasize the importance of parental consultation and involvement. This is followed up by Mr. Kgosiensho: "Do you think this young woman is merely just giving you trouble by accusing you for what you did?" He has to reply, "No." Mr. Kgosiensho attempts to use his failure to act properly to get him to accept the woman's claim: "Did you hear her saying that since you gave her a child you disappeared and broke your promise? Hadn't you better compensate her and stay away from her?" Mokwaledi still attempts to distance himself from the issue of compensation by stating, "I want to marry her." In response, Mr. Kgosiensho asks him, "Can marriage ever be set up by force? Can marriage be set up by this dispute? How do you think you can marry when a case about it is already on; do you think there is any chance to do so?" This emphasizes that when an action is stated in terms of compensation at the chief's kgotla, the parties' relationship is regarded as over. It is viewed as a social affirmation of breakdown. The man finally admits defeat and says, "No, I don't think there is any chance."

Mokwaledi is then asked, "Do you know your Kwena law?" He replies "I don't know it." This would be seen as an admission of weakness, as he is a member of the morafe. Mr. Kgosiensho starts to explain, "Kwena law in a case of seduction is when a person gives a girl a child outside the law." He is then interrupted by Mokwaledi, who claims, "I married her according to Tswana law and custom." He is reprimanded by Mr. Kgosiensho: "Did you hear this woman saying that you had a child with her by mistake because at the time plans for constituting marriage were under way and you then disappeared and that in her feelings she is not going to marry you anymore? You had better compensate her with eight head of cattle and you people part." Mokwaledi, however, will not give up his line of argument and states, "I had a child with her according to law, not outside the law, what do you mean by saying so? [i.e., that he did not]." In an attempt to support his claim he refers to the engagement presents and support given during and after confinement: "I had provided the initial property that is always given to an engaged woman, and at childbirth I gave support and did everything until she was out of confinement." Mr. Kgosiensho responds, "Did you hear in her statement that the arrangement was that you could live with her in the meantime by permission of both parents and that after plowing in January marriage was to take place? What made you not wait for that period?" Mokwaledi responds, "I did not wait because I and my parents were not ready for marriage." Mr. Kgosiensho tries once again to get him to see that he has no claim to marriage: "Do you think the idea of you being given special permission to live with the woman you proposed for marriage comes under any law, because that special permission was for just a short period until after plowing; is that the law?" Now that he is emphasizing that the permission was limited, Mokwaledi, however, remains obstinate: "That is not the law." Mr. Kgosiensho continues to show him that there is no marriage: "Do you see that that permission was not a law? When she took out your clothing and locked the hut you did not take any action because you were not yet married to her, do you see that point?" He responds, "Yes, I see that point."

APPENDIX D

Text for the Kgosidintsis' Hearing

Manaka made this opening statement to the members of Kgosing kgotla: "I've come to report that since 1980 I have been deserted by my husband. We have since our marriage been living peacefully together and we never experienced any misunderstandings and quarrels." She establishes, by implication, that she has fulfilled her marital role as wife and that all was well until, as she subsequently relates, the other woman appeared on the scene. She builds up to the fact that this woman is a widow by reference to her black clothing:

> In the middle of 1980, I noticed a woman. We were then living in teacher's quarters at Mahetlwe. What I noticed was that this woman in black clothes usually came to our dwelling house every day. She would tell my husband to go find some beer to drink and every time my husband would go with this woman into the village and return after sunset, at about 9 P.M. I was filled with much complaint and thought about this, and that was the beginning of our misunderstanding.
>
> I watched closely [and] then I discovered, with my own eyes, that my husband was using traditional herbs which are used for curing a woman after the death of her husband. I queried my husband about this practice, [but] he said, that the stuff they mixed with beer was not the herbs used for curing widows. I noticed that was not true, because he got sick as a result of using those herbs. One Mmabua [a woman] explained to me that the cause of his sickness was having sex with the widow.

Manaka reinforces this notion through Joel's refusal to have any medical treatment. She then goes on to show how she took appropriate action by consulting a relative who was also the headman of his ward: "At his refusal to see the medical doctor I reported to Victor Kgosidintsi [fig. 5, headman of the ward at that time]. Victor came to see my husband. He was surprised to find him sick." At this point Mr. Kgosiensho, hearing the dispute, interrupted, telling her to get to the point of her complaint. She continued, "After that I managed to get him to the doctor. He got better after medical treatment, and he went back to Mahetlwe, and after some time he told me that he wanted to marry another woman." At this point she reveals another source of tension in the relationship: "Then when I asked him why he wanted to marry the second woman, he told me he could not bear to stay with a woman who did not produce children. I told him my reason for not bearing children was because of a medical operation. Then my husband told me that he could do what he liked and that no one could stop him." Once again Manaka took appropriate action: "I then went to report the

253

situation to Victor Kgosidintsi, who sent for my husband, but my husband refused to respond to his call. He [Joel] then removed himself and went to stay in the dwelling house of the woman I have already mentioned." Not only does he fail to pay attention to his headman and relative, but he is presented as behaving in an unacceptable manner to his wife, treating her badly, in a rude and insulting manner: "Every time that he comes out of that woman's house he is very angry and hostile to me. I remember one day when he found me at our house, helping his own mother to bathe, he insulted me, saying that I was smelling under the armpits. Again I went to report the situation to Victor Kgosidintsi."

She then shifts the discussion to property matters: "After that I went back to Mahetlwe, where my husband and I stay. In the house I found that some of the household articles, such as dishes and basins, had been taken away by my husband's woman friend, who had also taken some chickens. When I queried this, he said that the articles I was asking about had been acquired by him at his own expense and that I had no business to be worried about them. Another complaint I have is that my husband has moved the cattle and small stock [goats] from my custody to the new woman's custody."

By the end of her statement she has managed to stress all Joel's defects while at the same time playing up her own behavior as an ideal wife. Such a wife is concerned when her husband is sick and consults his relatives and their local headman when they have real marital problems.

At this point, as in all such hearings, Joel as the other party is given an opportunity to question her. He goes straight to the heart of her allegations, beginning with property. He demands to know "who told you that I have taken the cattle from where I was caring for them to the cattlepost of that woman?" She responds, "You moved them in my presence," to which he responds, "Do you have any people to prove what you say?" She replies, "Any of the people at Mahetlwe Village can prove this."

He then shifts tack: "You say I have been using the medicine for boswagadi [to cure the widow]; do you say that you heard from one Mmabua that I was using boswagadi concoctions? Her reply establishes direct rather than hearsay evidence: "No, I saw you drinking the concoctions yourself."

Joel then shifts the subject and asks Manaka who gave her permission to raise the matter in the kgotla, to which she responds, "I had to report to Ramukwane [the senior wardhead for Mokgalo ward] after Victor Kgosidintsi. Bakwena Kgosidintsi reported the case to this kgotla."

He then raises the issue of marriage: "Do you have any witnesses to prove that I told you I was going to marry a widow?" She points to one of the court clerks present and says, "You told me, we were exchanging views and you told me in her presence that you were going to marry the widow woman."

Giving up on this line of questioning, he finally asks, "Do you have any proof that I have given some of the household articles to the widow and also some chickens?" She replies in the affirmative, and he gives up questioning her.

It is now time for the third party hearing the dispute to put his questions. In this case it is the deputy chief, Mr. Kgosiensho. His questions are geared to establishing the length of the relationship and the number of children that they have. He begins, "When were you married?" to which she replies, "We were married according to Tswana custom [meaning patlo] in 1956." Mr. Kgosiensho accepts this and inquires, "How many children?" to which she responds "seven" (who are still living). He then proceeds to try to interpret what is going on in the relationship: "By telling you that he wanted to marry the widow did your husband say he was going to divorce you?" She replies, "Yes." He then asks, "How many cattle and goats were there when he moved them from your kraal to the widow's kraal?" to which she answers, "There were thirty-five head of cattle and twenty-nine goats." He continues to try to itemize the property that has changed hands: "How many chickens did the widow remove from your place?" to which she replies "seven." He then asks, "How many cattle and goats are there today?" She is unable to answer this question: "I don't know, I have not seen them after plowing this year [sometime around January/February]." Aware of the problems of access that women face, he asks, "How far is the kraal in which the cattle are kept from you place?" to which she responds, "About one kilometer." Having established that distance is not an issue, he inquires if Joel's behavior is the problem: "Does you husband restrict you from going to the kraal where the cattle are kept at present?" Manaka affirms this, saying, "Yes, he does." Mr. Kgosiensho then asks a rhetorical question: "At the time of hearing this dispute today is your husband not staying with your at your dwelling house?" From what she has said in her earlier statements it is clear that this is not the case, but by raising this issue he is drawing attention to the fact that Joel is failing to act as a husband should: he might have a lover, but he should still live at home with his wife. Manaka is able to play on this, stating, "He doesn't stay with me in our dwelling house, he stays with the widow."

At this point, as it is late in the afternoon, the proceedings are adjourned until the next day, when Joel is given the opportunity to respond to Manaka's allegations. In his statement he attempts to discredit his wife and to provide an alternative version of the events already cited. He begins by trying to undermine her credibility. He maintains that far from acting appropriately with regard to reporting, she has prematurely raised the issue in the kgotla without having pursued it through the normal channels, thus needlessly exposing him to public humiliation. He states, "I just heard that the case between me and my wife has been brought to Kgosing ward, and my parents and my parents-in-law know nothing about it. From the very beginning it is I who reported the matter [marital discord] to my wife's parents, and we have not, as yet, met about it. I am surprised to find that it has been taken on at this level, officially, when it is still a family dispute which can be solved by our parents. I am very much ashamed of the action taken in this connection."

In contrast he tries to present Manaka as a brazen woman who does not act as a wife should: "My wife is not ashamed of scandalizing my name and saying anything undesirable to my feelings in public, like she is doing now." Not only that, but to make matters worse, she is a liar: "Even the statement she gave yesterday about me is a false statement. My wife knows very well that I respect her. Even the local people where we stay know so."

He attempts to shift the blame for what has occurred onto her: "She has suddenly changed this year. Her excuse is that I am married to a widow woman who she mentioned yesterday. It is false that my wife says that I've moved my livestock property to the kraal of the widow in question and also that I spend my earnings with that woman. That is not true. I've never given anything to that woman or any cow, not even money."

He turns the tables on Manaka, alleging that it is she who has appropriated another's property: "She went and confiscated some chairs from the house of that widow. She took away the chairs in the absence of the widow woman. There was a case about them which was heard at the kgotla."

He then challenges Manaka's other allegations: "There is no truth in what she was saying yesterday regarding my illness. As for goats and cattle, they had to go where that woman [the widow] stays because they were to be tended by the herd boys who were staying there. My wife knows very well that under this arrangement her own cattle and mine are kraaled together with the cattle belonging to the other woman, because of the herd boys who stay there." He goes on to reveal that far from being an unknown woman, the widow is in fact a friend of Manaka's whom Manaka asked to take care of him in her absence: "In her statement she says I am in love with the widow. What I know and she knows is that the widow in question has long been her close friend. Many people in the village where we stay can testify that they are friends and have been friends for a long time. It was according to my wife's instructions that when she came home to Molepolole, the widow woman should take care of me in her place. On her [Manaka's] return to Mahetlwe from Molepolole she began to say that I was married to that woman and has often insulted me about that woman." He attempts to bolster his position by commenting, "Some of the local people in the village of Mahetlwe are very much ashamed about her attitude to this situation."

He attempts to establish her as untrustworthy and thereby damage her credibility: "At the end of March this year I sent my wife to Molepolole with a check to cash for five hundred pula. I was sending her as normal because I trusted her. When she returned after having cashed the check, she never told me anything about the money, and I was very much ashamed. Out of that money I was going to pay some builders. Since then she has never shown me this money; I don't know what she has done with it. From that time I began to distrust her." He expands on this theme, presenting her as an unreliable person who is dangerous because she engages in physical violence. This is the reason that he gives for no longer living with her:

> At the beginning of the Easter holidays, on a Sunday afternoon, my wife assaulted me inside the kitchen when we were together. She closed all the doors and picked up an iron store opener [a crowbar; he then held this up for kgotla members to see] and hit me on the head. I can still feel the wound, it has not healed properly [and he pointed to a scar on his forehead]. I think that at that moment she intended to kill me. I fell on a burning stove and hurt my ribs. I think that they are fractured. In the fighting even the radio was broken into pieces, and when I fell with blood covering my face she sat on top of me. I held her arms because I realized that she wanted to strangle me.
>
> I was very much ashamed. We had never fought like that before. I show

you the shirt that I was wearing at the time [exhibited with blood on the collar and shoulder]. Another time I had to go to the widow's place where the herd boys were staying in order to ask them if all the cattle were together and if the borehole was in good running order. [The herd boys provide him with a legitimate reason for visiting the widow at her home. They are in fact her sons.]

My wife was not at our house [in Mahetlwe], she was in the village [Molepolole]. I left a message with the builders to tell her that I had gone to see the herd boys about the cattle. I found the senior herd boy and inquired about the cattle, and later the widow woman came in. We were inside the house and all of a sudden the door burst open and hit the lamp, which fell off the nearby table. When we asked who forces the door so terribly, the children said it was my wife. Then she ran away back to her house. I recognized her by her voice; she was insulting the widow and kept uttering insults until she got back to her house. Many people heard her that evening.

He comes to the crux of his narrative: "It was then, after all these incidents, that I told my wife that I was not willing to stay with her when she behaves like a beast. I am at this stage trying to keep away from her. When she is not at Mahetlwe, I stay in our premises there. When she is there I stay away." He ends his statement by placing the ball in his wife's court: "I don't know what my wife wants me to do now, because at the beginning of this year she told me that I will never have conjugal rights with her and saying that she is doing away with me altogether [i.e., divorcing him]." When a member of the audience interjects (as is common in such disputes) to say that perhaps she was just teasing him, he denies this, stressing that "traditionally it is well known that if a woman tells you that you are no longer going to have conjugal rights with her it means that she is no longer your wife and this has been the case for six to seven months now."

Not only does he try to turn the situation on its head and maintain that she is the one who has withdrawn from him, but he is adamant that he has not denied her any of her rights as a wife: "I don't know what she is actually accusing me of because she has all the rights. I allow her all the rights she is entitled to. She has a share of the property, food, and everything. I have no intention of divorcing her. If she wants a divorce, she may do it."

Manaka is then permitted to question Joel, and she begins by concentrating on her alleged friendship with the widow and the arrangements concerning the cattle. She attempts to undercut his allegations by stating, "Now that you say I am a friend of the widow woman, is it not me who refused when you recommended that we include her cattle in registering the herd for watering at a council borehole?" Joel, however, refuses to acknowledge this: "No, you never refused." However, she continues unperturbed, "What did you say when I refused?" to which he replies, "I explained to you that I am keeping my cattle with the widow woman because they are both to be looked after by her sons and the widow woman's kgotla men know of my application. They know that her cattle are kraaled with mine. The herd boys themselves are witnesses to this arrangement." Manaka comes at the issue of her relationship with this woman from another angle: "If she was my friend, why did this widow woman speak to you? Why did she consult with you on the registration of cattle at the council borehole without first consulting me?" He replies, "Because I am the owner of the cattle and am responsible for the upkeep of the kraal." Manaka concentrates on the cattle. She attempts to show why she would never be party to such an arrangement: "Since you say that I agreed that our cattle be herded together with those of the widow, why did I tell you that it was not good that your cattle, as a man of Mokgalo, should be herded together with cattle belonging to a woman of Goo mabe kgotla, which is a different and remote kgotla?" He admits that this issue was raised but says that it was not until a later stage: "You asked me after the cattle were herded together and you took them to the borehole." At this point she puts forward her objection to the arrangement: "Didn't I tell you that if this woman's cattle happened to be destroyed inside our herd, who would be responsible?" When he admits this and is cornered with the question "What grounds do you have for mixing the cattle together?" he responds, "The grounds are that the owners of the cattle know about the arrangement."

Manaka then adopts another line of questioning, which attempts to get him to admit that he has married the widow. If he does so, the issue of property may be raised; if he denies this, then he is at least liable to public censure for abandoning the marital home. Manaka (who suddenly refers to the widow by name) probes Joel: "You are denying that you are married to Bogadinyana. Why is it that you have moved to stay with her at her dwelling house?" Aware of what is at stake, Joel responds, "I am not staying at her home." Manaka then shifts the discussion to focus on their own relationship: "Since 1956, when you married me, up to today, have I ever assaulted or quarreled with you?" Joel admits, "We used to quarrel, but no fighting took place until this dispute erupted." In saying this he is acknowledging that there had been no real conflict in their lives until the appearance of this woman. Manaka plays on this: "What caused the fight where you were injured?" to which Joel is forced to respond, "The insults you often utter to me in connection with the woman we are talking about." Manaka then comes back to the issue of where he is living, but he continues to deny that he moved out to live with the widow, stating, "I moved out only after you assaulted me." Manaka challenges this: "You moved from our place in 1980 to the widow woman's place; it was before the assault. What were you afraid of in our dwelling house?" She is playing on the notion that a husband may not cease to live with his wife without good cause, and trying to establish that he has no such cause. She then tries to deal with his allegations that she was not behaving like a proper wife because she refused to have sex with him, and she tries to shift the blame onto him on the basis of his improper use of traditional medicine (which would justify such a refusal on her part): "Is it not me, who when you wanted us to have sex, told you I cannot accept because you have been drinking an African [traditional] medicine with the widow?" He will not be drawn into this and retorts, "You refused, on the pretense of herbs, when that was just an excuse." Once again Manaka comes back to his relationship with the widow. She does so in such a way that does not question his right to have a relationship with her but the way in which he does so: "Didn't I tell you that I did not like the practice of you staying with the widow woman and doing your washing there?" It is not appropriate for a husband to live full time with another woman, nor for him to allow such a woman to undertake tasks that should be carried out by his wife. In acting in this way he is undermining his wife's position. After another barrage of questions Joel finally gives up the pretense that he does not have a relationship with the widow.

The next interchange between husband and wife concentrates on the issue of reporting marital discord to the appropriate parties. Where there are real problems in a relationship, these should be reported to family members so that they can mediate between the parties or, failing that, bring the matter to the attention of the local headman. Reporting in this context is a means of establishing credibility for the allegations and is used as a means of upholding or undermining these allegations. Manaka, who is anxious to establish herself as the aggrieved party who tried to initiate discussion through the normal channels, now interrogates Joel along these lines: "Didn't I ask you to come and see the ward headman at Molepolole and you refused?" Joel will not be trapped: "I did not refuse. I said there was not time and that I would see him sometime later." This covers his position because he has not raised the issue with anyone. Manaka then shifts their interchanges to the subject of assault and attempts to establish that he has also acted aggressively: "Didn't you try to stab me with a knife sometime back?" Joel emphatically denies this: "I never; it was not me." However, she pursues the issue of assault: "Did you not beat me several times because of the widow when you came late at night?" Once again Joel states, "I never came to beat you." Manaka then attempts to explain her assault in terms of his prior behavior and the need for self-defense: "Don't you remember that I hit you when you were trying to strangle me?" He denies this but is brought up short by Manaka's reference to a witness: "Don't you remember one Mathwanye who tried to separate us?" to which he is forced to reply, "Yes, I remember." Manaka then refers to the kgotla's involvement in their problem: "After the assault, didn't you go and report to the chief's representative?" Joel tries to play this up saying, "Yes, I did . . . ," but Manaka takes the wind out of his sails by immediately responding, "What did the chief say when you told him?" Joel has to admit, "He did not say much," indicating a lack of support for Joel's position, but Joel manages to add, "He did say that you did not behave well." Manaka finally returns to the theme of his complete abandonment of her and the children: "Don't you remember telling me proudly that she [the widow] has completely taken you and that you would never return to me? Didn't you tell me last Wednesday I should get a husband to support our children?" When he denies this, she pushes the point home by saying, "Didn't I tell you that the children were starving and that if this was noticed by the public, you would be the person to blame and no one else?"

At this point, as is usual, the hearing is opened up to questions by kgotla members. Most of the questions in this case come from those who have the honorary status of court councillors. The first set of questions goes back to the issue of the check. Joel is asked, "Do you say at one time you gave your wife a check to cash?" Joel replies affirmatively and is immediately asked, "What was the value of that check?" to which he replies "five hundred pula, or more accurately, 495 pula 90 thebe." Having established the amount, one of the court councillors asks him, "Did you ever ask your wife where the money is for the check you asked her to cash?" Joel evades the answer, bringing his wife's conduct into the spotlight again by averring, "She assaulted me before I could ask her."

The councillor, however, persists: "What did she say when you asked her after she assaulted you?" and Joel this time states, "She told me that she had used the money." The councillor then seeks to establish the truth of these allegations by embarking on a line of questioning geared to establishing if Joel reported the matter to anyone. He begins with a rhetorical question: "Were you happy with what she did?" and having received the expected "No, I was not happy," immediately follows it up with the crucial question "What did you say to her parents?" Joel knows where this line of questioning is leading and responds, "I told her parents that I had a complaint against their daughter," and quickly adds, "We have never met since then" (implying that her parents have been at fault in not taking up the matter). However, the court councillor requires more detailed information and asks, "What action did your wife's brother take?" to which Joel responds, "He never acted after the report." The court councillor then seeks to find out how seriously Joel pursued this course of action: "How many times have you reported your misunderstanding with your wife to her parents?" Joel is forced to concede, "Twice only," but attempts to show that he has taken recent action: "The last time was last Sunday."

The court councillor then probes the nature of his relationship with Manaka: "Do you say you are not divorcing this woman, she is still your wife?" Joel agrees: "Yes I said so." Having accepted that he is still her husband, he is then asked why he does not behave like one: "If you are not divorcing her why do you say that you cannot bear to live with a dangerous person in one house?" Joel attempts to minimize what he has said on the basis that it was said in the heat of the moment, in response to his wife's assault on him: "I said it at that time when I was in pain and bleeding from the head wound she inflicted." He has managed to put the spotlight back onto Manaka. The court councillor appears to be sympathetic: "Were the wounds caused by her beating painful?" Joel affirms this but finds that this is just another way in which the court councillor has manipulated the discussion to bring it back to the issue of reporting. If the assault was so serious, surely he must have reported the matter to their parents: "Now that you say they were painful and you were sad about that, what action did you take as regards reporting to her and your parents?" Joel maintains, "I did report to my wife's parents about the question of assault." He is asked once again, "What action did they take?" and responds once again that "They took no action." The fact that there was no action is a difficult one, it suggests that either Joel is lying or that Manaka's family was not taking him seriously. He attempts to rectify this by placing the onus for action or for lack of it on her family. However, he is not allowed to get away with this, as the councillor persists, "Do you think it is good for a man to stay away from his wife when they are living in one village [i.e., next door to one another] for almost a year?" Joel still insists, "Yes there is a right to do so." However he is immediately asked, "Would you give us an example of someone in this community who ever did so?" He is unable to answer and has to admit, "I can't quote an example," but he still argues, "A married man has the right to do so."

His credibility is then approached from another angle with the focus placed on his relationship with the other woman. He is asked, "Can you tell me when your wife told you that the widow woman could do the cooking and washing for you while she herself was in Molepolole, did she also consent to your having sex with her?" Joel has to admit that "nothing was ever said about sexual rights."

The rest of the question period is taken up with trying to get Joel to admit that he has behaved inappropriately and that he is to blame for the situation that has arisen. He denies this and asserts that his wife was motivated by a desire "to kill me and enjoy the estate after my death." However, this is ignored, and the councillor reiterates once more, "If you had heeded your wife's warning [not to associate with the widow], do you think she would have assaulted you?" Joel attempts to salvage his position on the basis of pride: "I could not yield because of my wife's bad attitude of scandalizing my name. If she were to talk to me politely [i.e., if she would have recognized his authority] I would have listened."

At this point the role of questioning reverts to Mr. Kgosiensho. He asks "Is it true that you are in love with the widow?" When Joel says, "Yes," he is then put under pressure to accept that it is his behavior which has given rise to conflict: "Didn't you realize that once you fell in love with another woman there was going to be trouble and corruption in your family [life]?" He is forced to admit, "I knew that it would be so." Such an admission is taken one step further: "Do you think it is good to quarrel with your family because of a concubine?" (this is the role assigned to the widow by the kgotla, which never seriously considers her relationship with Joel to be a marriage). Joel, however, cannot accept this and makes a last attempt to put some of the blame on his wife: "I find it good [acceptable] on my side because of the attitude my wife takes." However, he is not allowed to get away with this: "Don't you think it is just for your wife to take the attitude she does? You stop doing what she dislikes and then take up the matter with the appropriate parents." Joel argues, "I did so, and she continued to be very hostile to me, and I cannot now bear her hostility." He is then asked outright, "Which would you prefer, to come in peace with your wife or to insist on keeping to your own life. Which do you think it is fair for a man to do?" He knows what the appropriate response must be but continues to try to transfer the spotlight from himself to Manaka: "I would stop dealing with the widow if my wife would lessen her hostility and talk to me about this affair in a formal and polite manner."

Mr. Kgosiensho then turns to question Manaka. He asks her, "Do you know that a married woman must obey her husband and that a husband is bound to obey her?" When she says yes, he turns to Joel and asks him, "Do you want this kgotla to reprimand her for the attitude she adopts towards you and leave you free of blame?" Joel responds "I don't suppose so." He knows what is at stake and from the way in which his allegations have been dealt with that there is little support for his position. Mr. Kgosiensho then asks Manaka if she wishes to make a final statement. Manaka makes her final comment: "According to my feelings I want my husband to stop being in love with the widow because by continuing the association the quarrels will never end between us and it is a public shame even to have it brought to the attention of staff in the department in which he is working." Joel also makes his final comment: "I've already said I'm not intending to divorce her. She is my wife. What I want is that she obeys my order and does not overrule everything that I want done."

APPENDIX E

Text for the Makokas' Hearing

Eva Makoka, like Manaka Kgosidintsi, set the hearing in motion with the claim "Since August last year [1981] there has been great misunderstanding between me and my husband. Our misunderstanding began when he was working in Francistown and bought a bedstead. I went to see him up there to find that he had sold the bedstead, and I inquired as to whom he had sold the bedstead, telling him I wanted to collect it and that I would refund the buyer the cost. My husband would not show me the person who had bought the bedstead. He would not even give me his name and would not take me to his place." She then raises the issue of lack of support: "I suggested to him that now that he was earning money he should help me buy food. He said he would not do so. He told me that he would share the food I buy [i.e., he would eat her food but not pay for it]." She then goes on to emphasize his odd behavior: "After that he began to behave strangely, for example, sometimes when we were in the lolwapa he would go into the house at bedtime without saying anything to me and lock me outside. That happened regularly." She finally gets to the issue of the other woman: "One day in November 1981 he told me he would like me to quit the dwelling house because he was going to marry another woman. I told him that I had nowhere to go because you married me and brought me here."

The third party hearing the dispute, Mr. Kgosiensho, goes straight to the heart of the matter. He asks Eva, "Do you think you disagreement is only caused by the question of the bedstead?" to which Eva replies cautiously, "No, I think it is only one of the causes of misunderstanding, because we have disagreed before on other things, for example, on the question of clearing land for plowing." However, Mr. Kgosiensho is not prepared to let the matter rest there and probes her directly: "Are you suspicious that you husband gave the bedstead to a woman with whom he might have been in love?" which opens up the space for this to be discussed. Eva seizes her chance: "Yes I'm suspicious that it is so because of the fact that he has chosen to sleep alone in another house." The questions continue to follow a predictable pattern.

When Patrick Makoka makes his statement, he, like Joel Kgosidintsi, seeks to lay the blame on his wife. It is much shorter than Eva's statement, but it highlights her failure to behave like a proper wife. He begins, "In the first place I state that my wife does not live often inside our courtyard. She wanders around whenever she chooses to do so. The second thing is that she never prepares bedding for me. The third thing is that she never cooks for me. She never washes for me. We often quarrel when I reprimand her from wandering about at night.

I often hear her knocking at the door when I am asleep. I often ask her where she is coming from at such a late hour [implying she must have been visiting a lover]." His statement continued in that vein. He also is subjected to a predictable form of questioning. For example, he is asked by Mr. Kgosiensho, "What action did you take when your wife was coming late at night or not staying at home?" and "Have you ever reported her behavior to her parents?"

APPENDIX F

Text for Mmathari's and Tshotego's Hearing

Mmathari's brother begins by explaining that the dispute must now be dealt with by Borakalalo ward because all other channels have failed: "It began in this way: My daughter referred this matter to me that she had no understanding with her husband. I told her that she should report the matter to her husband's parents. Then she told me that she had reported the matter several times to her husband's parents and they took no action. I told her if that is the case there are subwardheads and wardheads where you stay in Borakalalo, they are the people to report to when your parents-in-law do not listen to what you say."

He then proceeds to build up a picture, using the death of one of his sister's children to present the parents-in-law and their son in a very negative light and floating the possibility of improper use of traditional medicine before his audience: "Then it happened that my daughter's child got sick and died. This was reported to me when I was at Masimo. We came down with other members of the family to bury the child. To our surprise our daughter's parents-in-law were not there." This would be viewed as a serious breach of obligation on their part. He continues,

> As a result the funeral took place at our premises when it should have been at the husband's premises. I had to send word to call in the parents [parents-in-law]. They did not come down to the funeral and I had to decide to take the girl to go and be buried on my side, at my people's place. When we were burying the child I heard that our daughter's husband had a second wife. My daughter was crying at the funeral and she uttered that it was traditional medicine administered by the husband and the woman he loved [which had killed the child]. I reprimanded my daughter for uttering such words even if she was in sorrow.

This is an adept way of alluding to the possibility of an improper use of traditional medicine while at the same time denying any responsibility on the part of the speaker for such allegations, because he rebukes the woman who makes them. He then raises the issue of the other woman: "After the funeral, when Mmathari came to Borakalalo from Masimo she noticed that her husband was living with that woman. She reported the matter to Piet Pheko [a headman]."

He goes on to build up why the case must be dealt with here, not just on account of the other family's failure to respond, but also by presenting his Mmathari as someone who can no longer be controlled by his or Piet's authority:

Then my daughter said to me, if you are not going to take up a case against my husband, I am going to offer a fight to that woman because she is getting away with my husband. I told my daughter that if she did that it would mean contempt of authority in so far as Piet is concerned because the case had already been reported to him as an official. Against my advice she slipped off at night to come to Borakalalo. When she got here she searched for her husband only to find him in bed with the woman she was always complaining about. She found them fast asleep.

She stood for a few minutes. On the table beside the bed there was a radio which she took as an exhibit—here it is [he held it aloft]. She took her husband's shoes and a pair of his trousers and a sweater and a waistcoat and skirt belonging to the woman. She took these to the police [as evidence because] her husband always denied being in love with the other woman. The police then referred the matter to the senior wardhead here. He asked Mmathari if she had ever taken up her complaint with both [sets of] parents and the appropriate subwardhead. She had not done so, so the case was referred to the subward and I was asked to preside over it.

He relates how he handled the matter and lays great stress on the fact that he has been left with the couple's children to care for: "I arranged for the hearing by calling upon my daughter's parents-in-law. When we examined the case my daughter's husband admitted that he was in love with that woman. When he admitted that he was in love, the men listening to the case agreed that if he had a second wife he had better take the children back from under my care."

He then goes on to deal with the other woman: "Then I asked him [Mmathari's husband] to explain his intentions regarding the second woman. He told me that the other woman was just his nyatsi. I told him that he could not have two wives because he cannot even support one wife and children. I told him that I would not like it if he married the second woman. I went to my senior ward Goaramupi, where they advised me to report to Borakalalo."

At this point Mmathari's brother becomes quite dramatic, making references to her becoming temporarily "mad." This serves two purposes: it emphasizes the fact that she is beyond control and that the matter has got out of hand as well as raising the implication that this may well have something to do with the improper use of traditional medicine and its effects being transferred from child to mother. This is never expressly articulated, but the description of her temporary condition resonates with her being "possessed" or "bewitched," of which the audience would be well aware:

When I went home my daughter was mentally disturbed. She was tied up with leather thongs and I went back to Goaramupi and I told them that my daughter is mad now. They said that we should stop the case for a while and tell her parents-in-law about her illness. I told them that it was useless for me to go to her people because they never take any notice of me. After that I decided to go and tell them. They refused to come and see her. Her husband also refused to come and see her. I went back to Goaramupi again and told them that those people refuse everything. They said that was all right and that they were cutting their own throat. I nursed my daughter myself until she recovered.

Mr. Masimega pointed out to me that Mmathari and her family were Bakgalagadi and that this might account for the man's family's lack of interest in the marriage.

The issue of property is then raised together with a plea for something to be done about the children: "After my daughter recovered she slipped away again and came back to Borakalalo. When she returned that evening she told me that her husband had removed all her household utensils from the hut and that there were other people living in her house. She said she had asked the neighbors and they said that the house had been rented. I took the matter up to Goaramupi, and they sent me back to Borakalalo with a message to go ahead with the case and said that if they [Borakalalo kgotla] need us they can call us."

The matter is then taken up by Abraham, the wardhead, who, like Mr. Kgo-siensho in the chief's kgotla, pursues a certain line of questions. Once he establishes that the parties were married through patlo, he asks the woman, "During your lifetime before he [the husband] became interested in the second woman were you living happily?" Her response is in the affirmative, thereby implying that the blame for the breakdown lies with him: "Yes, it was not until he fell in love with the other woman that there was trouble." Abraham then asks a question relating to woman's clothing removed from her husband's hut, establishing that he had a lover. He asks, "Is it true that it was you who took away the articles shown here as an exhibit (woman's clothing)?" To this she responds, "Yes."

He then goes on to probe her attitude to the other woman. He states, "I heard that you would agree that your husband marries another woman as a second wife if that wife was younger than you?" To this she replies, "Yes, I would have no objection if the woman that he married was not older than myself." The reason for this is that according to custom a first wife should be older than the second wife because she is in a more senior position. It is hard for a first wife to wield the power due to her if the second wife is in fact older than she. Mmathari's response adheres to convention. She recognizes that a wife has very little influence over her husband taking another wife under the customary system, and that she must not therefore appear to be against it in theory, as this would set her up in the public eye as a difficult woman. However, she may oppose the individual who is selected on the basis of particular criteria, such as age, and thereby contest what is happening.

Abraham, having established that she accedes to her husband's relationship with the other woman—at least, that she agrees to marriage—then seeks to find out what can be done to restore their relationship. he asks, "If this kgotla could make an order that the property that was removed from your hut be restored and that the people who are renting be expelled, would you accept to live with this man as husband and wife?" She appears to agree by saying, "Yes." He then tries to see if this is genuine by asking, "Are you sure?" She responds, "Yes." He then tries to probe her attitude to the other woman. He asks, "Do you want your husband to be a polygamist?" She replies, "I've no objections." He is not satisfied that she really does agree and puts a series of propositions to her to establish her real views. He inquires, "If the second wife was about your age and she happens to be wild and burn your dwelling house would that be good for you?" As may be expected she responds negatively: "No, it would not be good." He pursues this line: "Now, if that would make you unhappy, if that wife could destroy your home, how could you be happy because you accepted that your husband could marry her?" She has to respond, "I would not be happy if the other woman could destroy my property." He then comes to the crux of the issue as he sees it: "Are you laying temptation for this kgotla [i.e., tempting fate] or your parents by saying that you are willing for your husband to have a second wife?" She says, "No." He then asks, "If the kgotla here made an order that the property which was removed from your huts be restored and that you and your children should go and live in your premises could there be no trouble after that?" She responds, "I do not know." She is thereby leaving the matter open for discussion.

Abraham then focuses his attention on the man and asks him a series of questions aimed at calling his behavior into question and showing how he has been at fault as a husband. He starts by underlining their relationship through the use of a rhetorical question: "What relation is this woman to you?" He replies as expected: "She is my wife." Abraham continues to underline the fact that he has failed to act properly as a husband by implying that his behavior denies such a relationship: "Are you not lying when you say that you are married to her?" He responds, "No, I'm not lying."

The next set of exchanges is aimed at showing him how he behaves inappropriately because they do not live together: "At the present moment where do you stay and where does she stay?" He responds, as Abraham knows he must, that they are living apart: "I stay here at home in Borakalalo, and she stays with her family at Masimo." Abraham then tries to bring out into the open the reason for the separation and who instigated it: "Did you give her permission to live with her parents?" He responds, "No, I didn't." Abraham then seeks to find out why this situation exists: "What caused her to stay with her parents and you to stay at home when she had been properly married by patlo?" He is emphasizing the fact that husband and wife are meant to live together. Tshotego tries to place the responsibility for their separation on his wife, in the same way that Mr. Makoka did: "I don't know the cause because she simply went off and left me to go and live with her parents."

Abraham switches his line of questioning to get Tshotego to recognize that his behavior with the other woman is inappropriate: "I'm a blind man [he is literally], but are the articles shown here your property?" He responds, "Yes, they are my property." Abraham then attempts to raise the issue of why they are there, as a sign of dispute in the relationship: "Is it normal that they should be in the kgotla here? Is it the first time that she has brought your personal effects to the kgotla?" He answers, "Yes." Abraham then works up to the significance of the articles and the fact that they have been acquired under circumstances showing that the man has acted inappropriately: "Have these things been collected from your home?" Tshotego replies, "No, they have not been collected from my home." Having been pushed into this admission, he is then asked, "From whose home have these things been confiscated?" He responds, "From my sister's home." Abraham seeks to emphasize the point: "In your married life do you sleep in your sister's hut rather than sleep in your hut with your wife?" Tshotego knows that this is not conventional behavior, so he attempts to justify himself by stating, "It was because my wife deserted me to go and stay with her parents." Abraham, however, is not prepared to accept his responses and directly challenges him by asking, "The articles here include a skirt, do you wear a skirt?" He is forced into an admission: "It belongs to the person that I am in love with." To push his point home Abraham says, "In this case do you realize that this skirt was collected with your personal effects from where you were sleeping with your nyatsi?" He responds, "Yes."

Having extracted this admission, Abraham seeks to deal with his conduct and how he has handled the difficulties in his relationship with his wife: "Why did you remove the household utensils from your home and then let it [without consultation, it is implied]?" to which Tshotego replies, "I did it because I was giving up hope that my wife would come home, and I took things to my nyatsi for safekeeping." He is, by this response, attempting to place responsibility for his behavior on his wife. This is not accepted by Abraham, who asks, "What law or custom were you following in taking such an action, in taking household property to another woman's home in the absence of your wife?" Tshotego remains obstinate: "I had given up hope because my wife had left me." In seeking to establish the veracity of this claim, as Mr. Kgosiensho did with Nyana's partner, Abraham asks, "Have you ever gone to your wife's parents to tell them that your wife has left you?" Tshotego attempts to show that he has acted properly by stating, "Yes, I have done so."

Abraham seeks to stress the point of good behavior: "If this kgotla would show you how to behave as a married man according to Tswana custom, what would you think of that, would you think that they were oppressing you?" He replies, "No." He must show respect for the kgotla.

Abraham then takes up Tshotego's claim that he has informed his wife's family of her behavior and seeks to show his skepticism of this claim by stating, "I heard you saying that you have been to report to your wife's family. If they did not take any action, what action did you take to report the matter to the kgotla here?" Tshotego finally has to admit, "I made no effort." There were mutterings by kgotla members at this admission. He is then asked by Abraham, "What do you think now; here is your wife who has reported a case to the kgotla; what do you think?" Tshotego cannot say he disapproves, because he has been shown to have acted improperly, so he says something noncommittal: "I think it is alright." Abraham wants more than this, so he presses the point: "Do you think that she has done something good for you?" He has to admit that she has acted correctly: "Yes, she acted wisely."

An exchange follows, based on an attempt to get the man to see that he is at fault and to alter his attitude. Abraham inquires, "Do you think your wife is fair?" Tshotego is then asked, "Do you find that you are in the wrong?" Tshotego will not admit this, but he does say, "If the kgotla finds me guilty, I cannot say that it is unfair." Abraham attempts to get him to recognize that he is at fault by dealing with the question of his living arrangements: "Did you build a house for your wife?" When Tshotego responds affirmatively, he is asked, "In your life [experience] do you know anything [reason] why a man would leave his dwelling place in his wife's absence to live somewhere else?" He must respond in conventional terms: "No." Abraham then tries once more to get him to admit that he is at fault: "In the kgotla's opinion you are guilty; is that fair to you?" Tshotego agrees with resignation, "The kgotla would not be unfair if they found me guilty [of being a bad husband]."

NOTES

PREFACE

1. A kgotla is the assembly center (both the physical location and the body of members) of a group of households presided over by a male headman or ward-head; in the past, but no longer, all household heads were related through the female line. It forms part of the organization of Tswana society that revolves around the construction of a morafe (usually glossed as "tribe," but see n. 6). Kgotlas are structured through a tightly organized hierarchy of progressively more inclusive administrative groupings, beginning with households and extending through wards, which are the major units of political and legal organization, to the morafe as a whole. A more detailed discussion of these relationships is provided at the beginning of chap. 2.

2. For an explanation of Tswana proper names see n. 5.

3. My visit to Botswana in 1981 formed part of a long-standing link between the University of Botswana, Lesotho, and Swaziland, now the University of Botswana, and the Edinburgh University Law Faculty. Students from the three countries were trained in Lesotho and came to Edinburgh for two years of their five-year legal training. The government of Botswana then decided that it was time to establish its own law department within the University of Botswana, and Edinburgh University assisted in the setting up of such a department in 1981.

4. I took that position because the member of the staff who had been teaching family law left to go into private practice.

5. In Setswana the prefixes "Ba" and "Mo" are the plural and singular modifiers of nouns designating persons, so "Bakwena" is the plural form of Kwena (Kwena people/persons) and "Mokwena" is the singular form (a Kwena person).

6. The Setswana words morafe and merafe are often glossed as "tribe" and "tribes," respectively. I prefer to use the terms "polity" and "polities."

7. This designation, established during the period of British colonial over-rule (1885–1966) to denote the official representatives of the morafe, including the kgosi (chief), continues to operate in Botswana since independence.

8. In 1981 the enumerated population for Kweneng District was 117,127, and for the village of Molepolole itself, 20,565. By 1991 the figures had increased to 169,835 for Kweneng District and 36,928 for Molepolole itself (Botswana 1991b, table 1, p. 7, and table 2, p. 8).

9. Since my research was completed these developments have included the building of a diamond-sorting plant in the village by the company Anglo Ameri-

can and the creation of a new government air force base several kilometers from the village.

10. Mr. Masimega was born on 24 October 1914. He grew up at his father's and grandfather's lands at Phatlhaneng and Mokgnono (about ten kilometers from Molepolole). When he was eleven, his father, Gofetakgosi, took him to the London Missionary Society school in Molepolole to be educated. He did well at school and after completing Standard 6 was appointed a teacher at second grade in 1935. He taught for three years and then took up a job at the hospital in Lobatse. He and his wife Virginia Kekgatlhege Masimega married on 31 December 1939. She is related to the Kwena ruling family, being the daughter of Moiteelasilo, brother of Kebohula (fig. 5). They had ten children together and by 1992 had seventeen grandchildren. In 1941, Mr. Masimega was called to work for tribal administration by Kgosi Kgari Sechele and served as tribal secretary under him and Neale Sechele from 1942 to 1963. Between the years 1946 and 1949 he served as a sergeant with the British High Commission Territory Corps in Egypt. In 1963 he retired from tribal administration and in the 1974 elections was appointed a district councillor, an appointment which he held for five years.

11. The word Kgosing is derived from the word kgosi, interpreted as "chief." Kgosing refers both to the chief's ward, which is the most senior of all Kwena wards in the morafe over which it presides, and to the chief's kgotla (often, loosely, called chief's court), which lies at the heart of Kgosing ward, representing the most senior of all the kgotlas within the ward itself. I use Kgosing to refer to the ward and chief's kgotla to refer to the court.

12. The role attributed to these forums within the national legal system is discussed in chap. 1 under "Upholding Divisions: The Old Legal Pluralism."

13. Simon Roberts became my Ph.D. supervisor and mentor in the United Kingdom.

CHAPTER ONE

1. Polygyny came under attack from missionaries who were active in the Protectorate from 1821 onward (Comaroff and Comaroff 1991:46–48). In their attempts to "colonize minds" (Ngugi wa Thiong'o 1986) they sought to eradicate what they considered to be "heathen" and "uncivilized" practices including polygyny and initiation ceremonies for boys and girls. Their influence and the means by which they sought to consolidate it, although not always successful, had an enormous impact which should not be underestimated (Comaroff and Comaroff 1991).

2. For a more detailed discussion refer to chap. 2, "The Household and Politics," "The Household and Economic Organization," and "Models of Tswana Kinship and Marriage."

3. Izzard (1985:264) observes that the majority of women in Botswana will be temporary or permanent female household heads (whether married or unmarried) at some point in their lives. *National Development Plan 1985–1991* (Botswana 1985 [hereafter NDP6]:9) notes that "women predominate among young adults and as heads of households." It also comments (p. 11) that "females headed a third of the households in urban areas and half in the rural areas."

4. In the past, women have very occasionally acted as regents for the morafe, but in these unusual circumstances they were seen to be fulfilling a male role.

5. My data and that of others (Kerven 1979a, 1979b) show that it is these households that have the necessary livestock to plow and can thus command the labor of other family members, or that can afford to hire whatever is necessary.

6. My own data from Mosotho kgotla show that women have a higher degree of education than men in the kgotla, but that is because a large number of the older men have no formal schooling at all.

7. Births to women between the ages of 15 and 19 increased by 43% between 1971 and 1981 (Botswana 1986:18), and a recent study (Botswana 1989:30) observes that the proportion of teenage mothers increased from 15% in 1971 to 24% in 1988.

8. Alexander (1991:34) notes that "the figures indicate that 80% of the drop-outs at secondary schools are girls and the majority of girls drop out due to pregnancy."

9. Although there has been a large expansion and diversification of the economy, women are still located primarily in traditionally designated female fields: nursing, teaching, and community service (Takirambudde 1991, cited in Stewart 1994:17). Although manufacturing has developed significantly, women remain marginal to mainstream enterprises such as textiles and garment making. Datta (n.d.) reinforces these findings: 30% of women are located in either domestic service or agricultural labor both of which represent the least-paid jobs (less than 175 pula per month), with no minimum wages or job security; the sectors of electricity and water, transport and communication, finance and business services, and mining and quarrying (on average 1,000 pula per month) account for only 6.8% of employment of women; finally, the only well-paid employment for women is in education, where approximately 13.5% of employed women are located. Even in the field of education the majority of women are employed as primary school teachers, the lowest-paid categories (salaries of less than 700 pula per month). UNICEF's report (1989) shows the gender disparities of formal sector employment even more starkly in the following ratios (men:women): in commerce 1.4:1 and in the construction sector 28.5:1. According to UNICEF (1989) the areas which are most likely to expand in the future (water and electricity, manufacturing, finance and business services, commerce and transport) represent the sectors where the ratios of males to females are the lowest, with the exception of transport. For further information see Stewart 1994.

10. The implication being that as the Nuer did not have law they were not therefore a civilized society, a claim which Evans-Pritchard contested.

11. S. represents the legal abbreviation for reference to a section of an act.

12. From 1885 until 1966, when it acquired its independence, Botswana was known as the Bechuanaland Protectorate and was subject to British overrule. During the Protectorate the common law was derived from the Roman-Dutch system operating in the Cape (Aguda 1973), which is now part of South Africa. This form of law had its roots in the Continental assimilation of Roman law at the time of its reception in Europe in the late medieval and early modern period (Hahlo and Kahn 1960). However, since the Cape was a British colony at the time of the Protectorate, some academics (e.g., Brewer 1974) have suggested that

because of the influence of English law principles in the 1800s, the term "Cape colonial law" is more appropriate for designating this body of law than Roman-Dutch law. While operative today in Botswana, Roman-Dutch law forms part of the common law together with legislation passed by the National Assembly. For a European lawyer this provides an unusual definition of common law that includes statutory provisions. Such a definition, however, is used to set up and distinguish common from customary law in Botswana.

13. Indeed, as the papers in the Mann and Roberts (1992) volume *Law in Colonial Africa* demonstrate, Africans actively engaged with law in all forums, and did so as much to enhance political maneuvering among themselves as with Europeans.

14. For example, through the mode of life exemption contained in s.2 of the Dissolution of African Marriages (Disposal of Property) Act [Cap.29:06] which provides for the application of common, rather than customary, law, with respect to the division of property on the dissolution of African marriages under certain circumstances.

15. For further information refer to J. L. Comaroff 1976.

16. The jurisdiction of the chief's kgotla is governed by the Customary Courts Act [Cap.04:05] and the Customary Courts (Procedure) Rules implemented under s.44 of that act. S.10 of the Customary Courts Act sets out the civil jurisdiction that applies to customary courts, and statutory instruments, such as no. 116 of 1976 and no. 18 of 1984 under the Recognition and Establishment of Customary Courts (Amendment) Notice, detail the limits of authority which apply to chiefs, senior chiefs' representatives, chiefs' representatives, and headmen. Their criminal jurisdiction is dealt with in s.11 of the Customary Courts Act and through statutory instruments such as no. 116 of 1976, which set out their powers. There are, however, certain types of cases both civil and criminal which are excluded from the jurisdiction of customary courts altogether, and these are set out in s.12 of the Customary Courts Act.

17. The extent of magistrates' courts' jurisdiction to apply customary law is uncertain; for discussions on this point see Himsworth 1972 and Bennett 1985.

18. S.36 of the Customary Courts Act [Cap.04:05] empowers the president to appoint a Customary Court of Appeal. The rules governing this court are contained in Statutory Inst. No. 3 of 1986, made through powers conferred on the Minister of Local Government and Lands by s.44 of the Customary Courts Act. However, this court operates at the level of a lower magistrate's court, and appeals from it go to the most senior magistrate's court or directly to the High Court (under the Customary Courts [Amendment] Act 1986).

19. For an account of the way in which disputing agencies associated with the kgotla system were incorporated into the national legal system of the Protectorate and their postcolonial characteristics see Roberts 1972b. For an account of the current structure of courts in the formal legal system of Botswana see Molokomme 1991:30–36.

CHAPTER TWO

1. These are Kgosing, Maunatlala, Mokgalo, Ratshosa (often referred to locally as Tshosa ward), Ntloedibe, and Borakalalo.

2. A cross-cousin of a person is the child of that person's parent's opposite-sex sibling; i.e., a man's mother's brother's or father's sister's daughter and a woman's father's sister's or mother's brother's son.

3. NDP6 comments that "females head a third of the households in urban areas and half in the rural areas" (p. 11). See also UNICEF (1989:61–62). The government's latest national development plan, NDP7 (Botswana 1991a [*National Development Plan 1991–1997*]), observes that "women headed 40% of households in urban areas and nearly half in the rural areas" (p. 9).

4. Kocken and Uhlenbeck (1980:59) observed that women tended to establish their own households at a later stage in the life cycle than their male counterparts. More recently Alexander (1991:17) noted that male heads of households are on average five years older than female heads in both rural and urban areas and that the average age for both female and male heads is eleven years higher in the rural areas than in the urban areas.

5. I use the term "household" to represent a physical entity or domain which is located in or associated with a kgotla.

6. The term "female-headed household," which appears in the literature on government planning and policy development in Botswana (Botswana 1982) is one which is the subject of some controversy (Peters 1983; Kerven 1984). I use the term "female-headed household" to denote those households associated with Mosotho kgotla in which women are in de facto control of the household and lands attached to it and where no adult male of equivalent generational status, whether husband, partner, or brother, was present at the time of research. In sixteen of the eighteen cases no adult male whatsoever was present (mainly due to migrant labor). In two cases, concerning widows, two young adult sons were present because they were unable to find work.

7. According to UNICEF (1989:58), "Female-headed households with no male present had an annual income less than one-half that of male-headed households, and just over half that of female-headed households with a male present." Given the range of factors affecting women's access to resources, the same report (p. 58) concluded that "household structure (male- or female-headed), is . . . an important predictor of poverty patterns." See also the study by Kossoudji and Mueller (1983:839). The government (NDP7:16–17) also documents that "households headed by women (which account for nearly half of all households) have generally lower incomes than male-headed households."

8. In the case of all thirty households, I have looked at the contributions made over time by absent household members (both women and men) as well as looking beyond the household itself to the broader family group and intra-household contributions, exchanges, and pooling of resources. For a detailed account of the history and developmental cycle of all households associated with the kgotla from 1937 to 1984 see A. Griffiths (1988a).

9. The national *Household Income and Expenditure Survey 1985/1986* (Botswana 1988c) shows that rural households depended on cash earnings and cash gifts to provide up to 50% of their income and support as compared with 23% derived from their own produce.

10. A situation analysis carried out by Maendeleo (Botswana) for UNICEF (UNICEF 1993:21) observed that "taking into account the lower incomes of fe-

male-headed households and their much lower cattle holdings it is clear that they constitute the majority of the poor and the poorest of the poor." The government notes that "35% of all farming households are female-headed, concentrated amongst the resource poor" (NDP7:242).

11. These findings may be contrasted with those of Murray (1981a) for Lesotho, where bohali (marriage payment) is more commonly used as a means of redistributing resources within the community.

12. Out of the ninety-two marriages involving sixty-one men and thirty-one women, bogadi featured in eight cases involving three women and five men.

13. 1977 Third Parliamentary Session, Hansard 59.

14. Christianity is very influential in Botswana (Comaroff and Comaroff 1991) and many Batswana are members of various churches, from the well-established Presbyterian, Roman Catholic, and Anglican denominations to the more prophetic sects that have developed a following over the years.

15. Otlhogile (1989:62) disagrees with me on this point. For him, "when a person enters into marriage under either system, he/she makes a *choice* of law" (emphasis added), and thus a person cannot truly "marry" under both systems, although he recognizes that "going through a second ceremony under either system with the same person is perfectly legal." When persons married under customary law also solemnize their marriage under the Marriage Act 1970 he interprets "solemnization" in this context to mean merely a celebration or ceremony, as it were, a symbolic affirmation only. I do not agree with this characterization. I argue that the choice of law is not limited in this way where a person is marrying the same person—in other words, that there is nothing in the Marriage Act which distinguishes between marriages which are constituted as such under the terms of this Act and those which represent mere formalities or celebrations. I argue that the second ceremony is not a mere ceremony but constitutive of marriage where it is registered under the common law system. If this were not so, and such a distinction could be made, this would cast doubt on the status of all registered marriages because the public would be unable to rely on the accuracy of the register and further inquiries would have to be made. The kinds of issues that are sparked by this debate on marriage reflect different perspectives on law—one which takes a flexible, integrative approach and another which thinks in terms of systems that are separate from one another and that give rise to "conflict" when they come into contact. This latter approach is in line with the old form of legal pluralism which endorses a dual systems theory of law.

16. In 1982 a preliminary survey carried out in the village with the help of Herman, Mr. Masimega's son, indicated a high incidence of marriage celebrated according to both common and customary law. This is borne out by data from Mosotho kgotla, where just over one-third of marriages (that is, thirty-five out of ninety-two marriages) involved patlo and a church or civil ceremony.

17. Out of the ninety-two marriages, eighty-six involved patlo. There were only six marriages where patlo did not feature and these involved five marriages by special license and one ordinary civil ceremony. Out of the thirty-five marriages that involved patlo and a common law component, sixteen involved a church ceremony, seventeen involved a civil ceremony, and two involved a special license. There were fifty-one marriages where patlo alone was involved.

18. Generation 2 (G.2) accounts for nineteen out of the sixty-one marriages, that is, almost one-third, and these marriages were entered into by thirteen men. Breaking the figures down in terms of generation, there are thirty-two marriages among the younger men in G.3 and ten marriages among the even younger men in G.4.

19. There were fifteen marital relationships among the women in G.3 and sixteen marital relationships among the women in G.4.

20. That is, seventy out of 103 relationships.

21. Out of the 103 other relationships, seventy involving fifty-six women and twelve men are no longer active; thirty-three are current involving twenty-two women and eleven men.

22. Twenty-seven women in G.3 compared with five men in G.3; twenty-six women in G.4 and seven men in G.4.

23. Nineteen relationships within the fleeting and brief categories and fourteen relationships in the intermediate and lifelong categories.

24. Only three out of twenty-one relationships fall within the more socially recognized intermediate and lifelong categories.

25. Out of 103 other nonmarital relationships only thirty-three are current.

26. Out of the twenty-two current relationships involving women, fifteen are associated with G.4 compared with seven in G.3.

27. In 1984 there were thirty women in childbearing relationships in G.3; among them there were fifteen formal marriages and forty other kinds of relationships including seven current relationships. In G.4 there were forty-six women in childbearing relationships; among them were sixteen formal marriages and thirty-nine other types of relationship including fifteen current relationships. By 1989 five out of the fifteen current relationships in G.4 had been converted into formal marriages.

CHAPTER THREE

1. This is because it was their leader Kgabo, the younger son of Tebele, who on his father's death seceded from the main group of Kwena living in the Transvaal under his brother Mogapa's control and led his group of followers into what is now Botswana and established them there (Sillery 1954:50; Schapera 1980; Ramsay 1991:51).

2. Under a mafisa arrangement, cattle are lent out in patronage to individuals who become clients under obligatory conditions which include mortgaging the clients' assets against the safety of the patron's property and interests.

3. For discussion of the transformations that have taken place see Silitshena 1978, 1982a, 1982b.

4. Household 4, which is physically present in the kgotla is not dealt with here, because it is in fact affiliated with the neighboring Moitlobo kgotla, which along with Mosotho and Motlabi kgotlas forms part of Basimane ward, a subward to Kgosing.

5. These were households 20–31.

6. These were households 12 and 5.

7. A Tswana household has at least two, ideally three, places of residence:

in the village, "at the lands," and (if cattle are owned) at a cattlepost. "The lands" are the household agricultural fields, assigned by the wardhead. In the past, male household heads divided their time between the cattlepost and the village, where they were required to participate in kgotla affairs; they were seldom at the lands, which were entrusted to women.

8. Nkadikang was at the mines from 1938 through 1960, Ntlogelang from 1945 until 1980, and Ramojaki from 1957 to 1970. Makokwe's youngest son, Aswa, left for the mines as soon as he was old enough and has never been heard of since. He is representative of a number of adults referred to by Schapera who became lost to a morafe through the course of migrant labor.

9. He is regarded as the youngest son because of Aswa's disappearance years ago.

10. In Ntlogelang's case some of these arrangements were with kin and others were not.

11. Nkgadikang (household 22), Ntlogelang (household 29), Morabane (household 23), and Ramojaki (household 24).

12. This was from Tsebekgale, who was the daughter of Godisaofe, brother to Tshitoeng (fig. 4a).

13. Of the 82% of women in G.3 who received some formal education, 59% of them attended primary school but did not complete it, 22% completed primary school, and 18% attended secondary school. This may be compared with the 85% of women in the younger generation (G.4), of whom 41% attended primary school but did not complete it, 16% completed primary school, and 41% attended secondary school.

14. Of the 33% of men in G.3 who received some formal education, 60% of them attended primary school but did not complete it, 20% completed primary school, and 20% attended secondary school. This may be compared with 39% of men in G.4 who received some formal education–38% of them attended primary school but did not complete it, 8% completed primary school, 38% attended secondary school, and 15% completed secondary school.

15. In Mosotho kgotla as a whole, 30% of women in G.3 and 29% of women in G.4 had to leave school because of pregnancy. Very few of these women ever returned to complete their formal education or turned to adult education to fill the gap.

16. Both married according to patlo, which was carried out in Koketso's case after the research visit in 1984, and which in Mmupi's case took place in 1989.

17. Compared with a 30% rate for women overall in Mosotho kgotla.

18. She is not unusual in this respect. Only 24% of women in G.3 have experienced any type of formal employment, compared with 62% of men in the same generation.

19. Among the younger women in G.4 only 31% have experienced some type of formal employment, compared with 51% of men in their generation.

20. This is a cow or heifer which is paid as compensation to the woman's family for "spoiling" her (through pregnancy) before serious marriage negotiations are underway.

21. ALDEP stands for the Agricultural Lands Development Economic Programme.

22. Nametso died of an illness in 1987, and Margaret was killed in a car crash in 1984.

23. This former "homeland" is now part of Northwest Province in post-apartheid South Africa.

24. On a return visit to Botswana in 1992 I discovered that Patricia had married according to common law and had a child.

25. See Ramsay (1991) for the use of Christianity in power politics among Bakwena.

26. Dr. Merriweather was informed in his capacity as minister of the London Missionary Society church in Molepolole. It was the practice at that time for any members of the congregation who became pregnant to report the matter to him.

27. It is a firmly held belief among certain congregations that people should not drink.

28. This is in accordance with the practice that when a woman becomes pregnant by a man from another tribal area the kgosi is approached before the parents of the man are contacted.

CHAPTER FOUR

1. For details of their duties see NDP7:445–72.

2. This is because the eldest son of Kgosi Bonewamang was too young to succeed to office when his father died in 1978.

3. Elsewhere in Botswana this is not always the case; for example, this was not Molokomme's (1991:5) experience in Kanye.

4. In 61% of cases, that is, 66 out of 109 situations that had arisen by 1984.

5. In 56% of cases, that is, thirty-seven out of sixty-six relationships.

6. That is, in six cases.

7. That is, in twenty-one out of thirty-seven cases.

8. These accounted for 27% of cases, or eighteen out of the sixty-six meetings.

9. That is, fourteen out of eighteen cases

10. That is in seventeen out of forty-three cases

11. This is something which Motzafi-Haller (1986) has also highlighted in her research.

12. This was the case in six out of forty-three situations where there was no contact.

13. In four out of six cases.

14. These claims are reinforced by written records in both the chief's kgotla and the magistrate's court which chart the increase.

15. Schapera's unpublished field notes on Bakwena compiled in 1937 support this claim.

16. A shebeen is an informal, unlicensed business enterprise, often run from home, that sells homemade beer.

17. She would of course have been turned away because a second child was involved.

18. This is on the basis that compensation is payable to the woman's guardian for her seduction whereas the claim for maintenance is specifically based on

the concept of support for the child or children concerned. However, s.13 of the Affiliation Act provides that "no court shall have jurisdiction in respect of a complaint under section three where proceedings by the complainant for substantially the same relief as provided by this Act had been instituted in relation to the same child in a customary court, and the final determination of those proceedings is still pending or has been made upon the merits." The effect of this section in the law is however still an open question (Molokomme 1991:75–76).

19. In the case of *Leepile v. Lejone* (MO 76/81) maintenance of twenty-five pula a month was awarded in the magistrate's court in the knowledge that an award for seduction had already been made by a customary court.

20. These views are in line with those expressed by the general public in response to the select committee's investigation into this issue in 1976, prior to the 1977 amendment to the Affiliation Proceedings Act.

21. Because this took place before my subsequent research in 1984, the case report written in Setswana was translated by Mr. Masimega and parties were later interviewed to elaborate on what had taken place.

22. Among her generation there are twenty-seven women including herself in this position, compared with fifteen who have had children only within formal marriage.

23. This was information acquired during the 1982 research period.

24. This practical approach to the problem of corroboration is one which is supported to varying degrees under Roman-Dutch law in South Africa (see S. v Swart 1965 [3] SA 454 [AD] and S. v Jeggels 1962 SA 704). However, the relationship between Roman-Dutch law and legislation such as the Affiliation Proceedings Act, representing different branches of the common law in Botswana, is a problematic one. Not only that, but according to Molokomme (1991:81), this relationship is further complicated by the uncertainty which currently surrounds the scope of the presumption of paternity under Roman-Dutch law in Botswana.

25. By the Affiliation Amendment Act 1977.

26. While the statute presents a time limit, under Roman-Dutch law, no such limit exists and a case can be brought at any time. The conflict between the two has been resolved in the High Court in favor of the statutory provision (*Makwati v. Ramohago*).

27. The case of *Makwati v. Ramohago* (unreported, civil appeal 7/1982), heard in the High Court on 16 September 1982 (Molokomme and Otlhogile 1987:21), was dismissed by the judge on the basis that the twelve-month limitation within which a complaint could be made was peremptory and not directory, with the result that the case, which was not raised within this period, was time barred.

28. It had in fact worked its way up through three kgotlas.

29. This statement is dubious, as in practice, it may last for years. However, in this case there was not the contact between the families that one would expect.

30. While Bakwena continue to follow this rule, another morafe, Bakgatla, awards compensation not only for the first, but for all subsequent pregnancies that a woman undergoes, since Linchwe Kgafela became kgosi in 1962 (Comaroff and Roberts 1977:110).

CHAPTER FIVE

1. This was a common practice because of the lack of facilities for training teachers in the Protectorate at that time.

2. For reasons that were unclear, this aspect of Manaka's allegations was ignored in the kgotla, and when she tried to revive discussion on this topic at the end of the dispute she was unsuccessful.

3. As this took place before my research visit in 1984, Mr. Masimega translated the case report, which was then supplemented by interviews with interested parties.

4. Unfortunately Joel Kgosidintsi was not available for comment on the relationship at any time during the research period.

5. Unfortunately Mr. Makoka was not available for comment on the relationship at any time during the research period.

6. Under this act a woman who is married according to common or customary law may apply for maintenance from her husband on her own behalf and that of her children, where he has deserted or fails to support her and their children.

CHAPTER SIX

1. In fact wards have only administrative powers and are no longer are empowered to levy fines, although Borakalalo appears to ignore this.

2. Disquiet was expressed about a division of property taking place at ward level in the House of Chiefs in 1982 when the preliminary research findings were discussed there. The point was made that traditionally such a division is only within the jurisdiction of the kgosi.

3. This was at an interview on 20 June 1982.

4. When interviewed on 20 June 1982.

5. Schapera's notes of June 1938 refer to the kgosi introducing the number of eight head of cattle as compensation for pregnancy as well as an award that might be made on divorce to deter husbands from leaving their wives. This was during a period when labor migration was increasing and the kgosi felt that his authority over the morafe was waning. His ruling was an attempt to reestablish control.

6. Comaroff and Roberts (1981:18) make this point more generally in relation to the nature of mekgwa le melao ya Setswana.

7. For the full text of this hearing refer to A. Griffiths 1989b.

CHAPTER SEVEN

1. This was known as the Married Women's Property Act but was changed to the Married Person's Property Act, as the reference to women in the title was apparently a draftsman's error (personal communication from Deputy Attorney General, 1984).

2. Although the official record refers to this case as Matrimonial Cause 106 of 1978, this is clearly inaccurate, as the Moisakamo case was in fact heard after the Molomo case and makes reference to it. In their casebook Molokomme and Otlhogile (1987:62) cite the date of the Moisakamo case as 23 September 1981.

3. Mr. Masimega commented in discussions years later that Murray's father

was a staunch Christian who believed that marriage must take place where pregnancy ensued in a relationship. He encouraged Murray to marry Gofetamang
even though she was not considered an ideal marriage partner for his son.

4. For a more detailed discussion of the third-party role see A. Griffiths
1986.

5. For a discussion of the two cases see A. Griffiths 1983.

6. All cattle are branded with marks that identify them as belonging to a
particular owner. Because men control the cattleposts, they are in a position to
change the brand of a particular animal and often do so—not only where there
wives are concerned.

7. Not only that, but as John Comaroff (personal communication, 14 July
1994) has observed, much of his research has been undertaken among Tswana-
speaking peoples who live in South Africa and who have experienced apartheid
under state law. In the context of his research, legal pluralism was not perceived
by Africans as representing any real form of choice among existing legal options
sanctioned by the state.

CHAPTER EIGHT

1. The position of Tswana women here may be contrasted with that of Her-
ero women in Botswana, who have an active relationship with and control
over cattle.

2. There have been debates about what form a feminist agenda should take.
In particular, heated discussions surround the issue of whether feminists should
engage with theory or work toward a feminist jurisprudence. These debates arise
due to concerns over the extent to which such scholarship will be co-opted by
"masculinist" ways of thinking and reproduce power relations set up by male
thought. While scholars such as MacKinnon (1983, 1987) continue to work with
theory, others such as Lahey (1985:538) vehemently reject such an enterprise.
Yet other feminists, such as Bottomley and Conaghan (1993), take exception to
the divide between theoretical and antitheoretical stances or between theory and
practice. Instead, they adopt a theoretical stance based on engagement which
allows for movement between theory and practice.

3. See Benda-Beckmann 1983 for a critique of the way in which legal norms
are conceptualized and the characteristics that are ascribed to their relationship
with human behavior.

4. Unity Dow, a Motswana and lawyer married to a man who is not a citizen
of Botswana, challenged sections 4 and 5 of the Citizenship Act 1984 on the
basis that they contravened section 3 of the Constitution of Botswana, which
confers rights and freedoms on individuals in Botswana. The basis of her challenge was that these sections, which provide that after 1985 the children of
women who are Batswana and married to noncitizens are not entitled to Botswana citizenship, discriminate against women who are married on the ground
of sex (and in effect, against the children of such women). These provisions do
not apply to the children of male Batswana married to noncitizens, who are entitled to full citizenship. The argument presented by the state in response to this
claim was that notwithstanding section 3, and section 15, which deals with discrimination, the Citizenship Act was not in contravention of the Constitution,

as the discrimination referred to in section 15 did not cover sex. The state argued the omission of sex from section 15 was deliberate policy, implemented in order to uphold the patrilineal structure of society in Botswana. For further details see *Unity Dow v. The Attorney General,* High Court Misca. no. 124/90, and *The Attorney General v. Unity Dow,* Court of Appeal, Civil Appeal no. 4/91. For local comment see the *Botswana Guardian,* 14 June 1991, and the *Botswana Gazette,* 19 June 1991. Sections 4 and 5 of the Citizenship Act have now been amended retrospectively by the Citizenship (Amendment) Act 1995 to ensure that children acquire citizenship of Botswana from either parent, by birth if they are born in Botswana, and by descent if born outside the country.

APPENDIX B
1. Transcript Case no. 1012/83. Heard 22 November 83.

REFERENCES

Abel, R. L. 1973. A Comparative Theory of Dispute Institutions in Society. *Law and Society Review* 8:217–347.

Adepoju, A. 1994. Women, Work and Fertility in Swaziland. In *Gender, Work and Population in Sub-Saharan Africa,* edited by A. Adepoju and C. Oppong, 157–172. Published on behalf of the International Labour Office, Geneva. London: James Currey; Portsmouth, N.H.: Heinemann.

Aguda, Justice A. 1973. Legal Development in Botswana from 1885 to 1966. *Botswana Notes and Records* 5:52–63.

Alexander, E. 1991. *Women and Men in Botswana: Facts and Figures.* Ministry of Finance and Development Planning, Central Statistics Office Gaborone: Government Printer.

Allison, C. 1985. Women, Land, Labour and Survival: Getting Some Basic Facts Straight. *Institute of Development Studies Bulletin* 16(3):24–30.

Allott, A. N. 1970. *New Essays in African Law.* London: Butterworths.

Allott, A. N., and G. R. Woodman, eds. 1985. *People's Law and State Law: The Bellagio Papers.* Cinnaminson, N.J.: Foris Publications.

Alverson, H. 1978. *Mind in the Heart of Darkness: Value and Self-Identity among the Tswana of Southern Africa.* New Haven, Conn.: Yale University Press.

Benda-Beckmann, F. von. 1983. Why Law Does Not Behave: Critical and Constructive Reflections on the Social Scientific Perception of the Social Significance of law. In *Papers of the Symposia on Folk Law and Legal Pluralism, XIth International Congress of Anthropological and Ethnological Sciences, Vancouver, Canada, April 19–23, 1983,* compiled by H. Finkler, 1:232–262. Ottawa: Commission on Folk Law and Legal Pluralism.

———. 1989. Scapegoat and Magic Charm: Law in Development Theory and Practice. *Journal of Legal Pluralism and Unofficial Law* 28:129–147.

Bennett, T. 1985. *Application of Customary Law in Southern Africa: The Conflict of Personal Laws.* Cape Town: Juta.

Bledsoe, C. 1990. Transformations in Sub-Saharan African Marriage and Fertility. *Annals of the American Academy of Political and Social Sciences,* July, 115–125.

Boateng, E. O. 1994. Gender-Sensitive Statistics and the Planning Process. In *Gender, Work and Population in Sub-Saharan Africa,* edited by A. Adepoju and C. Oppong, 88–111. Published on behalf of International Labour Office, Geneva. London: James Currey; Portsmouth, N.H.: Heinemann.

Boberg, P. Q. R. 1977. *The Law of Persons and the Family.* Cape Town: Juta.

Bohannan, P. 1957. *Justice and Judgment among the Tiv*. London: Oxford University Press for the International African Institute. (2d ed. published 1968.).

Botswana, Republic of. 1976. *The Rural Income Distribution Survey in Botswana 1974/75*. Ministry of Finance and Development Planning, Central Statistics Office. Gaborone: Government Printer.

———. 1982. *Migration in Botswana: Patterns, Causes and Consequences*. Final report of the National Migration Study, vol. 3. Ministry of Finance and Development Planning, Central Statistics Office. Gaborone: Government Printer.

———. 1985. *National Development Plan (NDP6) 1985–1991*. Ministry of Finance and Development Planning, Central Statistics Office. Gaborone: Government Printer.

———. 1986. *Botswana Country Profile*. Ministry of Finance and Development Planning, Central Statistics Office. Gaborone: Government Printer.

———. 1988a. *Education Statistics*. Ministry of Finance and Development Planning, Central Statistics Office. Gaborone: Government Printer.

———. 1988b. *Teenage Pregnancies in Botswana: How Big Is the Problem and What Are the Implications?* Gaborone: National Institute of Development Research and Documentation and the University of Botswana.

———. 1988c. *Household Income and Expenditure Survey 1985/1986*. Ministry of Finance and Development Planning, Central Statistics Office. Gaborone: Government Printer.

———. 1989. *Family Health Survey II 1988*. Edited by Lesetedinyana T. Lesetedi, Gaboratanelwe D. Mompati, Pilale Khulumari, Gwen N. Lesetedi, Naomi Rutenberg. Gaborone: Ministry of Finance and Development Planning, Central Statistics Office; Columbia, Md.: Institute for Resource Development/Macro Systems.

———. 1991a. *National Development Plan 1991–1997 (NDP7)*. Ministry of Finance and Development Planning, Central Statistics Office. Gaborone: Government Printer.

———. 1991b. *Population Census: Preliminary Results*. Ministry of Finance and Development Planning, Central Statistics Office. Gaborone: Government Printer.

———. n.d. a. *Kweneng District Development Plan 1977–1982*. Kweneng District Council and Kweneng District Development Committee. Gaborone: Government Printer.

———. n.d. b. *Kweneng District Development Plan for the Years 1986–87 and 1988–89*. Kweneng District Council and Kweneng District Development Committee. Gaborone: Government Printer.

Bottomley, A., and J. Conaghan. 1993. Introduction. In special issue: *Feminist Theory and Legal Strategy. Journal of Law and Society* 20(1):1–5.

Boyd, S. 1989. From Gender Specificity to Gender Neutrality? Ideologies in Canadian Child Custody Law. In *Child Custody and the Politics of Gender*, edited by C. Smart and S. Svenhuijsen, 126–157. London: Routledge.

Brewer, I. 1974. Sources of the Criminal law in Botswana. *Journal of African law* (18)1:24.

Brown, B. 1983. The Impact of Male Labour Migration on Women in Botswana. *African Affairs* 82(328):367–388.

————. 1985. *Report on the Child Maintenance Laws.* Gaborone: Women's Affairs Unit, Ministry of Home Affairs.

Cain, M., and K. Kulcsar. 1982. Thinking Disputes: An Essay on the Origins of the Dispute Industry. *Law and Society Review* 16(3):375–402.

Channock, M. 1982. Making Customary Law: Men, Women and Courts in Colonial Northern Rhodesia. In *African Women and the Law: Historical Perspectives,* edited by M. Hay and M. Wright, 53–67. Papers on Africa, no. 7. Boston: Boston University, African Studies Center.

————. 1985. *Law, Custom and Social Order: The Colonial Experience in Malawi and Zambia.* Cambridge: Cambridge University Press.

————. 1989. Neither Customary nor Legal: African Customary Law in an Era of Family Law Reform. *International Journal of Law and the Family* 3:72–88.

Collier, J. F., and M. Rosaldo. 1981. Politics and Gender in Simple Societies. In *Sexual Meanings,* edited by S. Ortner and H. Whitehead, 275–329. Cambridge: Cambridge University Press.

Collier, J., and J. Starr, eds. 1989. *History and Power in the Study of Law: New Directions in Legal Anthropology.* Ithaca, N.Y.: Cornell University Press.

Collier, J. F., and S. J. Yanagisako. 1987. Toward a Unified Analysis of Gender and Kinship. In *Gender and Kinship: Essays Toward a Unified Analysis,* edited by J. F. Collier and S. J. Yanagisako, 14–50. Stanford, Calif.: Stanford University Press.

Comaroff, J. L. 1973. Competition for Office and Political Processes among the Barolong boo Ratshidi. Ph.D. diss., University of London.

————. 1976. Tswana Transformations, 1953–1975. In *The Tswana,* by I. Schapera, 67–76. Ethnographic Survey of Africa, Southern Africa, pt. 3, edited by Daryll Forde. London: International African Institute.

————. 1980. Bridewealth and the Control of Ambiguity in a Tswana Chiefdom. In *The Meaning of Marriage Payments,* edited by J. L. Comaroff, 161–195. New York: Academic Press.

————. 1987. Sui generis: Feminism, Kinship Theory, and Structural "Domains." In *Gender and Kinship Essays toward a Unified Analysis,* edited by J. F. Collier and S. J. Yanagisako, 53–85. Stanford, Calif.: Stanford University Press.

Comaroff, J. L., and J. Comaroff. 1981. The Management of Marriage in a Tswana Chiefdom. In *Essays on African Marriage in Southern Africa,* edited by E. J. Krige and J. L. Comaroff, 29–49. Cape Town: Juta.

————. 1991 *Of Revelation and Revolution: Christianity, Colonialism, and Consciousness in South Africa.* Vol. 1. Chicago: University of Chicago Press.

Comaroff, J. L., and S. A. Roberts. 1977. Marriage and Extra-marital Sexuality: The Dialectics of Legal Change among the Kgatla. *Journal of African Law* 21:97–123.

————. 1981. *Rules and Processes: The Cultural Logic of Dispute in an African Context.* Chicago: University of Chicago Press.

Cooper, D. M. 1979a. *Migration to Botswana Towns: Patterns of Migration of Selebi-Pikwe Mine Workers prior to and including Coming to Pikwe.* National Migration Study Working Paper no. 3. Gaborone: Government Printer.

————. 1979b. *Economy and Society in Botswana: Some Basic National Socio-*

Economic Co-ordinates Relevant to an Interpretation of National Migration Statistics. National Migration Study Working Paper no. 2. Gaborone: Government Printer.

————. 1980. *How Urban Workers in Botswana Manage Their Cattle and Lands: Selebi-Pikwe Case Studies.* National Migration Study Working Paper no. 4. Gaborone: Government Printer.

————. 1982. *An Overview of the Botswana Class Structure and Its Articulation with the Rural Mode of Production: Insights from Selebi-Phikwe.*(Dated 1980.) Cape Town: Centre for African Studies, University of Cape Town.

Daniels, W. C. Ekow. 1975. The Effect of Marriage on the Status of Children in Ghana. In *Law and the Family in Africa,* edited by S. Roberts, 159–168. The Hague: Mouton.

Datta, K. n.d. *Research on Women in Economy and Its Impact on Policy Making in Botswana.* Gender Research Programme. Gaborone: University of Botswana and National Institute of Development Research and Documentation.

Delphy, C., and D. Leonard. 1992. *Familiar Exploitation: A New Analysis of Marriage in Contemporary Western Societies.* Cambridge: Polity Press.

Ehrlich, E. 1936. *Fundamental Principles of the Sociology of Law.* Translated by W. L. Moll. Harvard Studies in Jurisprudence, no. 5. Cambridge, Mass.: Harvard University Press. (Originally published 1913.)

Evans-Pritchard, Sir E. E. 1940. *The Nuer: A Description of the Modes of Livelihood and Political Institutions of a Nilotic People.* Oxford: Oxford University Press.

————. 1951. *Kinship and Marriage among the Nuer.* Oxford: Clarendon Press.

Field, R. F. 1982. Batswana Labour in South Africa: Migration to the Mines. In *Migration in Botswana: Patterns, Causes and Consequences.* Final report of the National Migration Study, 3:719–780. Gaborone: Government Printer.

Fineman, M. A. 1983. Implementing Equality: Ideology, Contradiction and Social Change—A Study of Rhetoric and Results in the Regulation of the Consequences of Divorce. *Wisconsin Law Review* 4:789–886.

————. 1991. Introduction. In *At the Boundaries of Law: Feminism and Legal Theory,* edited by M. A. Fineman and N. S. Thomadsen, xi–xvi. London: Routledge.

Fitzpatrick, P. 1984a. Traditionalism and Traditional Law. *Journal of African Law* 28:20–27.

————. 1984b. Law and Societies. *Osgoode Hall Law Journal* 22:115–138.

————. 1985. Review Article: Is It simple to Be a Marxist in Legal Anthropology? *Modern Law Review* 48:472–485.

————. 1988. The Rise and Rise of Informalism. In *Informal Justice?* edited by R. Matthews, 178–198. London: Sage.

————. 1991. The Abstracts and Brief Chronicles of Time: Supplementary Jurisprudence. In *Dangerous Supplements: Resistance and Renewal in Jurisprudence,* edited by P. Fitzpatrick. London: Pluto Press.

————. 1992a. The Impossibility of Popular Justice. In special issue: *State Transformation, Legal Pluralism and Community Justice,* edited by B. de Sousa Santos. *Social and Legal Studies: An International Journal* 1(2):199–216.

————. 1992b. *The Mythology of Modern Law.* London: Routledge.

Fortes, M. 1962. Introduction. In *Marriage in Tribal Societies,* edited by M. Fortes, 1–13. London: Cambridge University Press.

Galanter, M. 1981. Justice in Many Rooms: Courts, Private Ordering and Indigenous Law. *Journal of Legal Pluralism and Unofficial Law* 19:1–47.

Gluckman, M. 1950. Kinship and Marriage among the Lozi of Northern Rhodesia and the Zulu of Natal. In *African Systems of Kinship and Marriage,* edited by A. R. Radcliffe-Brown and D. Forde, 166–205. London: Oxford University Press for the International African Institute.

———. 1955a. *The Judicial Process among the Barotse of Northern Rhodesia (Zambia).* 2d ed. Manchester: Manchester University Press.

———. 1955b. *Custom and Conflict in Africa.* Glencoe, Ill.: Free Press; Oxford: Blackwell.

Goldschmidt-Clermont, L. 1994. Assessing Women's Economic Contributions in Domestic and Related Activities. In *Gender, Work and Population in Sub-Saharan Africa,* edited by A. Adepoju and C. Oppong, 76–87. Published on behalf of International Labour Office, Geneva. London: James Currey; Portsmouth, N.H.: Heinemann.

Griffiths, A. 1983. Legal Duality: Conflict or Concord in Botswana? *Journal of African Law* 27:150–161.

———. 1984. Support for Women with Dependent Children in Botswana. *Journal of Legal Pluralism and Unofficial Law* 23:1–15.

———. 1986. The Problem of Informal Justice: Family Dispute Processing among the Bakwena—A Case Study. *International Journal of the Sociology of Law* 14:359–376.

———. 1988a. Support among the Bakwena. In *Between Kinship and the State,* edited by F. von Benda-Beckmann, K. von Benda-Beckman, E. Casino, F. Hirtz, G. R. Woodman, and H. F. Zacher, 289–316. Dordrecht: Foris Publications.

———. 1988b. Law and the Family in Molepolole: A Study of Family Disputes in a Kwena village. Ph.D. thesis, University of London, London School of Economics and Political Science.

———. 1989a. Women, Status and Power: Negotiation in Family Disputes in Botswana. *Cornell International Law Journal* 22(3):575–622.

———. 1989b. The Legal Heritage of Colonialism: Family Law in a Former British Protectorate. In *Law and Anthropology: Internationales Jahrbuch für Rechtsanthropologie,* no. 4, edited by W. Bauer, 75–106. Vienna: VWGO-Verlag and Wissenschaftlichen Gesellschaften Österreichs; Hohenschäftlam: Klaus Renner Verlag.

Griffiths, J. 1979. The Legal Integration of Minority Groups Set in the Context of Legal Pluralism. Unpublished paper. (Revised as What Is Legal Pluralism, 1986.)

———. 1986. What Is Legal pluralism? *Journal of Legal Pluralism and Unofficial Law* 24:1–55.

———. 1992. Legal Pluralism and the Social Working of Law. In *Coherence and Conflict in Law,* edited by P. W. Brouwer, T. Hol, A. Soeteman, W. G. van de Velden, and A. H. de Wild, 151–176. Deventer: Kluwer Law and Taxation Publishers.

Gulbrandsen, O. 1980. *Agro-Pastoral Production and Communal Land Use.* Gaborone: Government Printer.

———. 1986. To Marry—or Not to Marry. *Ethnos* 51:7–28.

Guyer, J. 1981. Household and Community in African Studies. *African Studies Review* 24(2/3):87–137.

———. 1984. Naturalism in Models of African Production. *Man* 19(3):371–388.

Hahlo, H. R., and E. Kahn. 1960. *The Union of South Africa.* The British Commonwealth: The Development of Its Laws and Constitutions, edited by George W. Keeton, vol. 5. London: Stevens and Sons.

Harrington, C., and B. Yngvesson. 1990. Interpretive Sociolegal Research. *Law and Social Inquiry* 15(1):135–148.

Harris, O. 1981. Households as Natural Units. In *Of Marriage and the Market: Women's Subordination in International Perspective,* edited by K. Young, C. Wolkowitz, and R. McCullagh, 49–67. London: CSE Books.

Hay, M. J. 1982. Women as Owners, Occupants, and Managers. In *African Women and the Law: Historical Perspectives,* edited by M. J. Hay and M. Wright, 110–123. Papers on Africa, no. 7. Boston: Boston University, African Studies Center.

Himsworth, C. M. G. 1972. The Botswana Customary Law Act. *Journal of African Law* 16:4–18.

Hirschon, R. 1984. Introduction: Property, Power and Gender Relations. In *Women and Property: Women as Property,* edited by R. Hirschon, 1–22. London: Croom Helm Press; New York: St. Martins Press.

Holleman, J. F. 1973. Trouble Cases and Troubless Cases in the Study of Customary Law and Legal Reform. *Law and Society Review* 7:585–609.

Hooker, M. 1975. *Legal Pluralism: An Introduction to Colonial and Neo-Colonial Laws.* Oxford: Oxford University Press.

Ingstad, B. 1994. The Grandmother and Household Viability in Botswana. In *Gender, Work and Population in Sub-Saharan Africa,* edited by A. Adepoju and C. Oppong, 209–225. Published on behalf of International Labour Office, Geneva. London: James Currey; Portsmouth, N.H.: Heinemann.

Izzard, W. 1979. *Rural-Urban Migration of Women in Botswana.* Final fieldwork report for National Migration Study Botswana. Gaborone: Government Printer.

———. 1982. The Impact of Migration on the Roles of Women. In *Migration in Botswana: Patterns, Causes and Consequences.* Final report of the National Migration Study, 3:654–707. Gaborone: Government Printer.

———. 1985. Migrants and Mothers: Case-Studies from Botswana. *Journal of Southern African Studies* 11(2):258–279.

Kerven, C. 1979a. *Urban and Rural Female-Headed Households' Dependence on Agriculture.* For National Migration Study. Ministry of Finance and Development Planning, Central Statistics Office; Ministry of Agriculture, Rural Sociology Unit. Gaborone: Government Printer.

———. 1979b. *Rural-Urban Migration and Agricultural Productivity in Botswana.* For National Migration Study. Ministry of Finance and Development Planning, Central Statistics Office; Ministry of Agriculture, Rural Sociology Unit. Gaborone: Government Printer.

———. 1982. The Effects of Migration on Agricultural Production. In *Migration in Botswana: Patterns, Causes and Consequences.* Final report of the National Migration Study 3:526–622. Gaborone: Government Printer.

———. 1984. Academics, Practitioners and all Kinds of Women in Development: A Reply to Peters. *Journal of Southern African Studies* 10(2):259–268.

Kinsman, M. 1983. "Beasts of Burden": The Subordination of Southern Tswana Women, ca. 1800–1840. *Journal of Southern African Studies* 10(1):39–54.

Kocken, E. M., and G. C. Uhlenbeck. 1980. *Tlokweng, A Village Near Town.* ICA Publication no. 39 Leiden: Leiden University, Institute of Cultural and Social Studies.

Kooijman, K. F. 1978. Social and Economic Change in a Tswana Village. M. A. thesis, Leiden University.

Kossoudji, S., and E. Mueller. 1983. The Economic and Demographic Status of Female-Headed Households in Rural Botswana. *Economic Development and Cultural Change* 31(4)831–59.

Krige, E. J. 1964. Property, Cross-Cousin Marriage and the Family Cycle among the Lovedu. In *The Family Estate in Africa,* edited by R. Gray and P. Gulliver, 155–195. London: Routledge and Kegan Paul.

———. 1981. A Comparative Analysis of Marriage and Social Structure among the Southern Bantu. In *Essays on African Marriage in Southern Africa,* edited by E. J. Krige and J. L. Comaroff, 1–28. Cape Town: Juta.

Kuper, A. 1970. The Kgalagari and the Jural Consequences of Marriage. *Man,* n. s., 5:466–482.

———. 1975a. The Social Structure of the Sotho-Speaking Peoples of Southern Africa. *Africa* 45, pt. 1:67–81; pt. 2:139–149.

———. 1975b. Preferential Marriage and Polygyny among the Tswana. In *Studies in African Social Anthropology,* edited by M. Fortes and S. Patterson, 121–134. London: Academic Press.

———. 1978. Determinants of Form in Seven Tswana Kinship Terminologies. *Ethnology* 17(3):239–286.

———. 1982. *Wives for Cattle: Bridewealth and Marriage in Southern Africa.* London: Routledge and Kegan Paul.

———. 1987. The Transformation of Marriage in Southern Africa. In *South Africa and the Anthropologist,* edited by A. Kuper, 134–147. London: Routledge and Kegan Paul.

Lahey, K. 1985. Until Women Themselves Have Told All They Have to Tell. *Osgoode Hall Law Journal* 23(3):519–541.

Lamphere, L. 1974. Strategies, Cooperation, and Conflict among Women in Domestic Groups. In *Woman, Culture and Society,* edited by M. Z. Rosaldo and L. Lamphere, 97–112. Stanford, Calif.: Stanford University Press.

Lazarus-Black, M., and S. F. Hirsch. 1994. *Contested States: Law, Hegemony and Resistance.* After the Law series, edited by J. Brigham and C. B. Harrington. London: Routledge.

Leacock, E. 1978. Women's Status in Egalitarian Society: Implications for Social Evolution. *Current Anthropology* 19(2):247–275.

Livingstone, David. 1858. *Missionary Travels and Researches in South Africa.* London: Murray. (Reprint, New York: Johnson Reprint Corporation, 1971.)

―――. 1959. *Family Letters 1841–1856*. Vol. 1, *1841–1848*. Edited by I. Schapera. London: Chatto and Windus.

MacKinnon, C. 1983. Feminism, Marxism, Method and the State: An Agenda for Theory. *Signs* 8(2):635–658.

―――. 1987. *Feminism Unmodified: Discourses on Life and Law*. Cambridge, Mass.: Harvard University Press.

Maine, Sir Henry S. 1861. *Ancient Law: Its Connections with the Early History of Society and Its Relation to Modern Ideas*. 1st ed. London: J. Murray. (Reprinted as no. 734 in Everyman's Library. London: J. M. Dent and Sons, 1965.)

Mann, K. 1985. *Marrying Well: Marriage, Status and Social Change among the Educated Elite in Colonial Lagos*. Cambridge: Cambridge University Press.

Mann, K., and R. Roberts, eds. 1991. *Law in Colonial Africa*. Portsmouth, N.H.: Heinemann; London: James Currey.

Mautle, G. 1986. Bakgalagadi-Bakwena Relationship: A Case of Slavery, c. 1840—c. 1920. *Botswana Notes and Records* 18:19–31.

Minow, M. 1986. Consider the Consequences. *Michigan Law Review* 84:900–918.

―――. 1990. *Making All the Difference: Inclusion, Exclusion, and American Law*. Ithaca, N.Y.: Cornell University Press.

Merry, S. E. 1988. Legal Pluralism. *Law and Society Review* 22(5)869–901.

Molenaar, M. 1980. Social Change within a Traditional Pattern: A Case Study of a Tswana Ward. M. A. thesis, University of Leiden.

Molokomme, A. 1990/91. Family Law Reform in Botswana. *Journal of Legal Pluralism and Unofficial Law* 30/31:303–329.

―――. 1991. *"Children of the Fence": The Maintenance of Extra-marital Children under Law and Practice in Botswana*. Research report no. 46. Leiden: African Studies Centre.

Molokomme, A., and B. Otlhogile. 1987. *Cases on Family Law and Succession*. Gaborone: University of Botswana, Department of Law.

Moore, H. L. 1988. *Feminism and Anthropology*. Minneapolis: University of Minnesota Press.

―――. 1993. The Differences Within and the Differences Between. In *Gendered Anthropology*, edited by Teresa del Valle, 193–204. London: Routledge.

Moore, H. L., and M. Vaughan. 1994. *Cutting Down Trees: Gender, Nutrition, and Agricultural Change in the Northern Province of Zambia*. Portsmouth, N.H.: Heinemann; London: James Currey; Lusaka: University of Zambia Press.

Moore, S. F. 1978. *Law as Process: An Anthropological Approach*. London: Routledge and Kegan Paul.

―――. 1989. History and the Redefinition of Custom on Kilimanjaro. In *History and Power in the Study of Law*, edited by J. Starr and J. F. Colliers, 277–301. Ithaca, N.Y.: Cornell University Press.

Morton, F., and J. Ramsay. 1987. *The Birth of Botswana: A History of the Bechuanaland Protectorate from 1910 to 1966*. Gaborone: Longman.

Motzafi-Haller, P. 1986. Whither the "True Bushman": The Dynamics of Perpetual Marginality. In *Proceedings of the International Symposium on African Hunters and Gatherers*, edited by F. Rottland and R. Vossen, 295–328. Sprache and Geschichte in Afrika, vol. 7, no. 1. Sankt Augustin: Monastery of Sankt Augustin.

Murray, C. 1981a. The Symbolism and Politics of *Bohali:* Household Recruitment and Marriage by Installment in Lesotho. In *Essays on African Marriage in Southern Africa,* edited by E. J. Krige and J. L. Comaroff, 112–131. Cape Town: Juta.

———. 1981b. *Families Divided: The Impact of Migrant Labour in Lesotho.* Cambridge: Cambridge University Press.

Nangati, F. 1982. Early Capitalist Penetration: The Impact of Precolonial Trade in Kweneng (1840–1876). In *Settlement in Botswana,* edited by R. Hitchcock and M. Smith. Marshalltown: Heinemann.

Ncgoncgo, L. 1982a. Impact of the difaqane on Tswana States. In *Settlement in Botswana,* edited by R. Hitchcock and M. Smith, 167–171. Marshalltown: Heinemann

———. 1982b. Precolonial Migration in South-Eastern Botswana. In *Settlement in Botswana,* edited by R. Hitchcock and M. Smith, 23–30. Exeter, N.H.: Heinemann Educational Books.

Ngugi wa Thiong'o. 1986. *Decolonising the Mind: The Politics of Language in African Literature.* London: James Currey.

Obbo, C. 1980. *African Women: Their Struggle for Economic Independence.* London: Zed Press.

O'Donovan, K. 1985. *Sexual Divisions in Law.* London: Weidenfeld and Nicolson.

Okihiro, G. Y. 1976. Hunters, Herders, Cultivators, and Traders: Interaction and Change in the Kgalagadi, Nineteenth Century. Ph.D. diss., University of California, Los Angeles.

———. 1981. Population Change among the Kwena of Botswana. In *Proceedings of a Seminar Held at the Centre of African Studies Edinburgh University 24th and 25th April 1981,* edited by C. Fyfe and D. McMaster. Edinburgh: Centre of African Studies.

Okin, S. M. 1989. *Justice, Gender, and the Family.* New York: Basic Books.

Olsen, F. 1983. The Family and the Market: A Study of Ideology and Legal Reform. *Harvard Law Review* 96(7):1497–1578.

Oppong, C. 1994. Introduction. In *Gender, Work and Population in Sub-Saharan Africa,* edited by A. Adepoju and C. Oppong, 1–16. Published on behalf of International Labour Office, Geneva. London: James Currey; Portsmouth, N.H.: Heinemann.

Ortner, S. B. 1974. Is Female to Male as Nature Is to Culture? In *Woman, Culture and Society,* edited by M. Z. Rosaldo and L. Lamphere. Stanford, Calif.: Stanford University Press.

Otlhogile, B. 1989. Is Customary Marriage a "Union"? *Botswana Notes and Records* 21:61–66.

Parson, J. 1981. Cattle, Class, and State in Rural Botswana. *Journal of Southern African Studies* 7:236–255.

Parsons, Q. N. 1967. The Visit of the Chiefs to England. Thesis for diploma, Faculty of History, Edinburgh University.

———. 1977. The Economic History of Khama's Country in Botswana, 1844–1930. In *The Roots of Rural Poverty in Central and Southern Africa,* edited by N. Parsons and R. Palmer, 113–143. Berkeley and Los Angeles: University of California Press.

Pateman, C. 1988. *The Sexual Contract.* Stanford, Calif.: Stanford University Press.

———. 1989. *The Disorder of Women.* Cambridge: Polity Press; Oxford: Basil Blackwell.

Pateman, C., and M. L. Shanley, eds. 1991. *Feminist Interpretations and Political Theory.* Cambridge: Polity Press; Oxford: Basil Blackwell.

Peters, P. 1983. Gender, Developmental Cycles and Historical Process: A Critique of Recent Research on Women in Botswana. *Journal of Southern African Studies* 10(1):100–122.

Petersen, H. 1992. On Women and Legal Concepts: Informal Law and the Norm of Consideration. *Social and Legal Studies: An International Journal* 4(1): 493–514.

Pospisil, L. 1958. *Kapauku Papuans and Their Law.* Yale University Publications in Anthropology, no. 54. New Haven, Conn.: Yale University Press.

Radcliffe-Brown, A. R. 1950. Introduction. In *African Systems of Kinship and Marriage,* edited by A. R. Radcliffe-Brown and D. Forde, Oxford University Press for the International African Institute: London.

Ramsay, J. 1991. The Rise and Fall of the Bakwena Dynasty of South Central Botswana, 1820–1940. Ph.D. diss., Boston University.

Roberts, S. A. 1970. *A Restatement of the Kgatla Law of Domestic Relations.* Restatement of African Law Series. London: School of Oriental and African Studies.

———. 1971. The Settlement of Family Disputes in the Kgatla Customary Courts: Some New Approaches. *Journal of African Law* 15(1):60–76.

———. 1972a. *Restatement of African Law: Botswana: 1: Tswana Family Law.* London: Sweet and Maxwell.

———. 1972b. The Survival of the Traditional Tswana Courts in the National Legal System of Botswana. *Journal of African Law* 16(2):103–129.

———. 1977a. The Kgatla Marriage: Concepts of Validity. In *Law and the Family in Africa,* edited by S. A. Roberts, 241–260. The Hague: Mouton.

———. 1977b. Introduction. In *Law and the Family in Africa,* edited by S. A. Roberts, 1–14. The Hague: Mouton.

———. 1979. *Order and Dispute.* New York: St. Martin's Press.

———. 1991. Tswana Government and Law in the Time of Seepapitso, 1910–1916. In *Law in Colonial Africa,* edited by K. Mann and R. Roberts, 167–187. Portsmouth N.H.: Heinemann; London: James Currey.

Robertson, A. F. 1991. *Beyond the Family: The Social Organization of Human Reproduction.* Oxford: Polity Press.

Rosaldo M. Z. 1974. Woman, Culture, and Society: A Theoretical Overview. In *Woman, Culture and Society,* edited by M. Z. Rosaldo and L. Lamphere, 17–42. Stanford, Calif.: Stanford University Press.

Rwezaura, B. n.d. Uncovering Reality: Excavating Women's Rights in African Family Law. *Women and Law in Southern Africa Working Paper no. 7.* Harare: Women and Law in Southern Africa Project.

Sacks, K. 1979. *Sisters and Wives: The Past and Future of Sexual Equality.* Westport, Conn.: Greenwood Press.

Sanders, A. J. G. M. 1985a. The Legal Dualism in Lesotho, Botswana and Swaziland: A General Survey. *Lesotho Law Journal* 1:1–47.

———. 1985b. The Internal Conflict of Laws in Botswana. *Botswana Notes and Records* 17:77–87.

Santos, B. de Sousa. 1987. Law: A Map of Misreading—Toward a Postmodern Conception of Law. *Journal of Law and Society* 14(3):279–302.

Sarat, A., and S. Silbey. 1987. Critical Traditions in Law and Society Research. *Law and Society Review* 21(1):165–174.

Schapera, I. 1933. Pre-marital Pregnancy and Native Opinion: A Note on Social Change. *Africa* 6:59–89.

———. 1935. The Social Structure of the Tswana Ward. *Bantu Studies* 9:203–224. (Reprint, *African Studies* 31[1972]:91–109.)

———. 1938. *A Handbook of Tswana Law and Custom.* London: Oxford University Press for the International African Institute.

———. [1940] 1955. *Married Life in an African Tribe.* London: Faber.

———. 1943. *Native Land Tenure in the Bechuanaland Protectorate.* Alice: Lovedale Press.

———. 1947. *Migrant Labour and Tribal Life: A Study of the Condition of the Bechuanaland Protectorate.* London: OUP.

———. 1950. Kinship and Marriage among the Tswana. In *African Systems of Kinship and Marriage,* edited by A. R. Radcliffe-Brown and D. Forde, 140–165. London: Oxford University Press for the International African Institute.

———. 1952. *The Ethnic Composition of Tswana Tribes.* Monographs on Social Anthropology, no. 11. London: London School of Economics.

———. 1953. *The Tswana.* Ethnographic Survey of Africa, Southern Africa, pt. 3. (Reprint, London: International African Institute, 1976.)

———. 1956. *Government and Politics in Tribal Societies.* London: Watts.

———. 1957. Marriage of Near Kin among the Tswana. *Africa* 27:139–159.

———. 1963a. Agnatic Marriage in Tswana Royal Families. In *Studies in Kinship and Marriage,* edited by I. Schapera. Occasional Paper no. 16. London: Royal Anthropological Institute.

———. 1963b. Kinship and Politics in Tswana History. *Journal of the Royal Anthropological Institute* 93(2):159–173.

———. 1970. *Tribal Innovators: Tswana Chiefs and Social Change 1795–1940.* London School of Economics Monographs on Social Anthropology, no. 43. London: Athlone Press.

———. 1978. Some Notes on Tswana Bogadi. *Journal of African Law* 22(2): 112–124.

———. 1980. Notes on the Early History of the Kwena (Bakwena-bagaSechele). *Botswana Notes and Records* 12:83–87.

———. 1983. Tswana Concepts of Custom and Law. *Journal of African Law* 27:141–149.

Schapera, I., and S. A. Roberts. 1975. Rampedi Revisited: Another Look at a Kgatla Ward. *Africa* 45(1):258–279.

Shillington, K. 1985. *The Colonisation of the Southern Tswana 1870–1900.* Braamfontein: Ravan Press.

Silitshena, R. M. K. 1978. Notes on Some Characteristics of Population That Has Migrated Permanently to the Lands in the Kweneng District. *Botswana Notes and Records* 10:149–157.

———. 1982a. Population Movements and Settlement Patterns in Contemporary Botswana. In *Settlement in Botswana,* edited by R. Hitchcock and M. Smith, 31–43. Marshalltown: Heinemann.

———. 1982b. Migration and Permanent Settlement at the Lands Areas. In *Settlement in Botswana,* edited by R. Hitchcock and M. Smith, 220–231. Marshalltown: Heinemann.

Sillery, A. 1954. *Sechele: The Story of an African Chief.* Oxford: George Ronald.

Smart, C. 1984. *The Ties That Bind: Law, Marriage and Reproduction of Patriarchal Relations.* London and Boston: Routledge and Kegan Paul.

———. 1989. *Feminism and the Power of Law.* London: Routledge.

Snyder, F. G. 1980. Law and Development in the Light of Dependency Theory. *Law and Society Review* 14:723–804.

———. 1981a. Anthropology, Dispute Processes and Law: A Critical Introduction. *British Journal of Law and Society* 8:141–180.

———. 1981b. *Capitalism and Legal Change: An African Transformation.* New York: Academic Press.

———. 1983. *Three Paradigms in the Anthropology of Law.* Paper presented at Landbouwhoge School, Wageningen, Netherlands, on 15 April.

Solway, J. 1980. *People, Cattle and Drought in the Western Kweneng District.* Rural Sociology Report Series, no. 16. Gaborone:?

Stewart, R. 1994. The Economic Empowerment of Batswana Women: A Case-Study of Woman's Finance House, Botswana. M. A. thesis, Centre of African Studies, Edinburgh University.

Strathern, M. 1980. No Nature, No Culture: The Hagen Case. In *Nature, Culture and Gender,* edited by C. MacCormack and M. Strathern, 174–222. Cambridge: Cambridge University Press.

———. 1985. Discovering "Social Control." *Journal of Law and Society* 12(2): 111–129.

Timaeus, I., and W. Graham. 1989. Labour Circulation, Marriage and Fertility in Southern Africa. In *Reproduction and Social Organization in Sub-Saharan Africa,* edited by R. Lesthaeghe, 365–400. Berkeley and Los Angeles: University of California Press.

Tlou, T. 1972. A Political History of Northwestern Botswana to 1906. Ph.D. diss., Department of History, University of Wisconsin.

———. 1985. *A History of Ngamiland 1750 to 1956: The Formation of an African State.* Madison: University of Wisconsin Press.

Tlou, T., and A. Campbell. 1984. *History of Botswana.* Gaborone: Macmillan Botswana.

United Nations Population Fund (UNFPA). 1989. *Gender, Population and Development.* Report on the High-Level Seminar for Chiefs and District Commissioners. Edited by L. Divasse and G. Mookodi. Gaborone: Ministry of Labour and Home Affairs, Women's Affairs Unit.

UNICEF. 1989. *Children, Women and Development in Botswana: A Situational Analysis.* A consultant's report compiled for the joint GOB/UNICEF Programme and Planning and Co-ordinating Committee. Gaborone: UNICEF and Ministry of Finance and Development Planning.

———. 1993. *Children, Women and Development in Botswana: A Situational Analy-*

sis. Report prepared by Maendeleo (Botswana) for the Government of Botswana and UNICEF.

Vaughan, M. 1983. Which Family? Problems in the Reconstruction of the History of the Family as an Economic and Cultural Unit. *Journal of African History* 24:275–283.

———. 1985. Household Units and Historical Process in Southern Malawi. *Review of African Political Economy* 34:35–45.

Weizman, L. 1985. *The Divorce Revolution: The Unexpected Social and Economic Consequences for Women and Children in America.* New York: Free Press.

Whitehead, A. 1994. Wives and Mothers: Female Farmers in Africa. In *Gender, Work and Population in Sub-Saharan Africa,* edited by A. Adepoju and C. Oppong, 35–53. Published on behalf of International Labour Office, Geneva. London: James Currey; Portsmouth, N.H.: Heinemann.

Wilmsen, E. N. 1989. *Land Filled with Flies: A Political Economy of the Kalahari.* Chicago and London: University of Chicago Press.

Women and Law in Southern Africa Trust (WLSA). 1991. *Maintenance in Lesotho.* Maseru: WLSA.

———. 1992. *Maintenance Laws and Practices in Botswana.* Gaborone: WLSA, National Institute of Research and Documentation (NIR), University of Botswana.

———. 1994. *Inheiritance in Zimbabwe: Law Customs and Practices.* Harare: WLSA, SADES Trust.

Woodman, G. 1988. Unification or Continuing Pluralism in Family Law in Anglophone Africa: Past Experience, Present Realities and Future Possibilities. *Lesotho Law Journal* 4(2):33–79.

Wylie, D. 1991. *A Little God: The Twilight of Patriarchy in a Southern African Chiefdom.* Hanover, N.H.: Wesleyan University Press.

INDEX

The index includes individuals (listed by given name) and families mentioned in ethnographic accounts.

Tumagole, 72

UNFPA, 26
UNICEF, 26, 47, 273, 275

Vaughan, M., 15, 216, 219, 222
Victor Kgosidintsi, 101, 143

Wamakhyu, 55
Weizman, L., 238
Western/European form of law, 28–
    31, 33, 37, 112, 208, 213, 228,
    237
Western Transvaal, 18–19
Whitehead, A., 219
Wilmsen, E., 45–46, 65, 70
Witwatersrand, 19, 70
women
    and agriculture, 19, 25, 27, 47–48,
        52, 81, 85–87, 120, 131, 151,
        169, 178, 181, 223, 227

and cattle, 25, 85, 88, 95, 142, 169,
    177–178
domain of, 15–16, 42, 217–218,
    226
and law, 11–13, 36–38, 47, 58,
    113–114, 117, 119–121, 126–
    128, 131–133, 135–136, 150,
    157–160, 162, 165, 167, 171,
    176, 181, 183, 185, 187, 194,
    197, 208, 210, 212, 225, 229–
    230, 232–234, 236–238
networks of, 14, 27, 37, 51, 86, 88,
    101, 177, 181, 183, 223,
    226–227
Women and Law in Southern Africa
    Trust, 128, 229
Woodman, G., 17, 114, 159, 231
Wylie, D., 20

Zhu kinship, 45
Zimbabwe, 19